GW01158491

Southern Democrats in the
U.S. House of Representatives

Congressional Studies Series
Ronald M. Peters, Jr., General Editor

Southern Democrats in the U.S. House of Representatives

STANLEY P. BERARD

UNIVERSITY OF OKLAHOMA PRESS : NORMAN

Library of Congress Cataloging-in-Publication Data

Berard, Stanley P. (Stanley Paul), 1965–
 Southern Democrats in the U.S. House of Representatives / Stanley
P. Berard.
  p. cm. — (Congressional studies series ; v. 2)
 Includes bibliographical references and index.
 ISBN 0-8061-3305-8 (pbk.: alk. paper)
 1. United States. Congress. House. 2. Democratic Party (U.S.)
3. Legislators—Southern States. 4. Legislators—United States.
5. Southern States—Politics and government—1951– 6. United
States—Politics and government—1945–1989. 7. United States—
Politics and government—1989– I. Title: Southern Democrats in the
United States House of Representatives. II. Title. III. Series.

JK1319 .B47 2001
328.73'092'2—dc21

              00-064909

Southern Democrats in the U.S. House of Representatives is Volume 2 in the
Congressional Studies Series.

The paper in this book meets the guidelines for permanence and dura-
bility of the Committee on Production Guidelines for Book Longevity of
the Council on Library Resources, Inc.∞

1 2 3 4 5 6 7 8 9 10

CONTENTS

TABLES

PREFACE

This book studies the constituency basis of southern Democratic roll call voting in the House of Representatives from 1973 to 1997. Southern Democrats contributed substantially to the rise of partisanship in congressional policy making in the 1980s. The level of partisanship first evident in the late 1980s persisted throughout the 1990s and shows no sign of abatement early in the new century. This work makes the case that the increasingly partisan behavior of southern Democrats was the critical factor in the rise of congressional partisanship and that understanding the relationship between southern Democrats and their constituents provides the essential part of the explanation for their altered legislative behavior. The relevance of southern Democratic representative-constituency linkages to understanding congressional behavior persists beyond the initial partisan surge of the 1980s. Even after the 1994 elections sharply reduced their numbers and even after having become decidedly more partisan, southern Democrats remained a distinctive group within their party. Given the narrowness of the Republican majority since 1994, southern Democrats are often key actors in the formation of majority coalitions in the House.

A central assumption of this work is that the rate of roll call agreement of a legislator with his or her partisan colleagues is the result of the degree of similarity between their policy preferences. A further assumption is that preference similarity between legislators is associated with preference similarity between their respective constituencies. Thus the level of partisan behavior is associated with the degree of similarity of the members' constituencies within each party, as well as the degree of difference between the parties. The theory underlying this work is that the increase in southern Democratic partisanship was driven by a growing similarity between southern and northern Democratic constituencies. In short, southern Democratic representatives began voting more similarly to northern Democrats as their constituencies became less conservative and more like the constituencies of northern Democrats.

In elaborating this theory, I have emphasized that each member is responsive not to a single undifferentiated district constituency but to several constituencies that can be described much as Richard Fenno (1978) described them. Within each member's geographic constituency (the district), he will be particularly responsive to the reelection constituency (district voters who regularly support the incumbent or his party in general elections) and the primary constituency (reliable providers of material support in general elections and/or base of support in a contested primary election). A legislator's expressed preferences might be altered by a change in any one of these layered constituencies or more than one simultaneously. In the case of southern Democrats, three agents of change have each had a different combination of effects: urbanization has made southern geographic constituencies more similar to northern ones; the mobilization of black voters by the end of the 1960s has had implications for all three levels of constituency, especially reelection constituencies; and the rise of Republican competition has resulted in conservative white defections from reelection and primary constituencies, giving both a more liberal cast.

This work also emphasizes that although demographic variables can describe broad forces of change like the three northernizing agents I just described, they serve only as surrogates for constituent preferences. Using survey data to study constituent preferences, we find that the effects of the three northernizing agents have not been uniform across issues. Convergence in the attitudes of northern and southern Democratic reelection constituents occurred almost exclusively on economic issues and not on civil rights or cultural issues such as abortion or school prayer. This difference is reflected in greater partisanship among southern Democratic representatives on economic issues than on other issues. Still, southern Democratic representatives did move closer to northern Democratic positions in several issue areas for which there was little convergence between southern and northern Democratic reelection constituents. This reflects the influence of parts of the typical southern Democratic reelection constituency on particular issue areas: black constituents on civil rights issues and party activists (likely primary constituents) on cultural issues.

Geographic constituencies themselves are not uniform across the South. This study provides an alternative conceptualization of the geographic variation of political contexts in the South. On issues for which black voter mobilization makes the most difference to aggregate southern constituency opinion—economic and civil rights issues—the most conservative whites reside in those rural areas where the black population is most heavily concentrated. Southern whites with the least conservative economic attitudes reside in rural areas with sparse black populations. Urbanization represents a move away from this traditional association of racial context and white attitudes: in urban districts, more liberal whites tend to reside in areas with larger black populations. Yet urbanization is directly linked to more liberal attitudes among whites only on cultural issues. The impacts of urbanization and black voter mobilization on aggregate constituency attitudes depend on the urban and racial context of the district and on the issue being considered.

This study is based primarily on analysis of pooled cross sections of the National Election Studies (NES) time series and of congressional roll call voting using the collection maintained by the Inter-University Consortium for Political and Social Research (ICPSR). The pooled NES cross sections measure constituency opinion on a number of issues in the early 1970s, late 1980s, and early 1990s. The election-year surveys were pooled to generate reliable estimates of the public attitudes of various subsamples, for example, those who voted in congressional elections, divided into groups of reelection constituents by region and party (northern Democrats, southern Democrats, and Republicans) according to how they voted; political activists, classified into groups of primary constituents by region and party according to how they voted in congressional elections; southern Democratic reelection constituents grouped by race; and white southerners classified by the demographic characteristics of their congressional districts. I also computed southern Democrats' rate of support for the northern Democratic position on partisan roll call votes in eight issue areas for the 93d through 105th Congresses.

The combination of survey-based public opinion data with roll call voting data, both extending over a two-decade period, forms a unique contribution to the literature on partisanship in Congress and in elections as well as that on southern politics. This approach was inspired in large measure by David W. Rohde's (1991a, 1991b) work on partisanship in the U.S. House. This study adds to Rohde's work by giving closer scrutiny to changes in constituency attitudes in different issue areas and how issue differences are reflected in congressional behavior. It also has some important similarities to the work of James M. Glaser (1996). Glaser's case studies of southern congressional campaigns revealed how Democratic candidates were able to exploit issues successfully and turn back potential Republican gains. Glaser's analysis points to racial context as a critical factor shaping the coalitions that southern Democratic candidates can build and the issues they can exploit in doing so. This book complements Glaser's work in several ways. First, its use of roll call data allows the extension of Glaser's insights on the role of racial context across all southern congressional districts. Second, it refines the notion of racial context to include its different effects in rural and urban areas. Third, it adds a focus on representation in the House to Glaser's focus on campaigning in the district.

In addition, my use of roll call and public opinion data complements work by Nicol C. Rae (1994) that uses data from interviews with southern Democratic elected officials and party leaders to elaborate the pressures that have altered the role of southerners in the national Democratic Party. Finally, this study shares with work by Earl Black and Merle Black (1992) a concern with the role of the South in national politics. Black and Black chronicle the changing relationship of the South to each party's presidential election coalition, whereas I am concerned here with the changing relationship of the South to partisan policy coalitions within the House.

Several people provided valuable assistance, although they should not take the blame for errors of fact and judgment that remain. No one was more important to this project than Bill Keefe, who guided its development as a Ph.D. dissertation at the University of Pittsburgh. He shared and encouraged my own concerns with the connections between southern politics and congressional politics, and he constantly pushed me to clarify the issues that must be addressed in making those connections. None of this work would have been possible without him. Careful readers will note, however, that Bill Keefe had no influence on the writing of the preface.

I owe a considerable intellectual debt to David Rohde. His work on the roots of resurging partisanship in Congress illuminated the importance of studying southern constituencies in understanding contemporary congressional politics. He also provided encouragement and data for my work in revising and extending the study beyond the original dissertation.

As I worked on the dissertation, Guy Peters and Jon Hurwitz each read more than one draft of every chapter. Hurwitz was especially helpful in finding ways to refine several parts of the analysis, and Peters continually raised interesting and important empirical and theoretical points. Lee Weinberg also read the entire dissertation in progress, and his questions, suggestions, and encouragement were invaluable in its completion. Bert Rockman and Jeff Mondak read the completed dissertation and provided advice on which I relied heavily in transforming the dissertation into this book.

Ray Owen, chair of the political science department at the University of Pittsburgh, graciously facilitated access to computing accounts and facilities for the duration of this project. Li Tong of the Social Science Computer Research and Consulting Center (SSCRCC) at Pitt arranged the initial acquisition of NES and congressional roll call data from the ICPSR and provided technical assistance in using the data. ICPSR, NES, and the principal investigators for the NES share no responsibility for the use and interpretation of the data they have made available for this study.

Several other faculty and graduate students in political science at Pitt read and commented on particular chapters or on related conference or seminar papers, including Liz Adams, Simeon Brodsky, Damarys Canache, Annabelle Conroy, Paul Goren, David Fitz, Charles Gochman, Brooke Harlowe, Michael Margolis, Morris Ogul, Fiona Ross, Andrew Valls, and Anthony Zito.

Michelle Pupich, Marsha Tsouris, Donna Myers, Bea Kierzkowski, and Mary Ann Kaper—all on the office staff in Pitt's political science department when I studied there—provided help that was critical to completing this project and fulfilling other responsibilities. James Blessing, chair of the political science department at Susquehanna University, made his department's facilities available to me for work on this project during the summer months.

At Southern Arkansas University (SAU), two University Research Grants and the facilities of the Curtistine Walz Center enabled me to complete this book. James Willis and Don Watt, both of the history and political science department at SAU, provided substantial assistance and encouragement in acquiring necessary resources. Teresa Beaver, Floyd Smith, and Shaketha Ferguson, undergraduate students at SAU, helped by collecting data at SAU's Magale Library.

Several political scientists provided helpful advice and encouragement on parts of this project that I have presented at academic conferences over the years, including Sunil Ajuha, Tom Baldino, Doug Chaffey, Patrick Cotter, Keith Gaddie, Charles Prysby, David Rohde, Wayne Shannon, Henry Sirgo, Robert Steed, Andrew Taylor, Stephen Voss, and Cheryl Young. I am indebted to all of these people for sharing their insights with me.

The final version of this work was shaped by the comments of Keith Gaddie, Ron Peters, and two anonymous reviewers. Sheila Berg, Jean Hurtado, Alice Stanton, and Kimberly Wiar gave me guidance in preparing the manuscript for publication.

A few more people must be mentioned as playing a central role in shaping this book. The first political scientists to guide me were on the faculty at the University of Louisiana at Lafayette—known when I studied there as the University of Southwestern Louisiana (USL). Herbert M. Levine was the first to encourage me to write about politics and to provide guidance in how to do so. Janet Frantz, Tom Ferrell, and Donn Kurtz were also especially important mentors. These and many other professors at USL made lasting impressions that I hope are reflected in these pages.

Finally, I would like to extend my appreciation to Brooke Harlowe and to my parents, Lloyd and Mary Berard. In addition to providing guidance that can carry one anywhere through any endeavor, my parents were the first southern Democrats I ever met. Brooke has provided years of professional and personal companionship. She is a source of strength for me, and the depth of my gratitude to her cannot be measured.

*Southern Democrats in the
U.S. House of Representatives*

CHAPTER ONE

SOUTHERN DEMOCRATS AND PARTY GOVERNMENT IN THE HOUSE

The term "southern Democrat" once evoked an image of a conservative politician. As often as not, the attachment of southerners to the Democratic Party was grounded less in programmatic commitments than in loyalties that dated from a time when in most of the South the Democratic Party dominated electoral politics to the virtual exclusion of any other. This monopoly on political power meant that the champions of the political and social status quo in the South were Democrats. When northern Democrats began to press for national policies that promised to alter southern society in fundamental ways, the greatest resistance was from the southern wing of their own party. Today, the concept of the southern Democrat is still viewed by many in light of the role southern Democrats played during the 1940s, 1950s and 1960s as opponents of federal government involvement in social welfare policy and African American civil rights.

Through the early 1980s the unique relationship of southern Democrats to the national party system was reflected in the frequent occurrence in Congress of a "conservative coalition" of southern Democrats and Republicans in opposition to the policy preferences and initiatives of northern Democrats. This conservative coalition had wide-ranging influence on public policy, and one scholar referred to it as the "permanent majority" in Congress (Shelley 1983). The conservative coalition rendered the formation of partisan Democratic majorities less likely, even though the Democrats held a majority of the seats in each chamber in most of the Congresses from the 1930s through the 1980s. Along with the gradual decentralization of power in the House after the 1910 revolt against Speaker Joseph Cannon and the erosion of party organizations' role in mobilizing voters in congressional elections, the divergence of policy preferences in the Democratic party was a major factor contributing to the long-term decline of partisanship in congressional policy making during the twentieth century.

Since the 1980s, however, the decline in partisanship in Congress has been reversed and party politics have come to play a crucial role in congressional policy making. The resurgence of partisanship in the House has been especially dramatic. One illustration of the decline and resurgence of party politics in the House is the party unity data in table 1.1. Party unity votes—those roll call votes pitting a majority of Democrats against a majority of Republicans—were not more than 48 percent of all House roll call votes from the late 1960s to 1982. In fact, party unity votes appeared only about 37 percent of the time in 1980–82. In every year since 1983, however, party unity votes have been not less than 47 percent of House roll calls.[1]

Not only did partisan coalitions begin to occur more frequently on roll call votes, but leaders within each party became more active in shaping the substance of the policy agenda and strategies for achieving legislative goals on the floor. Recent scholarship emphasizes that increased partisanship on the House floor reflects to a substantial degree the increasing aggressiveness, and success, of party leaders in promoting policy priorities. Institutional changes in the House laid essential groundwork for this expanded exercise of party leadership. House reforms during the 1970s empowered individual members and party leaders at the expense of committee chairs, enabling each party's leaders to pursue policy goals as agents

TABLE 1.1
Partisan and Conservative Coalitions
in the House of Representatives, 1971–1998

YEAR	PARTY UNITY VOTES	CONSERVATIVE COALITION VOTES	PARTY UNITY SCORES			
			SOUTHERN DEMOCRATS	NORTHERN DEMOCRATS	ALL DEMOCRATS	REPUBLICANS
1971	38	31	48	83	72	76
1972	27	25	44	82	70	76
1973	42	25	55	86	75	74
1974	29	22	51	84	72	71
1975	48	28	53	85	75	78
1976	36	17	52	85	75	75
1977	42	22	55	82	74	77
1978	33	20	53	79	71	77
1979	47	21	60	82	75	79
1980	38	16	64	83	78	79
1981	37	21	57	84	75	80
1982	36	16	62	88	77	76
1983	56	18	67	89	82	80
1984	47	14	68	88	81	77
1985	61	13	76	90	86	80
1986	57	11	76	90	86	76
1987	64	9	78	92	88	79
1988	47	8	81	91	88	80
1989	55	11	77	90	86	76
1990	49	10	78	90	86	78
1991	55	9	78	89	86	81
1992	64	10	79	90	86	84
1993	65	7	84	92	88	87
1994	62	7	83	91	88	87
1995	73	18	75	87	84	93
1996	56	11	76	87	84	90
1997	56	9	78	88	85	91
1998	50	8	79	89	86	89

SOURCE: *Congressional Quarterly Almanac*, various years.

of the party caucus. At the same time, it is generally accepted that the increased similarity of goals and preferences within each party caucus represents a critical change in the context within which House leaders can deploy these resources (Rohde 1991b; Sinclair 1995).

Southern Democrats are the group of representatives for whom the rise of partisanship entailed the greatest behavioral change. Because the behavior of representatives is linked in some way to the preferences and characteristics of those they are elected to represent, the behavioral change among Southern Democrats can be traced to the change in their constituencies. It is this connection that I explore here.

SOUTHERN DEMOCRATS AND THE CONGRESSIONAL PARTY RESURGENCE

The emergence of the conservative coalition of southern Democrats and Republicans coincided with the decline of partisanship as a prominent feature of congressional politics. Likewise, the surge of partisanship in the House coincided with the declining influence of the conservative coalition. In the House, appearances of the coalition among roll call votes declined from 21 percent in 1981 to 8 percent in 1988.[2] Since 1988 the coalition has appeared on more than 11 percent of roll calls only once (column 2 of table 1.1).

The decline of the conservative coalition occurred at a time when southern Democrats were increasingly supportive of their party's positions on House and Senate roll call votes. The third column of table 1.1 reports annual mean party unity scores for southern Democrats in the House, that is, the percentage of party unity votes on which they voted with their party. Party unity votes are roll calls on which a majority of all Democrats votes against a majority of Republicans. House southern Democrats were substantially more supportive of their party's positions in the late 1980s than they had been in the early 1970s. Before 1979 they had voted with the party no more than 55 percent of the time; after 1979, their party unity scores dropped below 60 percent only once; and in every year after 1985 southern Democratic party unity was at least 75 percent.

The coincidence between the rise of partisanship among southern Democrats and the decline of the conservative coalition can be documented more precisely by modeling each of the two trends using a time series intervention analysis. The first year of each Congress beginning with the 94th (i.e., 1975, 1977, and so on, to 1991) was entered as an intervention variable in a regression analysis of each time series in table 1.1 for the years 1973–92. For example, years preceding 1975 had a value of zero for the 1975 intervention, while 1975 and later years took a value of one. These nine intervention variables were the independent variables in regression models of annual conservative coalition appearances and party unity scores. The results of several such models are reported in table 1.2.

Table 1.2 shows that the first substantial decrease in conservative coalition appearances in the House occurred in 1979, with another large decrease in 1985. When scholars and journalists began to pronounce the conservative coalition practically dead in the late 1980s (e.g., Ehrenhalt 1987), they were commenting on the culmination of a trend that had begun during the Carter presidency. Likewise, southern Democrats' party unity scores showed their first substantial increase in 1979, followed by large increases in the mid-1980s.

This coincidence between the rise of southern Democratic partisanship and the decline of the conservative coalition can be explained in terms of the preferences of southern Democrats on issues that produce a partisan split in Congress. By definition, both conservative coalition and party unity votes are partisan in nature. In a vote on which a majority of northern Democrats are in opposition to a majority of Republicans, the behavior of southern Democrats determines whether the vote will meet the definition of a conservative

TABLE 1.2

Interruptions in Time Series of House Partisanship, 1973–1992

		PARTY UNITY SCORES			
	CONSERVATIVE COALITION VOTES	SOUTHERN DEMOCRATS	NORTHERN DEMOCRATS	ALL DEMOCRATS	REPUBLICANS
Constant	23.50****	53.00****	85.00****	73.50****	72.50****
1975	-1.00 (-.052)	-.50 (-.014)	.0000 (.000)	1.50 (.078)	4.00* (.434)
1977	-1.50 (-.104)	1.50 (.056)	-4.5*** (-.506)	-2.50* (-.173)	.50 (.072)
1979	-2.50 (-.199)	8.00*** (.343)	2.00 (.258)	4.00** (.317)	2.00 (.332)
1981	.0000 (.000)	-2.50 (-.114)	3.50** (.483)	-.50 (-.042)	-1.00 (-.177)
1983	-2.50 (-.217)	8.00*** (.374)	2.50* (.352)	5.50*** (.476)	.50 (.091)
1985	-4.00 (-.340)	8.50*** (.389)	1.50 (.207)	4.50*** (.382)	-.50 (-.089)
1987	-3.50 (-.278)	3.50* (.150)	1.50 (.193)	2.00 (.159)	1.50 (.249)
1989	2.00 (.139)	-2.00 (-.075)	-1.50 (-.169)	-2.00 (-.138)	-2.50 (-.362)
1991	-1.00 (-.052)	1.00 (.028)	-.50 (-.042)	.0000 (.000)	5.50** (.597)
R^2 (adjusted)	.70***	.97****	.88****	.95****	.55**

NOTES: Entries are unstandardized regression coefficients. Standardized coefficients are in parentheses.

**** $p < .001$
*** $p < .01$
** $p < .05$
* $p < .10$

coalition appearance or a party unity vote. As more southern Democrats vote with the northern Democrats on partisan issues, it is reflected both in reduced appearances of the conservative coalition and increased party unity scores for southern Democrats. House southern Democrats preferred Republican positions less often and northern Democratic positions more often after 1979 than before.

The changing behavior of southern Democrats necessarily played a crucial role in the resurgence of partisanship in the House during the 1980s. Table 1.2 reveals that Republicans became substantially more supportive of their party's positions in 1975 and 1991, but the noticeable increase in overall House partisanship during the 1980s was not associated with a significant change in Republican roll call behavior. To the extent that the rise of partisanship in the House was a matter of party members more frequently voting with their party majority, it was primarily a Democratic phenomenon. Further, it was primarily a southern Democratic phenomenon. Among Democrats, the change in the rate of partisan voting among southerners was far greater than that among northerners. The timing of southern Democrats' increase in party unity matches closely the timing of the overall increase in party unity among Democrats in the House. The intervention analyses in table 1.2 reveal precisely the same results for all House Democrats as for southern Democrats: the first substantial increase in party unity occurred in 1979, with further increases in 1983 and 1985.

One can infer from the close similarity of the two trends that the rising party unity of House Democrats since 1979 reflects primarily the increasing partisanship of southern Democrats. In fact, in a regression model predicting House Democrats' average party unity scores from the scores of northern and southern Democrats, change in party unity among all House Democrats is far more closely associated with change in southern Democratic than northern Democratic scores. As revealed in table 1.3, this result is especially the case for the years 1979–86, when most of the increase in roll call partisanship occurred.

TABLE 1.3

Northern and Southern Contributions to
Rising Democratic Party Unity in the House

	ANNUAL MEAN DEMOCRATIC PARTY UNITY	
	1973–1992	1979–1986
Southern Democratic party unity (Annual mean)	.732**	.837**
Northern Democratic party unity (Annual mean)	.292**	.185
R2 (adjusted)	.98**	.97**

NOTES: Entries are standardized regression coefficients.
** p < .001

INFLUENCES ON SOUTHERN DEMOCRATIC PARTISANSHIP IN CONGRESS

Agendas, Preferences, and Partisanship

So far, I have made the case that most of the surge in partisanship on House roll calls in the 1980s was a result of the changing behavior of southern Democrats. This does not necessarily mean that increasing House partisanship reflects constituency-driven change in Southern Democrats' policy preferences. To begin making the case that changing southern Democratic partisanship was constituency driven, let us distinguish between two factors that influence the formation of legislators' preferences. First, legislators bring with them from outside the institution motivations, values, and attitudes that condition their behavior in the legislature. These motivations, values, and attitudes shape members' preferences on specific decisions that face the legislature. Becoming a candidate for the office involves a fair degree of self-selection, which introduces considerable variation into the range of goals and preferences that might be represented. At the same time, the election process enforces a degree of congruence of members' preferences with the values and attitudes of their constituents, to the extent that organizations, activists, and voters provide and withdraw support to candidates on the basis of the preferences they represent in office. In the language of formal approaches to the study of legislatures, constituency-driven preferences are exogenous to the legislative process: they are given a priori, not contingent in any way on the interaction of members in the institution.

If preferences displayed by members in the legislature are not entirely exogenous, then they are at least in part endogenous. Preferences are endogenous to the extent that they derive from the choice situations presented to the members in the legislature rather than from the motivations, values, and attitudes the members bring in from outside the institution. The importance of endogenous preference formation to explaining legislative behavior is illuminated by making a distinction between underlying preferences and revealed preferences. The revealing of members' preferences in roll call votes occurs in response to the choices generated by the strategic interaction among various agenda setters. Bill sponsors, committees, and party leaders structure roll call alternatives by drafting bills, scheduling votes, and setting procedures for debate and amendments. The issues that come to a vote and the content of the bills that are considered are the product of procedures determined in the legislature. Thus endogenous factors determine what roll calls will occur and what preferences will be revealed. In exercising influence over the agenda, a given member may be willing to act against her own preferences on some issues in return for moving legislative outcomes on other issues closer to preferences she holds more intensely.

Furthermore, the expression of preferences in roll call voting is only the end-point of a legislative process that contains multiple opportunities for endogenous influence on members' *underlying* preferences. The exchange of information about policy choices among legislators, interest groups, and government agencies is part of the agenda-setting process. Detailed issue-oriented learning and policy development occurs via contacts among the members most interested in a given issue, both informally and formally, in committee and subcommittee mark-ups. Although each member's level of participation in agenda-setting activities across different issues is determined by a mix of personal and constituency factors, participation can also shape a member's preferences (Hall 1995).

Even if we could retain the assumption that members' underlying preferences are entirely exogenous, members' revealed preferences are determined in part endogenously. Revealed preferences result from the interaction between members' underlying preferences and an agenda that is endogenous to the legislature. It is theoretically quite possible that the altered behavior of southern Democrats was produced not by constituency-induced changes in their underlying preferences but by changes in the relationship of those preferences to the alternatives presented in Congress. Here we will consider two sources of agenda change that very likely increased the attractiveness of partisan alternatives for southern Democrats, quite apart from any constituency-induced change in their own underlying preferences. Even taking into account the dynamics of agenda setting, however, the conclusion remains unavoidable that constituency-induced change in southern Democrats' preferences is fundamental to explaining the partisan resurgence in the House.

Partisan Agenda Setting in the House

Institutional reforms in the House set the stage for party leaders to play a much more active role in setting the agenda and manipulating outcomes. House reform occurred in the context of an institution that until the early 1970s invested substantial policy-making power in the hands of conservative southern Democratic committee chairs who attained their positions due to their longevity of service there. Party reform was undertaken by liberal Democrats in the House for the express purpose of "creat[ing] a situation in which liberal policy proposals would win more often" (Rohde 1991b: 19). By granting the Democratic caucus more influence in selecting the members and chairpersons of committees and subcommittees and by enhancing the role of the party leadership in setting the House agenda, the reforms created a situation in which the liberal majority of the party could use institutional rewards to elicit party unity. The Democratic majority in the House could thus be harnessed for the purpose of pursuing a more liberal policy agenda.

Empowered by the House reforms, Democratic leaders took actions to facilitate members' support of party positions in cases in which such support could be electorally costly otherwise. Several instances can be cited during the 1980s in which southern Democratic representatives clearly were influenced by the ability of party leaders to provide both cover and rewards for supporting the party. At the same time, members who strayed too far from the party line could potentially be denied transfers to desirable committees or advancement to committee leadership posts. The House reforms thus helped to facilitate the partisan surge among southern Democrats.

However, in another institutional context, the Senate, southern Democratic partisanship increased without substantial change in the power of party leaders (table 1.4). Senate procedures and rules have always given party leaders less formal authority and fewer power resources than are available to the House Speaker and party leadership. If anything, the House reforms of the 1970s accentuated the differences in the formal structure of leadership between the two chambers, since comparable efforts to empower party leaders to promote the policy priorities of the party caucus were largely absent in the Senate. Even so, southern Democratic senators were somehow compelled to increase their support of party positions just as their colleagues in the House were.

TABLE 1.4

Southern Democratic Party Unity Scores, 1971–1998

YEAR	HOUSE	SENATE
1971	48	56
1972	44	43
1973	55	52
1974	51	41
1975	53	48
1976	52	46
1977	55	48
1978	53	54
1979	60	62
1980	64	64
1981	57	64
1982	62	62
1983	67	70
1984	68	61
1985	76	68
1986	76	59
1987	78	80
1988	81	78
1989	77	69
1990	78	75
1991	78	73
1992	79	70
1993	84	78
1994	83	77
1995	75	76
1996	76	75
1997	78	77
1998	79	85

SOURCE: *Congressional Quarterly Almanac,* various years.

We can make a more precise comparison of the House and Senate trends with the time series intervention method used earlier. Comparing intervention models of southern Democratic party unity in the House and Senate, we find that 1979 marks the beginning of the partisan surge in both chambers (table 1.5). House southern Democrats were at first slower than their Senate colleagues to move closer

TABLE 1.5

Interruptions in Time Series of
Southern Democratic Party Unity Scores, 1973–1992

	HOUSE	SENATE
Constant	53.00****	46.50****
1975	-.50	.50
	(-.014)	(.014)
1977	1.50	4.00
	(.056)	(.148)
1979	8.00***	12.00**
	(.343)	(.507)
1981	-2.50	.00
	(-.114)	(.000)
1983	8.00***	2.50
	(.374)	(.115)
1985	8.50***	-2.00
	(.389)	(-.090)
1987	3.50*	15.50***
	(.150)	(.655)
1989	-2.00	-7.00
	(-.075)	(-.258)
1991	1.00	-.50
	(.028)	(-.014)
R^2 (adjusted)	.97****	.85****

Notes: Entries are unstandardized regression coefficients. Standardized coefficients are in parentheses.

**** $p < .001$
*** $p < .01$
** $p < .05$
* $p < .10$

to majority positions within the party. The two time series differ in another way: additional substantial increases did not occur in Senate party unity until 1987, after the major surge in the House had been completed. Republican control of the Senate in 1981–86 could certainly have reduced the incentives of southern Democrats to support party positions, even as their counterparts in the House continued to move in a partisan direction. The fact remains, however, that something other than empowered party leadership caused Senate southern Democrats to increase their support of party positions, suggesting that House partisanship too was driven by other factors.

To what extent was the growing partisanship of the House southern Democrats a product of empowered House leadership, and to what extent was it the product of the forces moving Senate southern Democrats to greater partisanship? The first column of table 1.6 reports a regression model of the annual mean House southern Democratic party unity scores with two independent variables: party unity among Senate southern Democrats and among House northern Democrats. The standardized regression coefficient for Senate southern Democrats is greater than that for House northern Democrats. Factors affecting the behavior of southern Democrats in both the House and the Senate (e.g., constituency change in the South) were more important sources of change in partisanship among House southern Democrats than were factors within the House affecting both northern and southern Democrats (e.g., the exercise of party leadership), although internal factors in the House were a contributing factor. In the Senate, by comparison, party influences affecting both northern and southern Democrats appear to have played no role in southern Democrats' rising partisanship.

The increasing party support among southern Democrats, occurring as it did in both the House and the Senate, is the result of forces acting on southern Democrats in both chambers. Change in the constituencies shared by southern senators and representatives is a likely source of partisan change in both the House and the Senate.

TABLE 1.6
Southern Democratic Party Unity in the House and Senate

	ANNUAL MEAN SOUTHERN DEMOCRATIC PARTY UNITY	
	HOUSE	SENATE
Southern Democratic party unity (Other chamber)	.547**	1.010**
Northern Democratic party unity (Same chamber)	.468*	-.161
R^2 (adjusted)	.86**	.74**

NOTES: Entries are standardized regression coefficients.
       ** $p < .001$
       * $p < .01$

Preference Change among Nonsouthern Members

The policy goals and political imperatives that drive the behavior of individual members of Congress have their ultimate origins in the nature of the constituencies from which those members are drawn. Whatever structure is imposed by legislative institutions on the expression of member preferences, those preferences are rooted in the politics of particular congressional districts. Different groups of similar congressional districts may experience varying kinds of political change at different times. Change that is isolated to one sub-set of districts can alter the types of legislative coalitions the members from those districts are willing to enter. If members of Congress have become more willing to enter partisan coalitions on legislative matters, it has probably happened because the electoral coalitions sending members of the same party to Congress have become more similar. The similarity of electoral imperatives between northern and southern Democrats is greater than it once was, and the similarity between southern Democrats and Republicans has become less.

This study is based on the assumption that the main impetus to the convergence of northern and southern Democratic roll call voting has been a liberalization of the coalitions that elect southern Democrats to Congress. Yet greater partisanship in Congress could just as well have resulted from electoral change in the North. If changing electoral imperatives over time cause both northern Democrats and Republicans to take more conservative positions in the legislature, southern Democrats could appear to have become more "liberal" without having actually changed at all.

Shifting policy perspectives among northern Democratic and Republican legislators seem to be rooted in the shifting support coalitions that typically characterize each party's electoral base. In the postwar period a steady decline has occurred in the degree to which partisanship in U.S. presidential and congressional elections divides along economic class lines (Ladd 1978; Petrocik 1981; Dalton 1988: 153–60). The decline of class differences in partisanship can be traced in part to the large influx of Democrats into the ranks of the middle classes following World War II and in part to the rise of a new set of issues. Differences between the parties persist in the attitudinal tendencies of their supporters on economic issues, but new partisan distinctions have emerged on various social, moral, and cultural issues such as abortion, crime, school prayer, and gun control. The electoral activism of organized political movements concerned with such issues has been aligned in an increasingly partisan manner: liberal social activists have become an important element of Democratic coalitions, and conservative social activists are emerging as a potent force in Republican politics.

How are these electoral trends reflected in the policy orientations of Republican and northern Democratic members of Congress? Most telling has been the declining influence of liberal Republicans in the congressional party. Fewer liberal Republicans are now elected to Congress, and their seats have been taken by socially liberal

Democrats (Rae 1989). The ranks of conservative Republicans have grown, and part of the conservative movement is infused with the political agenda of the Christian right (Rohde 1991b: 121–27). At the same time, northern Democrats entering Congress since the 1970s have been more concerned with the efficiency and effectiveness of government programs than with maintaining the liberal zeal of the Great Society or the New Deal (Rohde 1991b: 48–50). Thus since the early 1970s simultaneous rightward movements of the congressional parties have occurred on economic matters. Over roughly the same period, social issues have increasingly been debated on partisan lines in Congress. It is entirely conceivable that the rightward movements of northern Democrats and Republicans on economic questions could account for the greater partisanship of southern Democrats, even as the widening split between northern Democrats and Republicans on social issues provides a more durable basis for the occurrence of the conservative coalition of southern Democrats and Republicans.

The absence of any substantial effect of these factors on the level of cohesion among House Republicans or northern Democrats is telling, however. Certainly, these changes in Republican and northern Democratic electoral coalitions altered the possibilities for legislative coalition building with southern Democrats. It is unlikely, however, that any changes in northern constituencies that were sufficient to produce the behavioral changes among southern Democrats could have also produced the paucity of aggregate behavioral change that occurred among northern Democrats and Republicans. In any case, the changes in the electoral coalitions of northern Democrats and Republicans are marginal, representing new alignments superimposed on the preexisting New Deal economic alignment. Change in the policy preferences of southern Democrats is far more likely than change among northern Democrats and Republicans to account for the magnitude of change in southern Democrats' partisanship in the House.

SOUTHERN DEMOCRATS, REPRESENTATION, AND PARTISANSHIP

Representatives and Constituents

I have now established empirical grounds for the assumption that the partisan surge in the House in the 1980s was due primarily to the changing behavior of southern Democrats and that we should seek first to explain this behavioral change with reference to changes in representative-constituency relations. This brings us to the core question of this study: To what extent and in what respects does the increased preference for partisan outcomes expressed by southern Democrats in roll call votes reflect observable changes in the preferences and characteristics of their constituencies?

The issue of how closely legislators' preferences map onto those of their constituents is of considerable interest from the perspective of a simple normative model of representation that many democratic theorists share, either implicitly or explicitly: preferences expressed by legislators should be representative of the preferences of constituents. Yet we are faced with the issues of defining the constituency and ascertaining whether the linkage between constituency and representation is a one-way relationship.

If for no reason other than her own reelection, the legislator does well to ask, frequently if implicitly, Whom do I represent? Who are my constituents? The constitutional order in the United States establishes an electoral relationship between individual members and citizens who inhabit geographically bounded constituencies. Now, we will leave aside the observation that a candidate's ability to mobilize votes in a geographic district depends in part on her ability to recruit support and resources both within and outside the district (Herrnson 1996). It is quite likely that the acquisition of campaign resources results in members' being obligated to represent constituencies that are outside the district or whose memberships overlap with district boundaries, but members do not appear to view their constituencies this way. Even as interest groups and parties pursue national strategies in deploying campaign resources, the social and demographic characteristics of districts and the distribution of preferences within districts constitute the milieu from which congressional candidates are drawn and within which they must win the votes of a plurality of the electorate. Members represent geographically bounded constituencies.

Still, these geographically bounded districts should not be viewed as undifferentiated masses of constituents. Multiple constituencies are embedded in each member's district, and assessments of the nature of representation will likely have to take account of this. Richard Fenno (1978: 8–18) described the embedded constituencies that were typical of House members he observed in their districts. Geographic constituencies encompass entire district electorates. The reelection constituency is the portion of the district electorate that regularly supports the representative in general elections. The primary constituency consists of groups that are the representative's strongest supporters and is most likely to provide campaign resources at election time. In contested primaries the primary constituency is the core of the representative's support. The reelection or primary constituency can be an amalgam of groups with varying preferences or with differing priorities among issues. A representative will find herself in greater agreement or in closer communication with some groups in the district than with others.

While attempting to associate member roll call voting with constituency attitudes or characteristics, it is important to keep in mind that member preferences are not entirely exogenous to the legislative process. Let us take that observaton a step further. Not only does the political process in the legislature, and among political elites more generally, influence the content of legislators' preferences. There is substantial evidence also that the relationship between the positions taken by elites (including legislators) and the attitudes of the mass public (i.e., constituents) is often a reciprocal one (Kuklinski and Segura 1995; Hill and Hurley 1999). Elites take positions and pursue policies in response to changes in public opinion (Stimson 1991; Page and Shapiro 1983, 1992). At the same time, changes in aggregate public opinion show an association with changes in government policies (Stimson 1991; Page and Shapiro 1992), and elite cues can be shown to play a large role in the formation of mass attitudes (Zaller 1992). In partisan realignments, mass voting behavior responds to changes in both the salience of issues and the alignment of political elites (Sundquist 1983; Carmines and Stimson 1989).

Interactions with constituents provide an opportunity for legislators to "explain" their votes (Fenno 1978; Kingdon 1989; Bianco 1994). These explanations provide information with which constituents adjust their attitudes toward issues, incumbents, or parties (Carmines and Kuklinski 1990). On issues that are highly salient and that define the differences between the political parties, the behavior of legislators can alter the attitudes of the mass public. The emergence of a new salient issue on which elites split on party lines will induce some individuals to adjust their attitudes in the direction of those of their own party, while others will respond by sorting themselves into new party attachments (Carmines and Stimson 1989; Adams 1997). Legislative behavior can thus be the cause as well as the result of change in the preferences of members' reelection and primary constituencies.

These considerations are relevant to a central concern of this study, the relative influence of constituency and party in member behavior. Party and constituency often have been regarded as competing influences: when party and constituency pressures on a member of Congress are in conflict, he or she is more constrained to follow constituency preferences than party cues (Kingdon 1981). The partisan surge of the 1980s thus raises several questions. Is the partisan surge the product of (1) more empowered party leadership, (2) greater consistency between constituency and party pressures, or (3) some combination of the two? I proceed under the assumption that we should look first to assessing the degree to which increased southern Democratic partisanship reflects greater consistency between constituency and party pressures.

Individual Members and Aggregate Change:
Member Replacement and Adjustment

The relationship between individual members and the changing aggregate partisan behavior of southern Democrats might be characterized in some combination of three ways, in each of which constituency change is a progressively more important and proximate explanation of changing partisanship. First, a simple replacement of the most conservative southern Democrats by Republicans (or their defection to the Republican Party) could account for all of the increase in mean partisanship among the remaining southern Democrats in the absence of any fundamental change in their constituencies. Second, increased aggregate partisanship could be the result of more recently elected cohorts of southern Democrats being more liberal than their predecessors. This would imply that incumbency advantages and candidate recruitment processes play a decisive role in the character of a given district's representation and that fundamental constituency change has at best an indirect influence on southern Democratic partisanship. Third, behavioral change by incumbent members of Congress could account for greater partisanship among southern Democrats, indicating a response by sitting officeholders to political change. To the degree that behavioral change among incumbents is an important source of the increased partisanship of southern Democrats, it strengthens the case for scrutinizing constituency change in the South as the explanation for increased partisanship.

Behavioral change of the magnitude necessary to produce the partisan changes witnessed among southern Democrats is rarely observed in Congress. Representatives typically display a high degree of consistency in their roll call voting over time (Clausen

1973: 70–77; Asher and Weisberg 1978; Stone 1982; Kingdon 1989: 274–278; Poole and Rosenthal 1997). As a result, rapid change in the dominant congressional roll call coalition is normally associated with a "critical election," in which one or more social groups switch party allegiance and party control of Congress changes hands. Changes in public policy are associated with the change in party control, and these changes serve to reinforce the new partisan loyalties in the electorate (Key 1955; Burnham 1971; Brady 1978). New members are important actors in partisan change in Congress, because (1) they are likely to be members of the new majority party replacing members of the old majority party and (2) they are more likely than incumbent members to be sensitive to the issue concerns of groups that are new to their party's coalition, since their electoral victories are more likely to have depended on their party's new constituencies. Thus critical elections not only produce a new party balance in the Congress but also infuse Congress with new definitions of the policy stands that distinguish the parties (Brady 1978).

Applying the critical election model of congressional party politics to the more gradual partisan surge of the late 1970s and 1980s, one might expect that new members were the dominant source of the aggregate increase in partisanship among southern Democrats. New cohorts did contribute to the higher average partisanship, to be sure. Republicans were more likely to replace conservative than liberal southern Democrats, and later entering cohorts of southern Democrats tended to have more liberal voting records than earlier cohorts (Bullock 1981; Shaffer 1987; Whitby and Gilliam 1991; Hood and Morris 1998).

Cohort effects notwithstanding, however, a large component of the change in southern Democratic roll call voting came through the changing behavior of sitting representatives. David W. Rohde (1989: 140–41) has analyzed the effects of behavioral and membership change on the party unity scores of southern Democrats who served between 1977 and 1985 (the period of major increase in partisanship among southern Democrats); he observed a combination of behavioral change within cohorts and greater partisanship of new cohorts. The forty-one southern Democrats whose service began in 1977 or before and who served the entire 1977–85 period increased their average party unity score from 57 in 1977 to 69 in 1983 and 70 in 1985. The eleven members of the 1978–79 cohort of southern Democrats demonstrated a similar increase, from 59 in 1979 to 64 in 1983 (63 in 1985). The average party unity among the six southern Democrats entering in 1980–81 increased from 47 in 1981 to 52 in 1983 and 1985. The 1983 and 1985 cohorts of southern Democrats, totaling twenty-four members, entered the House with average party unity scores of 71 in their first terms. These members were more partisan on average than previous cohorts in 1985, with an average party unity score of 72 compared to 67 among the fifty-eight incumbents from previous cohorts. Before 1983, however, new cohorts can account for none of the increase in partisanship, as those of 1979 and 1981 were less partisan than those entering in 1977 and before. Behavioral change within cohorts is absolutely essential for explaining the partisan trend in the period 1977–83. These observations support the notion that the movement of southern Democratic representatives toward the positions of their northern colleagues reflects an adjustment by both incumbents and new members to a fundamental change in southern politics.

SOUTHERN DEMOCRATS AND THEORIES OF PARTY IN CONGRESS

The party's role in the representation of constituent preferences is inextricably tied to its role in the legislative process. Among the approaches to legislative parties that find currency among congressional scholars today, this book fits the "conditional party government" approach (Rohde 1991b: 31–34). The assertion that a given legislature is characterized by "party government" implies that partisan institutions and strategies are central in the formation of public policy. The theory of conditional party government holds that party government—the empowerment of party leaders by party members to influence legislative outcomes—will occur under specified conditions.

The existence of relative preference homogeneity among party members is central to the conditional emergence of party government in Congress. In either house of Congress, to the extent that conflict among preferences within the majority party is low and that conflict between the parties is high, the necessary conditions for party government are satisfied. These conditions make it likely that party members, particularly of the chamber majority, will empower their leaders to pursue a partisan agenda and to sanction party members who hamper that agenda significantly.[3] Such outcomes were evident in the House Democratic caucus during the 1980s (Crook and Hibbing 1985; Rohde 1991b), as well as in the Republican caucus after that party won a House majority in 1994 (Aldrich and Rohde 1995, 1996a, 1996b; Rohde 1995a).

Other theories explain the organization of Congress with little reference to parties. Some depict the congressional policy-making process as designed to facilitate the distribution of benefits as widely as possible among members. Sometimes referred to as distributive theories of congressional organization, these approaches explain the formation of committees and the fashioning of rules as mechanisms to promote the goal of efficient logrolling among members with salient interests in different policy domains (e.g., Shepsle 1979; Weingast 1979; Weingast and Marshall 1988). An alternative approach, informational theory, explains the committees and procedures of Congress as designed to maximize expertise in specific jurisdictional areas by providing incentives to individual members to specialize and perform legislative work (e.g., Gilligan and Krehbiel 1989, 1990; Krehbiel 1991). In neither of these approaches are party organizations typically depicted as playing an independent role in governing Congress. In the distributive approach, party leadership is at best a set of roles that maintain the committee logrolling structure (Mayhew 1974). In the informational approach, parties are simply epiphenomena, reflective of the distribution of exogenous policy preferences (Krehbiel 1991, 1993).

Note that partisan outcomes reflecting within-party agreement and interparty difference in the underlying preferences of members can be predicted without any reference to legislative parties as having an independent influence (Krehbiel 1991, 1993). However, approaches that ignore the role of party in the legislature ignore two critical facts. First, revealed member preferences are not entirely exogenous to the legislative process, and a prominent organizational feature such as party leadership can thus influence member behavior independently of other preference-forming influences. Second, constituency attitudes are not necessarily ordered on a single ideological dimension, a point that is clearly relevant to the behavior of southern Democrats. Rather than simply assume that party has no independent influence and that partisan roll call voting simply reflects members' placement on a single liberal-conservative spectrum, theories of legislative behavior should allow for the possibility of an independent role for party.

Conditional party government specifies that the members of the legislative party are likely to empower party leaders under conditions of intraparty homogeneity of preferences. Holding similar preferences gives party members an incentive to empower party institutions within the legislature because of (1) the potential instability of outcomes when preferences are ordered on more than one dimension and/or (2) the existence of a collective action problem in which individual legislators gain by defecting from a position that is in the collective interest of a group (Aldrich 1995: 28–45). The first of these conditions, known as Arrow's paradox (Arrow 1951), is a well-known result of the formal approach to social choice. A number of theories are devoted to the role of legislative organization in overcoming the potential inability of majorities to produce stable legislative outcomes. Among the possible means depicted in distributive theories for enforcing collective outcomes on behalf of legislators are the committee system and its associated norms of reciprocity (respect for committee jurisdictions) and universalism (pass all projects; Weingast 1979). Another possible means of enforcing collective outcomes is empowering party leaders. The conditional party government approach holds that legislative party members in substantial agreement on a salient policy dimension (and facing opposition from outside the party) are likely to empower their party leaders to enforce the party's collective interests.

Changes over time in interparty and intraparty differences among members of the legislature are driven primarily by changes in the degree of difference among members' constituencies. This tenet of the conditional party government approach is especially important in the American context of weak parties and "candidate-centered politics" (Wattenberg 1991). In the absence of strong party organizations able to impose sanctions in the electoral arena, the conditions for party government in Congress rest squarely on the degree of similarity between legislators' typical constituents of their attitudes toward issues.

In assessing this similarity across districts, it is crucial to take account of the different subsets of constituents within districts (Fiorina 1973; Rohde 1991a). Similarity of constituency attitudes among legislative party members may derive from similarity of their geographic, reelection, or primary constituencies (Fenno 1978: 8–18). Changes in the degree of similarity among a legislative party's geographic constituencies—entire district electorates—can be produced by cultural or demographic change or by the replacement of one party by another in a group of similar districts. Within each geographic constituency, competition between the two parties in congressional elections produces an election or reelection constituency for each party. Changes in the degree of similarity among a legislative party's reelection constituencies are instrumental in altering the degree of intraparty homogeneity among its members: two representatives are more likely to exhibit similar legislative behavior when their reelection constituents hold similar attitudes (Fiorina 1973). Interparty difference and intraparty homogeneity of members' primary constituencies can be similarly altered by electoral change. Even in the absence of change in the geographic constituencies of members, changes in the distribution of policy preferences between the reelection constituencies of the two parties in some districts can alter the homogeneity of member preferences within one or both legislative parties.

The conditional party government approach suggests that partisanship can vary not only over time but also across issue dimensions at a given point. If my description of constituent attitudes in the South turns out to be correct, southern Democrats are closer to northern Democrats on some issues than on others. In this situation, empowered partisan leadership may play a role. A purpose of the legislative party is to enforce outcomes agreed on by party members with regard to some overriding principle and to discourage members from defecting in order to pursue favored outcomes on secondary dimensions (Aldrich 1995b: 37–45, 77–82). On salient issues for which intraparty agreement is low, however, it is more difficult for party leadership to overcome incentives to defect. The effective exercise of party leadership consists in part in understanding when such incentives are insurmountable. For instance, Rohde (1991b) documents several instances in which Democratic leaders in the House took pains to structure alternatives so that on some bills southern Democrats could take positions favored by some constituents back home without jeopardizing the final content of party-endorsed legislation.

We should find, then, that the propensity of southern Democrats to support partisan outcomes varies across issue areas, as well as according to district characteristics that render their constituencies more or less similar to those of northern Democrats. At the same time, we can expect a degree of slippage in the connection between constituency attitudes and party support, caused by the exercise of party leadership or by the influence of partisan ties on member attitudes. If representatives' behavior has a reciprocal impact on constituency opinion, we can also project that partisan roll call votes on salient issues may reinforce or create new partisan divisions within district electorates.

CATALYSTS OF
CONSTITUENCY CHANGE

Assessing the connection between constituency change and roll call change among southern Democrats requires (1) describing the parameters of change and continuity in the preferences and characteristics of southern Democrats' constituencies over the two decades from the early 1970s to the late 1980s; and (2) describing the parameters of change and continuity in roll call voting over the same period, in the process assessing how closely the southern Democratic partisan surge maps onto observable constituency change. For the first task, Rohde's (1991a) study of the constituency roots of the increased southern Democratic partisanship provides a useful point of departure. He describes three transformations in southern politics during the last thirty years that have resulted in greater similarity between the South and the North in the electoral coalitions that support Democratic representatives. First, the mobilization of large numbers of previously disfranchised African American voters in the 1960s and 1970s, and their strong tendency to vote Democratic, made the geographic and reelection constituencies of southern Democrats more liberal. Second, the urbanization of the South, coupled with Supreme Court decisions in the 1960s that outlawed large disparities within states in congressional district population, increased the similarity of southern Democratic districts to those of northern Democrats. Third, the rise of the Republican Party in much of the South was associated with the movement of the South's most conservative voters and politicians out of the

Democratic Party to the Republican Party, rendering the reelection constituencies of southern Democrats more liberal. Together, these three factors created greater similarity of southern with northern Democratic geographic, reelection, and primary constituencies and made it more likely that southern and northern Democratic preferences in Congress would be similar.

What is the relationship between these three transformations of southern congressional electorates and the preferences of southern Democrats' constituents? Much of the literature related to this question appears to suggest that all three are unambiguously associated with more liberal policy preferences: African Americans are more liberal than whites, urban residents are more liberal than rural residents, and Democrats are more liberal than Republicans. In examining data on constituent preferences, however, we find that the truth of all three of these statements depends on the issue area. We also find that the South exhibits geographic variation in the effects of these three forces on aggregate constituency preferences.

Black Voter Mobilization

It is generally accepted that the African American mobilization has had a liberalizing effect on southern constituencies, particularly the reelection and primary constituencies of Democrats. In the South as well as outside it, substantial interracial differences occur on economic, social welfare, and race-related questions (Lamis 1984: 218–21; Black and Black 1987: 216–19; Lublin 1997: 73–76, Whitby 1997: 8–9). Such is not the case across all issue areas, however. On several noneconomic issues—including abortion, women's rights, prayer in public schools, and military spending—the attitudes of southern blacks and whites tend to be similar (Lamis 1984: 221–24; Black and Black 1987: 216–19).

The impact of African American mobilization on aggregate constituency preferences is likely to vary not only across issues but also across districts with different racial composition. Conservative political attitudes and behavior in the South have been associated historically with higher concentrations of African Americans in the local population (Wright 1977; Knoke and Kyriazis 1977; Huckfeldt and Kohfeld 1989; Giles and Buckner 1993; Giles and Herz 1994; Glaser 1994). This relationship was reflected in Congress, where districts with larger black populations formed the geographic base of southern conservatism at midcentury (Key 1949: 378–82) and well into the 1980s (Combs, Hibbing, and Welch 1984; Whitby 1985).

Urbanization

Urbanization is often cited as a liberalizing force in southern politics. Indeed, nontraditional social influences characteristic of more urban environments—particularly education and the mass media—provide a powerful challenge to traditional agents of socialization in the South (Reed 1972). Urbanization can be more credibly linked to racial and social liberalism than to economic liberalism, however. In fact, lasting Republican success in congressional elections first became evident in urban areas, where support for Republicans was linked to higher economic status rather than to racial or social conservatism (Strong 1956, 1960; Seagull 1975; Black and Black 1987: 264–77). Thus we see that the effect of urbanization on particular members' constituencies may vary not only according to the urban or rural geography of a district, but also according to the issue area.

Recent studies also suggest that urbanization has had the effect of reversing the "black threat" effect on white attitudes. Whereas an association between black population and white conservatism exists in rural areas, the association appears to be reversed in urban areas (Voss 1996). If such is the case, then geographic variation in constituency preferences amomg rural or urban districts is potentially as important as urban-rural differences.

Republican Realignment

Regarding the rise of Republicanism in the South, it is indeed the case that the gradual defection of whites from the Democratic to the Republican Party resulted in the southern parties being divided along lines of economic status and issue attitudes, with the Republicans attracting more conservative and upper-status whites (Black and Black 1987, 1992; Carmines and Stanley 1990; Nadeau and Stanley 1993). By the late 1980s this gradual transformation appears to have been substantially complete in its redefinition of the partisan coalitions in the South. We should note, however, that the issue basis of the realignment was limited to economic matters: social and racial issues had no bearing on white southerners' party identification or presidential voting (Prysby 1989; Abramowitz 1994).

The secular realignment of southern whites' party identification was accompanied by Republican presidential candidates winning all of the South's electoral votes in 1984 and 1988 and losing only Georgia in 1980. The realignment of political offices proceeded at a much slower pace at lower electoral levels, however (Bullock 1988). Democrats were most likely to retain House seats, often with little or no opposition, in places where Republican growth was slowest— nonurbanized areas, especially those with large populations of African Americans. These were the most conservative geographic constituencies in the South, and Democrats representing such districts typically experienced a much smaller degree of liberalization of their primary and reelection constituencies than those representing other types of districts.

LINKING CONSTITUENCY CHANGE
TO CONGRESSIONAL BEHAVIOR

Multiple Issue Dimensions

Most studies of the linkage between southern constituency characteristics and roll call voting fail to explicitly take account of the full range of issue and geographic variation in constituent attitudes. With regard to issue variation, studies that focus on the impact of demographic variables on roll call change typically rely on a single indicator of party support or ideological positioning, such as party unity scores, ratings from the Americans for Democratic Action (ADA), or the NOMINATE scores developed by Keith T. Poole and Howard Rosenthal. However, given the differences across issues that one can expect to find in the attitudes of southern Democrats' constituents, it is a mistake to rely solely on a unidimensional approach. In chapter 4, I assess whether roll call change has occurred at different rates in different issue areas.

Even in the days of the conservative coalition, southern Democrats showed greater support for northern Democratic positions in the economic realm than on other issues (Key 1949; Sinclair 1977, 1981; Brady and Bullock 1980, 1981). During the Reagan years, coinciding with the partisan surge of the 1980s, North-South differences among House Democrats occurred substantially more often on defense policy than on other issues (Rohde 1994a, 1994b). Nicol C. Rae's (1994: 65–110) interviews with southern Democratic representatives and senators, most of which were conducted in 1990, reveal that the southerners identified most closely with the national party's positions on economic and civil rights issues and were far less comfortable with the party on moral and cultural issues. This evidence suggests that issue differences in southern Democratic partisanship in Congress developed in a manner similar to the issue differences in the definition of partisan reelection constituencies.

The Influence of District Characteristics

A proper test of the linkage between district-level variables and southern Democratic roll call behavior requires three determinations that have been neglected by recent studies: (1) whether the effects of Republican competition and African American concentration have increased over time, (2) whether the effect of African American population varies between urban and nonurban districts, and (3) whether differences occur across issue areas in these relationships.

We must assess change in these relationships over time, because during the period from the late 1970s to the late 1980s—when the partisan surge in southern Democratic behavior occurred—most of the variation in the independent variables is cross-sectional. The African American share of the electorate and the degree of Republican penetration in congressional elections were at fairly constant levels in this period. The two voting rights revolutions—the registration of African American voters and the drawing of minority-majority districts—occurred, respectively, before and after the partisan surge in the House. Likewise, the two major expansions of Republican contestation rates and vote share in congressional elections occurred in the 1960s and in the 1990s. In the late 1970s and 1980s, southern Democratic reaction to white defections from and black additions to their reelection constituencies must be conceptualized not as a response to the phenomena but as an increase in responsiveness to them.

Two recent models address the impact of Republican competition and African American concentration on liberal roll call voting by southern Democrats in the House. One is a time-series cross-section model that addresses whether southern Democrats were responding to demographic change in the 1980s but not whether southern Democrats were becoming more responsive to demographic variables (Hood and Morris 1998). The other is a cross-sectional model that employs too few cross sections to make comparisons across the entire period of the partisan trend (Fleisher

1993). Neither of these studies addresses the potential interaction of urban and black population. The distribution of white conservatism and the impact of urbanization on traditional channels of attitude formation in the South suggest that African American population should be associated with more liberal roll call voting among urban representatives, but with more conservative voting among rural representatives. Such a relationship had been noted in studies of roll call voting during the 1970s and early 1980s (Combs, Hibbing and Welch 1984; Whitby 1985, 1987).

THE ROLE OF SOUTHERN DEMOCRATS AFTER THE 1990s

The behavior of southern Democratic representatives during the partisan surge raises critical questions of legislator-constituent relations. Yet what is the relevance of the partisan trend among southern Democrats, largely completed by the end of the 1980s, for understanding Congress after the year 2000? After the 1992 election, the impetus to draw majority-minority districts produced an increase in the number of African Americans among southern Democrats in Congress from 5 to 17, while the number of white southern Democrats declined from 80 to 68. African American Democrats support party roll call positions at high rates, typically above 90 percent, and exhibit far less variation in partisanship than do white Democrats. The results of the 1994 election and its aftershocks further reduced the number of white southern Democrats. After the 1996 elections, 39 white Democrats represented southern congressional districts, along with 16 black Democrats and 82 Republicans. The 1994 election also took both houses of Congress out of Democratic control, making the 55 southern Democrats a small minority in the House, with a numerically much smaller impact on partisan outcomes and without the formal role they once held in majority party governance.

On initial reflection, the diminished numbers of southern Democrats in the House arguably makes a study of the roots of their increased partisanship a matter of purely historical interest. However, aside from its historical importance in establishing the environment for a more partisan congressional politics, the shifting behavior of southern Democrats remains directly relevant to understanding the creation of congressional majorities. Three interrelated factors that persist in the aftermath of the monumental electoral changes assure this relevance.

First, prospects are strong that Democrats will continue to be competitive in southern congressional elections in the forseeable future and white Democrats will continue to constitute a substantial portion of the southern congressional delegation. The 1994 election was critical with regard to the composition of the southern congressional delegation, but the party balance has returned in subsequent elections to fluctuating within a fairly narrow range. No net change occurred in the partisan distribution of southern House seats in 1998.

Second, white southern Democrats continue to display moderate behavior in the House, and substantial variation continues to exist among white southern Democrats in their degree of support for partisan roll call outcomes. In 1998 white southern Democrats averaged an adjusted party unity score of 74, compared to 93 for black southern Democrats. Southern Republicans averaged 8 percent support of the Democratic position on party unity votes. Party unity among white southern Democrats ranged from 23 to 98 percent, with a standard deviation of 17. This deviation is relatively large, compared to 6 for black southern Democrats and 4 for southern Republicans. Thus white Democrats as a group continue to hold a moderate position in southern congressional politics, while the propensity of particular white southern Democrats to cross party lines is highly variable (see also Black 1998: 605–7).

Third, southern Democrats will continue to exert critical influence on the formation of congressional majorities despite their reduced numbers, because of the close partisan balance in Congress that has resulted from the electoral changes of the 1990s. In the 102d Congress, the Democrats held 267 seats, about their average for the ten Congresses preceding the 1994 election, and they held 257 seats in the 103d. On a party line vote, the Democrats could win with as many as 39 of their members defecting to the minority. The size of the Republican majorities since the 104th Congress has been far smaller. After the 1994 election, the Republicans controlled 231 seats, a total that dwindled to 228 after 1996 and 223 after 1998. Both the closeness of these Republican majorities and the prospect that small electoral shifts could return Democrats to a similarly narrow majority status heighten the importance of southern Democrats in the creation of policy majorities, even as their numbers are reduced and their ideological distance from other Democrats has narrowed. The distance has narrowed, but it has not disappeared, and it may be as crucial as ever in a congressional politics characterized by sharply divided and closely competitive parties.

CHAPTER TWO

SOUTHERN GEOGRAPHIC CONSTITUENCIES

The research design pursued here tests a constituency-driven explanation of roll call partisanship among southern Democrats in the House of Representatives. The design entails two central tasks. The first is to establish the contours of southern Democratic constituency attitudes. Critical elements of this task are determining the variation in typical attitudes across different types of geographic constituencies, defining the issues on which partisan reelection constituencies are differentiated, and identifying potentially unique attitude formations typical of the primary constituents of southern Democrats. The second task is to test a set of hypotheses linking constituency variation to roll call partisanship. These hypotheses are discussed below, in chapters 4 and 5.

THE LIBERALIZATION OF SOUTHERN GEOGRAPHIC CONSTITUENCIES

It is frequently hypothesized that the mobilization of African American voters and the urbanization of southern congressional districts played crucial roles in the liberalization of southern Democrats' roll call voting. The Voting Rights Act gave additional impetus to efforts to register blacks in the South, and voter registration rates among African Americans increased rapidly in the late 1960s. In the eleven-state South, black voter registration increased from 29.5 percent in 1962 to 64.5 percent in 1970. As a proportion of the African American voting-age population, black registration rates fluctuated between 53 and 66 percent during the 1970s and 1980s (Timpone 1995: table A1).

The urbanization of southern congressional districts also received a major impetus in the 1960s as a result of congressional redistricting related to the "one person, one vote" decisions of the Supreme Court. In *Wesberry v. Sanders* (1964), the Supreme Court ruled it unconstitutional for states to underrepresent urban areas in drawing congressional district boundaries. Several states had permitted large disparities in population between districts, either by design or by neglect. By the end of the 1970 redistricting cycle, urban populations were more proportionately represented in congressional districts. Thus the reapportionment revolution of the 1960s combined with continued growth and subsequent redistricting since then have increased the weight of urban constituents in state congressional delegations and within congressional districts (Keefe and Ogul 1964: 76; Schwab 1988: 77–78; Rohde 1991a: 6).

As indicators of the liberalization of southern congressional constituencies, black mobilization and urbanization have both cross-sectional and temporal dimensions. My research design gives prominence to the cross-sectional dimension. In their temporal dimension, urbanization and black mobilization are seen as having created constituencies that are more liberal since the 1980s than they were in the 1960s. By adding liberal voters to what had been predominantly white conservative constituencies, these two forces created constituencies that were in the aggregate less conservative over time.

Some scholars have deduced from this temporal logic that roll call voting became more liberal in direct relation to increases in urban population and black voter registration (Hood and Morris

1998; Hood, Kidd, and Morris 1999). Such a hypothesis carries the temporal logic a bit far, however. Black voter registration had stabilized well before the beginnings of the southern Democratic partisan surge in the late 1970s, and the African American population of the typical district has not changed markedly since the 1960s (although the cross-district variation changed dramatically in the 1992 round of redistricting). As for urbanization, any effects it may have on constituency preferences cannot be efficiently represented in the House until after reapportionment and redistricting based on the next census, because it is only after the next census that the most rapidly growing areas will be proportionately represented in the House delegations of the various states.

In fact, before testing the relationship between African American and urban population and roll call voting—whether as a temporal or a cross-sectional hypothesis—we need to more closely examine the assumptions on which these hypotheses are based. In their cross-sectional dimension, the urbanization and black mobilization hypotheses are based on the assumption that African Americans have more liberal policy preferences than whites and that urban dwellers are more liberal than rural dwellers. These assumptions are fundamental to the demographic explanation of southern constituency change. The fundamental task in this chapter, then, is to closely examine the assumptions about the political preferences of white and black southerners in urban and rural settings. Would geographic constituencies deprived of their African American or urban constituents have been as likely to support the level of partisanship that southern Democrats were displaying by the late 1980s?

To answer no to this question would be fundamentally correct, but it would mask some important caveats. To the extent that the mobilization of black voters had a liberalizing influence on aggregate constituency attitudes in the South, it was with respect to questions of economics and race and not with respect to social issues such as abortion or prayer in public schools. Furthermore, the impact of African American citizens on politics was not a simple function of their numerical strength across congressional districts. On those issues on which black voter mobilization made the greatest difference for overall constituency attitudes, the most conservative whites clearly resided in rural districts where black population is most heavily concentrated. These congressional districts also had the lowest black voting rates in the late 1980s. Yet until 1994 they were the districts most likely to send Democrats to Congress.

To the extent that urbanization represents the geographic concentration of better-educated and more affluent whites, it is a distinct indicator of more liberal environments on social issues. At the same time, urbanization is associated with more conservative orientations among whites to government economic programs. Further, the relationship between black population and white attitudes in urban areas is the reverse of that in rural districts. In urban districts, more liberal whites tend to reside in areas with higher proportions of African Americans, reflecting to some degree the differences between suburban and center-city political environments. Hence, black voter mobilization and urbanization are not uniformly liberalizing influences on geographic constituencies in the South; their impact varies by issue and by demographic characteristics of the district.

RACE AND POLITICAL ATTITUDES IN THE SOUTH

Perhaps the most important outcome of the civil rights era was the incorporation into southern electorates of a large proportion of the black voting-age population. Black voter registration rates in the eleven-state South increased from 29.1 percent in 1960 to 63.7 percent in 1988; the white registration rate in 1988 was 67 percent (Conway 1991: 108). It is commonly argued that this expanded black electorate has altered the overall balance of opinions among southern voters in a liberal direction compared to what it had been before passage of the Voting Rights Act.

Whites and blacks differ substantially in their political and social attitudes, particularly regarding civil rights, economic, and social welfare policies (Lublin 1997: 73–76; Whitby 1997: 8–9). African Americans are substantially more likely to support liberal positions on economic and social welfare questions. Substantial interracial differences exist on such issues even at higher levels of income and social status (Gilliam and Whitby 1989). Although there are diverse attitudes and perspectives among the African American public, the variation is small in comparison to the differences between blacks and whites in their views of the role of government in the distribution of wealth and opportunity and the degree of progress in civil rights.[1]

It is easy to infer that in contemporary southern politics the liberalism of the total electorate varies with size of the black electorate. We should recognize, however, that the addition of black voters to southern congressional electorates has had a liberalizing effect on the balance of opinions only on some types of issues. Substantial differences exist between the opinions typical of blacks and whites on economic matters and on questions regarding civil rights and racial equality. In the South, substantial interracial differences occur on economic, social welfare, and race-related questions (Lamis 1984: 218–21; Black and Black 1987: 216–19). However, the central tendencies of the attitudes of blacks and whites have been found to be similar on several issues: abortion, women's rights, prayer in public schools, environmental protection, combating drugs, and military spending (Lamis 1984: 221–24; Black and Black 1987: 216–19). We might collectively characterize these latter issues as "noneconomic." If among southerners black and white opinions are more alike regarding some issues than others, then the mobilization of black voters has varying implications for different issue areas: the liberalizing influence of the black vote may be greater with respect to economic and civil rights issues than noneconomic issues.

Table 2.1 compares the attitudes of blacks and whites in the South on fourteen items asked by the National Election Studies (NES) in 1984–90. Table A.1 in the Appendix contains the text of these questions. On most of the issue items, black respondents hold substantially more "liberal" positions than whites. On items asking respondents to place themselves on a seven-point scale, blacks are typically closer than whites to the end of the scale that indicates support for government-run health insurance, agreement that government should guarantee citizens jobs and a good standard of living, support for busing if it is necessary to achieve school integration, support for government assistance to minorities, and opposition to increased spending on defense. Blacks are less likely than whites to respond that the position of blacks in society has advanced "a lot" recently, that civil rights leaders are pushing "too fast" for change, that government should not allow integration of schools, or that the federal government is too powerful.

The survey items on which blacks and whites differ substantially encompass an array of concerns centered on the role of government in the economy and in race relations. The magnitude of these differences, particularly with respect to questions involving race, suggests that the incorporation of blacks into southern electorates should be critical to the substance of southern representation in Congress: If legislators are responsive to something like the median voter of their respective districts, then black electoral participation will exert pressure on southern representatives to support more liberal positions in the realms of economic and civil rights policy.

Three of the items in table 2.1 are conspicuous in that they do not follow the same pattern as the rest: First, little apparent difference exists between blacks and whites in their position regarding women's role in society. Second, blacks are slightly less likely than whites to respond that abortion should always be legal. Third, and most striking, is that blacks are somewhat more likely to support allowing public school personnel to lead students in prayer. If

TABLE 2.1

Political Attitudes of Blacks and Nonblacks in the South, 1984–1990

| | MEANS | | |
| | WHITES | BLACKS | DIFFERENCE (WHITES-BLACKS) |
ITEM			
Liberal-conservative	4.44	4.06	0.38**
(7-point scale)	(1210)	(298)	
Government health insurance	4.14	3.56	0.58*
(7-point scale)	(544)	(157)	
Government guarantees jobs			
and standard of living	4.49	3.05	1.44**
(7-point scale)	(1391)	(455)	
School busing	6.26	4.87	1.39**
(7-point scale)	(197)	(45)	
Government aid to minorities	4.83	3.31	1.52**
(7-point scale)	(1640)	(523)	
Government services spending	4.10	5.06	(-0.96)**
(7-point scale)	(1535)	(454)	
Defense spending	4.22	3.79	0.43**
(7-point scale)	(1572)	(438)	
Change position of Negro	51.3	24.2	27.10**
(% responding "a lot")	(1041)	(335)	
Civil rights leadership	38.9	9.0	29.90**
(% responding "too fast")	(1017)	(324)	
Government allow school integration	60.3	13.4	46.90**
(% no)	(292)	(112)	
Government in Washington too strong	67.3	43.5	23.80**
(% yes)	(312)	(69)	
Abortion	31.0	25.7	(5.30)*
(% for "always legal")	(1846)	(587)	
School prayer	77.2	89.0	-11.80*
(% "allow")	(351)	(100)	
Women's equal role	2.88	2.94	-0.06
(7-point scale)	(1053)	(308)	

NOTES: *N* is in parentheses below each entry. In the difference column, parentheses indicate items for which a lower score or the reported category represents a more "conservative" response.
** $p < .001$.
* $p < .01$.

anything, blacks are less "liberal" than whites on these three questions. The pattern suggests that, with respect to issues that address questions of religious and social values, black political empowerment is not a force compelling change in the values articulated by southern political leaders. One can infer that black electoral mobilization has led to a liberalization of southern congressional electorates with respect to economic policy and civil rights, but one cannot draw such an inference with regard to noneconomic or social issues.

THE INTERACTION OF URBANIZATION AND TRADITIONALISM

The mobilization of African American voters was accompanied by changes in the social context in which the political attitudes of whites are formed and expressed. Many of these changes are encompassed by the term "urbanization." Urbanization is associated not only with the attitudes of whites but also with variations in the political context in which mobilized black voters must attempt to influence representation.

In confronting the question of how urbanization has changed politics in the South, one must confront common assumptions concerning the impact of the social and economic environment on political systems. Explanations of the convergence of southern and northern political patterns often rest on the notion that fundamental political change is caused (or at least indicated) by the urbanization of the South. It seems prudent to expect the social and economic upheaval that constitutes the process of urbanization to be associated with changes in the interests, attitudes, and organizational forms that are reflected in political activity. However, it is quite a leap from this expectation to the conclusion that the urbanization of the South, occurring at a different place and time from that of the North, would result in nearly identical patterns of politics.

V. O. Key was perhaps most prominent among the scholars who drew the line of inquiry into the political consequences that could be anticipated from the economic and social correlates of urbanization in the South. It is natural that more recent scholars who observe a temporal association between urbanization and political change in the South would be guided by Key's example. Urbanization was seen by Key as indicative of the degree of diversification of the southern economy due to industrialization. He anticipated two consequences of economic change for the political system: a diversification of the economic interests achieving representation and the organization of working-class interests through the growth of unionization.

The first of these two consequences amounts to the emergence of a more pluralist politics in the South. The expansion of economic concerns beyond the traditional nexus of large-scale agriculture and finance multiplies the potential conflicts over the role of government in the economy, both among the new industrialists and between industrial and more traditional economic interests. The diversification of economic interests, necessarily accompanied by the diversification of the sources of financial and other campaign support, widens the range of policy views represented in political competition (Key 1949: 673–74).

Key and others anticipated that industrialization would be accompanied by the expansion of labor organization in the South, which would serve as a vehicle for injecting lower-class interests into the new pluralist politics. At the time Key wrote, organized labor was becoming an integral part of the effort to expand political participation among blacks and working-class whites, and this role continued through the civil rights period (Bass and DeVries 1976: 392–96). The ability of labor to organize voters in some urban areas and the emergence of a class politics with the rise of presidential Republicanism in the 1950s suggested the outlines of a political system in which the interests of "those who have less" were represented in opposition to the interests of the "haves."

Given the patterns of economic and political development in the South since the 1950s, one should ask whether the linkages between the two have been precisely as anticipated. In many respects, Key's prognosis was remarkably perceptive. Economic development in the South indeed appears to be associated with a marked increase in the variety of economic interests having the motivation and resources to influence government. Agricultural and other primary product concerns must now compete with industrial and commercial interests in shaping public policy, and different industrial and commercial concerns often make competing demands on government (Black and Black 1987: 24–25, 31–32).

The impact of economic development on the political debate in the South is reflected in the ideas that have been expressed in politics.[2] Considerable evolution occurred in this regard from the early part of the century to the 1980s. In the early 1900s the "New South" movement—which was promoted by the small-town governing class—placed an emphasis on concentrating capital in a low-wage economy (Billings 1979; Weiner 1982; Cobb 1982, 1984). This vision applied to the relations between white labor and capital; traditional southern cultural patterns of racial and class relations were not to be sacrificed to the goal of economic progress (Cash 1941: 179–85). Earl Black and Merle Black (1987) apply the label "conservative modernization" to this orientation to economic progress.[3]

There were at least two critiques of the conservative vision of modernization in the South: populist and progressive. The populist appeal saw the redistribution of resources to the lower classes (of whites at least) as a much greater imperative than economic progress. Without some active redistribution of resources, pursuit of the goal of economic development, especially as the conservatives articulated it, would only perpetuate the misery of the poor (Palmer 1980). The influence of this appeal on southern political discourse in the twentieth century was sporadic, and perhaps more evident in election campaigns than in public policies.[4]

The progressive vision of modernization became more influential as the isolation of the southern labor market was eroded and
the conservative path to modernization appeared less viable (Wright
1986: chap. 8). Progressive elites sought to break the bonds of
traditionalism, which they saw as impeding the development of a
skilled labor force and of an entrepreneurial class. Progressivism
did not contemplate direct redistribution of resources to the poor.
Instead, progressives viewed upgrading the labor force and
achieving high rates of economic growth as a means of solving the
region's poverty (Black and Black 1987).

Progressivism came to replace conservatism as the dominant
southern approach to economic development. This evolution was
testament to the impact of industrialization on political debate in the
South. It indicated, however, that debate on economic issues was to
a large extent limited to the concerns of business-oriented elites. By
the 1980s southern politics had not fully realized the expectation that
labor unions and other working-class organizations would emerge
to represent the economic interests of the lower classes. Even as the
size and composition of the southern workforce became comparable
in broad terms to the northern labor force, unionization rates
remained very low in most southern states (Black and Black 1987:
64–66), and the AFL-CIO continued to play a small and inconsistent
role in financing congressional campaigns (Theilmann and White
1990). In several areas organized labor appeared to have influence
in matters of public policy and to be able to deliver blocs of votes, but
it may have been more effective in reinforcing patterns of black
political organization than in mobilizing working-class whites (Bass
and DeVries 1976: 392–96). Here it should be noted that on average
there are greater differences in the South between working-class
whites and blacks than between working-class and upper-class
whites with respect to economic ideology and issue attitudes (Black
and Black 1987: 66–72, 213–19).

The failure of labor to take a stronger role in the politics of the
industrial era in the South is perhaps explainable in part by the

peculiar pattern of southern industrialization. Industrial and urban development in the South have coincided in time, but virtually no association exists between levels of urbanization and the location of industrial employment. Southern industrial concerns are just as likely to be scattered about the rural areas as they are to be located in urban centers. Decentralized employment is particularly characteristic of the low-wage and small-scale industries that have been prominent in the economic development of the South (Black and Black 1987: 32–33).

If urbanization in the South has been weakly associated with the concentration of the industrial working class, it has been more strongly associated with the concentration of the middle class employed in commercial pursuits. One might well expect to find among more urbanized electorates in the South a more diverse set of perspectives on economic development than in less urban areas, but one should not necessarily expect to find generally more favorable attitudes toward lower-class interests among urban residents. As a matter of fact, the increased incomes that accompany middle-class employment in urban areas are likely to be associated with lower support for programs involving government spending, particularly to redistribute income.

If it is not unreasonable to anticipate an association between urban residence and conservative attitudes on economic issues, how is it that urbanization is typically connected in theory to the liberalization of politics? The economic transformation characteristic of urban areas in the South alters not only the balance of economic interests but also the context in which attitudes are formed on social and racial matters. Social and racial liberalism rest on the emerging economy's need for a pool of well-educated labor and resident management and on its reliance on labor and capital markets that are far more integrated with those of the national and international economy than in the past (Wright 1986: chap. 8).

Relatively high average levels of education are thus a critical characteristic of the new urban South. The impact of education on political attitudes is not beyond debate. Does education lead to greater tolerance of social and racial differences (Stouffer 1955; Prothro and Grigg 1960)? Or does education instead enhance the capacity of group members to understand and defend their own economic and political interests, as opposed to the interests of other groups (Jackman and Muha 1984)? For whites in the modern South, these two results are not contradictory. Educated urban whites are likely to comprehend that their economic standing is not threatened by black gains in basic civil rights and social relations, particularly since the legacy of segregated workforces and educational systems has left blacks in a poor position to compete in a rapidly changing economy. Moreover, the better educated understand the link between the quality of race relations and the willingness of northern capital and personnel to migrate South. The same goes for the importance of maintaining a social environment that does not repress cultural or religious differences. These are critical issues given the dependence of the industrial and commercial sectors of the southern economy on infusions of outside capital and expertise. Educated whites are the likeliest participants in the urban economy. Maintaining the unattractive aspects of southern tradition is not in their interest (Wright 1986: 257–69).

Aside from the independent role it potentially plays in the development of political tolerance, educational opportunity constitutes one of a number of challenges in the urban environment to traditional channels of political learning in the South. John Shelton Reed (1972: 84–87) develops the idea that persistence and change in the maintenance of the distinct value orientations of southern culture can be explained by reference to the competing socializing influences: religion and family versus education and mass media. More liberal social and cultural attitudes not typically a part of traditional southern outlooks are associated with the displacement of southern religion as a socializing influence by other more "modern" agents of socialization. Urbanization entails the multiplication of modern influences. Nonfundamentalist denominations are likely to be more visible, mass media outlets are more numerous, and education is more attainable in urban areas. The presence of forces that can potentially undermine individuals' integration in and commitment to a religious denomination can potentially reduce the role of religious outlook as a cue or organizing principle for political values and attitudes.[5]

Reed (1972) and others have emphasized religion as an especially important agent of socialization in the South. Christian fundamentalism is in a particularly strong position in southern culture, compared to other regions. A study by Ted Jelen (1982) seems to indicate that nonreligious influences and attachments are less able to withstand the influence of fundamentalism in the South than elsewhere in the United States. In the South, children of parents with no church affiliation were far more likely to adopt fundamentalism than children of parents affiliated with a nonfundamentalist faith. No such differences in the proclivity to adopt fundamentalism occurred among nonsoutherners (Jelen 1982: 76–85).

It is frequently observed that particular variants of religiosity are associated with lower levels of tolerance of groups whose culture or political beliefs place them outside the mainstream (Stouffer 1955). The fundamentalist outlook and affiliation with Protestant evangelical denominations are associated with conservatism on a range of issues, especially social issues (Wald 1997: 179–88, 201). Historically, religion has reflected itself in various ways in southern political patterns. For instance, southern counties with higher rates of Baptist church membership among whites had lower rates of black voter registration before the voting rights era (Matthews and Prothro 1966: 129–30). A connection between religious fundamentalism and social conservatism also is evident in more recent studies of southerners, particularly convention delegates in both political parties (Steed, Moreland, and Baker 1990).

Bringing together the attributes of income, education, and religion, figure 2.1 summarizes the likeliest paths by which urbanized

Figure 2.1   Urbanization and the Attitudes of Southern Whites

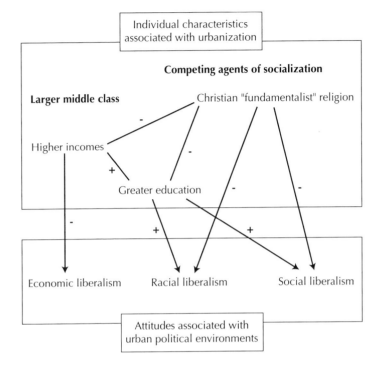

political contexts might be associated with peculiar attitudinal patterns among white southerners. In short, urban contexts should be associated with more liberal white attitudes on social and racial issues. Yet urban political settings should not necessarily be characterized by more liberal economic attitudes. In fact, urban areas in the South may be bastions of economic conservatism.

URBANIZATION AND SOUTHERN GEOGRAPHIC CONSTITUENCIES

To investigate the impact of urbanization on the typical attitudes of southern geographic constituents, I have divided the southern white voters in the combined NES sample for 1984–90 into two groups: one residing in congressional districts having urban populations above the mean for all southern districts and the other in districts with urban populations below the southern mean.[6]

Table 2.2 compares the attitudes of white southerners in these two groups. The figures depict an association between urban contexts and liberal attitudes among whites on four items. These items include only one of the four questions that more or less directly address race but all three of the questions used here to tap attitudes on "social" issues: respondents in more urban districts were less likely to think that civil rights leaders were attempting to move too fast to achieve their goals, less likely to believe that prayer should be allowed in public schools, more likely to feel that abortion should always be legal, and more inclined to answer that women's social roles should be equal to men's.

Only two other items listed in table 2.2 display substantial differences in attitudes between respondents from rural and urban districts: urban residents tended to place themselves farther than did rural residents from responding that spending should be increased on government services and that government should guarantee everyone a job and a good standard of living. It appears

TABLE 2.2

Urbanization of Congressional District and Political Attitudes of Southern Whites, 1984–1990

| ITEM | URBAN POPULATION OF CONGRESSIONAL DISTRICT (RELATIVE TO MEAN) | | DIFFERENCE (ABOVE - BELOW) |
	ABOVE	BELOW	
Civil rights leadership (% responding "too fast")	32.6 (534)	46.0 (483)	-13.40***
Abortion (% for "always legal")	35.0 (999)	26.3 (847)	(8.70)***
Women's equal role (7-point scale)	2.75 (571)	3.03 (482)	-0.28*
School prayer (% "allow")	74.0 (204)	81.6 (147)	-7.60*
Government health insurance (7-point scale)	4.06 (291)	4.23 (253)	-0.17
Government allow school integration (% no)	58.4 (154)	62.3 (138)	-3.90
Government in Washington too strong (% yes)	66.3 (184)	68.8 (128)	-2.50
Defense spending (7-point scale)	4.20 (875)	4.25 (697)	-0.05
Change position of Negro (% responding "a lot")	51.1 (548)	51.5 (493)	-0.40
Government services spending (7-point scale)	3.98 (856)	4.24 (682)	(-0.26**)
Government guarantee job and standard of living (7-point scale)	4.59 (757)	4.38 (634)	0.21*
School busing (7-point scale)	6.37 (116)	6.11 (81)	0.26

TABLE 2.2 (continued)

ITEM	URBAN POPULATION OF CONGRESSIONAL DISTRICT (RELATIVE TO MEAN)		DIFFERENCE (ABOVE - BELOW)
	ABOVE	BELOW	
Liberal-conservative	4.47	4.40	0.07
(7-point scale)	(698)	(512)	
Government aid to minorities	4.86	4.79	0.07
(7-point scale)	(899)	(741)	

NOTES: N is in parentheses below each entry. In the difference column, parentheses indicate items for which a lower score or the reported category represents a more "conservative" response.
*** $p < .005$.
** $p < .01$.
* $p < .05$.

that, to the extent that the urbanization of congressional districts is related to the economic attitudes of whites, the association links urban residence to greater conservatism.

Urban political settings in the South are associated with conservative economic attitudes and liberal social attitudes. The theoretical discussion above suggests that the pattern of opinion in urban districts can be explained with reference to the demographic attributes of the individuals who reside there. Table 2.3 shows that among southern whites included in the 1984–90 NES surveys, those respondents with college educations and with incomes in the upper third of the national sample comprise a substantially larger portion of the population of urban districts than of rural ones. Only a slightly lower percentage of urban than of rural respondents identify themselves with a fundamentalist denomination.[7] One must proceed with caution in concluding that more urbanized electorates in the South are less susceptible to fundamentalist socializing influences, but one can reliably conclude that the relatively

TABLE 2.3

Demographic Characteristics of White Respondents
by Level of Urbanization of Congressional District, 1984–1990

ITEM	URBAN POPULATION OF CONGRESSIONAL DISTRICT (RELATIVE TO MEAN)		DIFFERENCE (ABOVE - BELOW)
	ABOVE	BELOW	
College education (%)	38.5 (1023)	31.0 (864)	7.50*
Income (% in upper 1/3 of national sample)	29.8 (934)	22.0 (799)	7.80*
Religion (% fundamentalist)	41.8 (760)	45.1 (617)	-3.30

NOTES: N is in parentheses below each entry. In the difference column, parentheses indicate items for which a lower score or the reported category represents a more "conservative" response.
  * $p < .0001$.

wealthy and better-educated middle-class southerners are more likely to reside in urban districts than in rural ones.[8]

INDIVIDUAL ATTRIBUTES AND THE ATTITUDES OF SOUTHERN WHITES

Are the demographic attributes associated with urbanization also associated with political attitudes? Higher levels of education are clearly linked to more liberal responses on a range of survey items, all of which concern social or racial matters (table 2.4). In contrast, the college educated are the most conservative group on three economic questions: government spending, national health insurance, and the role of government in guaranteeing jobs and living standards.

TABLE 2.4

Political Attitudes of Southern Whites by Level of Education, 1984–1990

	LEVEL OF EDUCATION		
ITEM	BELOW HIGH SCHOOL	HIGH SCHOOL	COLLEGE OR ABOVE
***Abortion	15.2	27.6	42.7
(% for "always legal")	(276)	(918)	(646)
***Women's equal role	3.57	3.06	2.39
(7-point scale)	(148)	(513)	(392)
***School prayer	87.2	84.8	62.7
(% "allow")	(47)	(178)	(126)
***Change position of Negro	61.7	54.7	42.8
(% responding "a lot")	(149)	(501)	(388)
*Civil rights leadership	40.1	43.3	32.7
(% responding "too fast")	(147)	(210)	(125)
***Government services spending	4.46	4.29	3.77
(7-point scale)	(193)	(715)	(624)
***Government health insurance	3.26	4.04	4.51
(7-point scale)	(65)	(256)	(223)
***Government guarantee job and standard of living	4.13	4.37	4.77
(7-point scale)	(196)	(656)	(536)
Government in Washington too strong	64.5	65.0	69.6
(% yes)	(31)	(123)	(158)
School busing	6.19	6.39	6.10
(7-point scale)	(26)	(103)	(68)
Government allow school integration	61.9	62.1	56.9
(% no)	(42)	(132)	(116)
**Defense spending	4.12	4.35	4.09
(7-point scale)	(186)	(751)	(629)
**Liberal-conservative	4.08	4.52	4.43
(7-point scale)	(106)	(534)	(567)
*Government aid to minorities	4.70	4.95	4.71
(7-point scale)	(213)	(792)	(629)

NOTES: N is in parentheses below each entry.
*** $p < .001$.
** $p < .01$.
* $p < .05$.

The pattern of association between survey responses and income is similar (table 2.5). Respondents with high incomes are the most liberal group with respect to the role of women, abortion, and the extent of progress that has occurred in black civil rights. The highest incomes are accompanied by the most conservative responses on items involving economic concerns: government spending, national health insurance, government guarantees of jobs and living standards, and government aid to minorities. Comparing the impact of education and income, one finds both associated with more liberal attitudes on racial issues and especially on social issues but with more conservative attitudes on economic issues.

The impact of religious affiliation follows a different pattern (table 2.6). On all but two of the fourteen survey items examined here, fundamentalists gave more conservative responses than other southerners, although the difference attains statistical significance on only seven of them. The seven items include all three of the religious/social questions, three of the items on race (including the "government aid to minorities" item), and the question on health insurance.

Fundamentalist religion, low levels of education, and lower incomes all tend to be accompanied by greater conservatism on social and racial issues. This pattern emerges fairly clearly in tables 2.4 through 2.6, and one might expect it given the interrelationships among education, religion, and income. Among the southern whites in the 1984–90 NES samples, higher education is positively associated with having an income in the upper third of the national sample ($r = .32$). Membership in a fundamentalist denomination has a negative correlation with both college education ($r = -.11$) and high income ($r = -.14$).

The demographic correlates of economic attitudes are less easily summarized than racial and social attitudes. Consider the question of government-provided health insurance. It makes sense that people with higher incomes are less likely to favor a government role in health insurance, since such a policy is less likely to serve

TABLE 2.5

Political Attitudes of Southern Whites by Income Level, 1984–1990

| ITEM | INCOME RELATIVE TO NATIONAL SAMPLE | | |
	BOTTOM THIRD	MIDDLE THIRD	TOP THIRD
***Abortion	22.9	34.2	40.2
(% for "always legal")	(638)	(211)	(448)
***Women's equal role	3.43	2.70	2.39
(7-point scale)	(341)	(375)	(254)
*Change position of Negro	53.9	50.7	46.6
(% responding "a lot")	(336)	(351)	(130)
School prayer	79.2	76.4	72.6
(% "allow")	(106)	(123)	(84)
School busing	6.40	6.19	6.10
(7-point scale)	(50)	(74)	(50)
***Government services spending	4.47	4.05	3.72
(7-point scale)	(487)	(518)	(416)
***Government health insurance	3.46	4.08	4.79
(7-point scale)	(154)	(199)	(152)
***Government guarantee job and standard of living	4.03	4.47	5.14
(7-point scale)	(457)	(464)	(359)
**Liberal-conservative	4.22	4.47	4.54
(7-point scale)	(313)	(423)	(379)
***Government aid to minorities	4.56	4.98	4.94
(7-point scale)	(535)	(557)	(429)
Government in Washington too strong	67.1	65.1	69.1
(% yes)	(73)	(126)	(97)
Civil rights leadership	38.4	41.4	35.8
(% responding "too fast")	(323)	(350)	(274)
Government allow school integration	58.8	60.4	59.3
(% no)	(97)	(91)	(86)
Defense spending	4.10	4.30	4.23
(7-point scale)	(471)	(554)	(426)

NOTES: *N* is in parentheses below each entry.
      *** $p < .001$.
      ** $p < .01$.
      * $p < .05$.

TABLE 2.6

Political Attitudes of Southern Whites by Religious Affiliation, 1984–1988

	RELIGIOUS AFFILIATION	
ITEM	FUNDAMENTALIST OR EVANGELICAL PROTESTANT	OTHER
***Abortion	20.2	36.8
(% for "always legal")	(584)	(758)
***Women's equal role	3.25	2.66
(7-point scale)	(359)	(445)
**School prayer	88.7	72.6
(% "allow")	(150)	(179)
***Change position of Negro	58.4	46.3
(% responding "a lot")	(358)	(434)
***Civil rights leadership	47.2	31.3
(% responding "too fast")	(345)	(435)
***Government aid to minorities	5.00	4.61
(7-point scale)	(512)	(677)
**Government health insurance	4.43	3.94
(7-point scale)	(228)	(285)
Government guarantee job and standard of living	4.70	4.46
(7-point scale)	(423)	(537)
Government allow school integration	74.6	60.5
(% no)	(71)	(76)
School busing	6.38	6.25
(7-point scale)	(69)	(114)
Defense spending	4.39	4.24
(7-point scale)	(509)	(656)
Liberal-conservative	4.57	4.41
(7-point scale)	(394)	(513)
Government services spending	4.06	4.01
(7-point scale)	(485)	(650)
Government in Washington too strong	67.2	67.7
(% yes)	(125)	(167)

NOTES: N is in parentheses below each entry.
  *** $p < .001$.
  ** $p < .01$.
  * $p < .05$.

their economic interests. Individuals with college educations are also less supportive of government-provided health coverage, perhaps because the college educated have higher incomes. Yet fundamentalists, who tend to have less education and lower incomes, are also less supportive of national health insurance than are other respondents.

On the question of the government's role in providing jobs, responses follow a pattern similar to the ones regarding health insurance: conservatism is associated with higher incomes and higher education, but also with religious fundamentalism. The same can be said of the "government aid to minorities" question, except that no clear association occurs between education and support or opposition to programs benefiting blacks. Responses are clearly associated with income: people with higher incomes are less supportive of the government taking extensive action in this area. Yet fundamentalists, who are less likely than other southerners to have high incomes, are also less supportive of government aid to minorities. Fundamentalism contributes to a conservative outlook on economic issues and thereby appears to strengthen the links between economic conservatism and racial and social conservatism.

To the extent that urbanization represents the geographic concentration of better-educated and more affluent whites, urban political contexts in the South are characterized by a relatively more liberal environment on racial and social matters—but by a relatively more conservative orientation to government programs. One supreme irony is that the whites with the greatest material stake in maintaining at least the appearance of racial harmony also have the greatest material stake in limiting government spending on social welfare and job creation. This tension complicates the creation of black-white coalitions in urban areas just as surely as more overt racial differences do in the countryside.

URBANIZATION AND THE PERSISTENCE OF
THE BLACK BELT

In the South conservative racial attitudes among whites were historically associated with the proportion of blacks in the local population (Glaser 1994). If the effect of the Voting Rights Act has been to achieve black voter mobilization rates comparable to those of whites in each political jurisdiction, then the largest increments of black voters have been added to the electorate in precisely those jurisdictions where the white electorate is most conservative. The base of southern conservatism in Congress at midcentury was that set of districts with the larger black populations (Key 1949: 378–82, 670). The most conservative political behavior has tended to come from whites living in areas with many blacks (Knoke and Kyriazis 1977; Wright 1977; Huckfeldt and Kohfeld 1989; Giles and Buckner 1993; Giles and Hertz 1994).

Table 2.7 is one more illustration of the association of white conservatism with black population. Three of the fourteen survey items examined show a statistically significant difference in political attitudes between whites who reside in districts with relatively large black populations and whites from districts with relatively few blacks.[9] All three of the items concern racial issues: whether civil rights leaders are pushing too fast for change, whether public schools should be integrated, and how much the government should help minorities to get ahead. This evidence confirms a link between white conservatism on racial issues and the numerical size of the black population in the congressional district.

Such results confirm the "racial threat" hypothesis—that white support for racial conservatism is correlated with the size of the black population. Recent tests of the racial threat hypothesis in voting behavior suggest that the impact of racial context on issue attitudes should be reexamined. On the basis of models that include an interaction term for percent black and percent urban, D. Stephen

TABLE 2.7

Political Attitudes of Southern Whites by Level of Black Concentration in Congressional District, 1984–1990

ITEM	BLACK POPULATION OF CONGRESSIONAL DISTRICT		
	ABOVE MEAN	BELOW MEAN	(ABOVE - BELOW)
Civil rights leadership	46.4	33.6	12.80***
(% responding "too fast")	(427)	(590)	
Government allow school integration	66.9	55.6	11.30**
(% no)	(121)	(171)	
Government aid to minorities	4.95	4.75	0.20**
(7-point scale)	(675)	(965)	
School busing	6.45	6.14	0.31
(7-point scale)	(78)	(119)	
Government guarantee job and standard of living	4.60	4.42	0.18
(7-point scale)	(575)	(816)	
Defense spending	4.30	4.16	0.14
(7-point scale)	(654)	(918)	
Women's equal role	2.97	2.82	0.15
(7-point scale)	(436)	(617)	
Government in Washington too strong	71.1	64.7	6.40
(% yes)	(128)	(184)	
Government health insurance	4.17	4.12	0.05
(7-point scale)	(226)	(318)	
Government services spending	4.08	4.11	(-0.03)
(7-point scale)	(640)	(898)	
Change position of Negro	52.5	50.4	2.10
(% responding "a lot")	(438)	(603)	
Abortion	29.2	32.3	(-3.10)
(% for "always legal")	(759)	(1087)	
Liberal-conservative	4.43	4.45	-0.02
(7-point scale)	(504)	(706)	
School prayer	76.9	77.5	-0.06
(% "allow")	(147)	(204)	

NOTES: N is in parentheses below each entry. In the difference column, parentheses indicate items for which a lower score or the reported category represents a more "conservative" response.
*** $p < .001$.
** $p < .05$.

Voss (1996) finds that white support for David Duke in statewide elections in Louisiana was consistent with the racial threat hypothesis only in more rural parishes. In the most urban parishes, greater black concentration is associated with lower support for Duke among whites. This finding is consistent with a finding from outside the South—that whites living in more racially heterogeneous contexts in New York City were more likely than those living in neighborhoods with a larger white population to support the mayoral candidacy of David Dinkins (Carsey 1995).

The finding that black population is associated with white liberalism in urban areas might be expected, because in areas of greater residential mobility, where individuals are more likely to choose their social context, people choose contexts in which they are comfortable. Racial conservatives would be more likely to choose contexts with fewer members of other races. This process is one more way, in addition to the distribution of incomes, education, and religious affiliation, in which urbanization removes southern politics from its traditional context.

How does urbanization alter the relationship of racial composition of the population to white political attitudes? The data in table 2.8 address this question. To produce the table, southern white respondents to the 1984–90 NES surveys have been grouped into four categories according to whether their congressional district is above or below the mean urban population for southern districts and whether it is above or below the mean black population. (See the Appendix for a list of southern congressional districts represented in the NES samples in 1984–90.) The evidence indicates that the geographic basis of conservatism in the South is still to be found in rural districts with large black populations. On ten of the fourteen NES items reported in table 2.8, low-urban high-black districts were home to the most conservative white respondents; on the remaining four items, the mean response of these respondents ranked second in conservatism among the four district types.

The pattern occurring among rural whites from areas populated by relatively few blacks is strikingly different. Whites from districts

TABLE 2.8

Urbanization, Black Population, and Political Attitudes of Southern Whites, 1984–1990

| ITEM | URBAN AND BLACK POPULATION OF CONGRESSIONAL DISTRICT (RELATIVE TO MEANS) | | | |
| | HIGH URBAN | | LOW URBAN | |
	HIGH BLACK	LOW BLACK	HIGH BLACK	LOW BLACK
School prayer (% "allow")	74.3 (70)	73.9 (134)	79.2 (77)	84.3 (70)
*Abortion (% for "always legal")	35.7 (381)	34.6 (618)	22.8 (378)	29.2 (469)
*Civil rights leadership (% responding "too fast")	29.7 (202)	34.3 (332)	61.3 (225)	32.6 (258)
*Women's equal role (7-point scale)	2.55 (217)	2.88 (354)	3.38 (219)	2.75 (263)
*Government health insurance (7-point scale)	3.76 (109)	4.24 (182)	4.56 (117)	3.96 (136)
*Government allow school integration (% no)	56.1 (57)	59.8 (97)	76.6 (64)	50.0 (74)

Defense spending (7-point scale)	4.18 (321)	4.21 (554)	4.41 (333)	4.11 (364)
*Change position of Negro (% responding "a lot")	46.6 (208)	53.8 (340)	57.8 (230)	46.0 (263)
*Government aid to minorities (7-point scale)	4.74 (331)	4.93 (568)	5.15 (344)	4.49 (397)
*Government guarantee job and standard of living (7-point scale)	4.47 (288)	4.67 (469)	4.73 (287)	4.09 (347)
*Government services spending (7-point scale)	4.10 (323)	3.91 (533)	4.07 (317)	4.40 (365)
Liberal-conservative (7-point scale)	4.42 (265)	4.50 (433)	4.44 (239)	4.38 (273)
Government in Washington too strong (% yes)	68.8 (64)	65.0 (120)	73.4 (64)	64.1 (64)
School busing (7-point scale)	6.61 (36)	6.26 (80)	6.31 (42)	5.90 (39)

NOTES: N is in parentheses below each entry.

* $p < .001$, analysis of variance.

in the "low-urban low-black" category are the least conservative of the four groups of respondents on nine of the items. On three other items, low-urban low-black areas rank next to last in conservatism, and their mean scores are more similar to the mean scores of the urban categories than to the scores of rural high-black districts. On only two items do the two categories of rural district have similar levels of conservatism: whether prayer should be allowed in public schools and whether abortion should be legal. On all the other questions that deal with civil rights and economic matters, white attitudes in rural areas tend to be more conservative in those places with relatively large black populations.

Looking at the "high-urban" columns in table 2.8, the attitudes of whites in both urban categories are less conservative than the attitudes of whites in both rural categories only on the items concerning school prayer and abortion. Urbanization is most clearly linked to liberalism on these two questions. The association between urbanization and liberal attitudes that appears in table 2.2 with respect to the pace of civil rights demands and women's equality disappears if one removes the peculiarly conservative districts of the rural black belt from the analysis.

Where urbanism appears in table 2.2 to be linked to conservative attitudes—on issues of government spending and government efforts to create jobs—the linkage can be traced to the peculiarly liberal character of the residents of districts in the "low-urban low-black" category. On these economic issues, white urban residents appear to be more like people in the old black belt areas than like people from the hills.

What does this distribution of attitudes imply for the linkage that has been drawn between the size of the black population and the conservative attitudes of whites? The only items in table 2.8 for which both of the "high-black" categories are more conservative than both of the "low-black" categories are the questions on school busing and the power of the federal government. In these two cases, the differences across groups are not large enough to inspire confidence given the small number of respondents. By contrast, the substantially large associations in table 2.7 between black population and white conservatism reveal themselves in table 2.8 to be artifacts of the particularly high level of conservatism in high-black rural congressional districts.

Two of the survey items—on school prayer and abortion—demonstrate a direct relationship between urbanization and liberalism, and two items—on the power of the federal government and school busing—suggest a direct relationship between black population and white conservatism. Leaving aside these four issues, the ten items that remain include all of the economic items and most of the civil rights items. For these items, in rural areas black population is directly associated with white conservatism; in urban areas black population is directly associated with white liberalism. The respective relationships are quite substantial in rural areas but much smaller in urban areas.

"Black threat" is associated with white conservatism in rural areas but not in urban areas. Where the black threat hypothesis holds, it extends to economic issues as well as questions purely of race. Why does the black threat hypothesis hold in rural but not urban areas? Because the more vulnerable economic positions in the economy (i.e., working-class jobs) are distributed evenly across rural and urban contexts, the association of black threat with white conservatism is likely to be at least attenuated in those areas where less vulnerable jobs are more concentrated—urban areas. Yet the association between black population and white conservatism is not merely attenuated in urban areas, it is reversed in most of the instances reported in table 2.8.

URBANIZATION AND BLACK INFLUENCE
IN CONGRESSIONAL ELECTORATES

Given the persistence of historic attitudinal patterns among whites in black belt districts, one must return to the question of the impact

TABLE 2.9

Reported Voter Turnout in Congressional Elections
(NES 1984–1990)

	URBAN AND BLACK POPULATION OF CONGRESSIONAL DISTRICT (RELATIVE TO MEANS)			
	HIGH URBAN		LOW URBAN	
ITEM	HIGH BLACK	LOW BLACK	HIGH BLACK	LOW BLACK
Blacks	51% (250)	24% (68)	28% (275)	36% (25)
Whites	38% (397)	44% (635)	40% (384)	36% (480)
All respondents	42% (722)	41% (714)	35% (663)	36% (511)

NOTE: *N* is in parentheses below each entry.

of black voter mobilization on southern elections. In addition to the evidence that whites in the black belt are less sympathetic to the policy positions of blacks than are whites in the cities, there is also considerable evidence of the importance of urban context in providing the organizational resources for black mobilization. If white conservatism persists in the black belt, so might the relative difficulty of bringing a large portion of the black voting age population to the polls.

Blacks are underrepresented in the congressional electorate in those districts with the most conservative white populations. Among respondents to the 1984–90 NES surveys, 28 percent of eligible black voters reported having participated in the congressional election, compared to 40 percent of whites from those districts (table 2.9). Where blacks are most numerous in the rural South, their political influence is doubly limited by the greater conservatism of the white electorate and low rates of black voting participation. In marked contrast to the black belt districts, the city districts with large black populations had the highest rate of reported black voting—51 percent, compared to 38 percent among whites. These districts also happen to be home to the most liberal whites.

The influence of blacks in urban congressional electorates probably comes close to varying in proportion to their share of the voting-age population. In rural areas the association is more complex. Lower turnout rates and white electorates that are apparently less receptive to black opinion than whites in urban areas produce a situation in which greater black population is potentially associated with more conservative representation. As the potential black vote approaches 50 percent of the electorate, however, the most conservative white voters can be more easily marginalized by a combination of the most liberal white voters with black voters.

CONCLUSION: SOCIAL CHANGE AND SOUTHERN POLITICAL ATTITUDES

We can draw several conclusions concerning the likely impact that black voting rights and urbanized constituencies have had on southern electoral politics. To the extent that black voters have had a liberalizing influence on the median attitudes in the electorate, it is with respect to questions of economics and race and not with respect to social issues. Also, the impact of black citizens on politics is likely not to be a simple function of their numerical strength in a given place, especially in rural areas. Consistent with historical patterns, whites are clearly most conservative in those rural areas where black population is most heavily concentrated. It is in these same areas that black voting rates are lowest.

Urbanization is associated with several deviations from traditional southern political patterns. Table 2.10 summarizes the most important features of mass political variation across southern congressional districts. Among those congressional districts with

TABLE 2.10

Race and Observed Political Patterns in Congressional Districts

DISTRICT CHARACTERISTICS		BLACK VOTING RATE IN CONGRESSIONAL ELECTIONS	TYPICAL WHITE ATTITUDES (RANK: 1 = MOST LIBERAL; 4 = MOST CONSERVATIVE)		
PROPORTION URBAN	PROPORTION BLACK		ECONOMIC ISSUES	RACIAL ISSUES	SOCIAL ISSUES
<52%	<18%	36	1	1t	3
<52%	>18%	28	4	4	4
>52%	<18%	24	3	3	2
>52%	>18%	51	2	1t	1

relatively large black populations, electoral participation among blacks occurs at a much higher rate in urban districts than in rural districts. This pattern was linked earlier to the observation that, among whites, the marked conservatism of residents of the black belt has no equal in urban areas. At the same time, the liberal economic attitudes associated with upland rural areas in the South are also tempered in urban areas. Urbanization seems to be associated with the concentration of pockets of economic and racial conservatism in suburban areas where few blacks live. In that respect, the distribution of conservative attitudes among whites in urban areas is similar in the North and the South. Northernization does not amount to liberalization, however. Only on social issues is urbanization unambiguously associated with liberal attitudes among whites in the South.

The patterns displayed in table 2.10 should have clear implications for the association of district variables with the roll call voting of southern House members. Urbanization and black population interact in a manner such that black population is associated with conservatism in rural areas and with liberalism in urban areas. To the extent that roll call patterns diverge across issue areas, the interactive effect of urban and black population should be strongest in predicting roll call votes when race is an issue. The urban-black interaction should also show a strong association with economic issues. On social issues the interaction should be weakest, and urbanization should be the strongest predictor of roll call liberalism.

Before assessing House members' roll call votes, however, we must add an important dimension to our picture of constituency change in the South: the redefinition of southern Democrats' reelection constituencies. Demographic change in southern congressional electorates had a liberalizing effect on Democratic politics only through the sorting of southern Democratic congressional voters into partisan groupings differentiated by issues. Chapter 3 outlines the parameters of that issue-based partisan sorting.

CHAPTER THREE

CHANGE IN REELECTION AND ACTIVIST CONSTITUENCIES

A key component of the northernization of the constituencies of southern Democrats was the impact of Republican competition on the composition of their reelection and primary constituencies. In this chapter, we find a shift from the early 1970s to the late 1980s in the attitudes typical of southern Democratic reelection constituents, a shift that placed southern Democrats closer to northern Democratic than Republican constituents. This transformation occurred mostly with respect to economic issues, however, and not racial or social issues, on which southern Democratic reelection constituents still were not distinguishable from Republicans in the late 1980s. The same basic pattern held for southern Democratic primary constituents, except that they showed signs of leftward movement in the late 1980s on abortion. In general, these trends continued into the 1990s. Thus the conditions for partisan behavior by southern Democrats in the House were not equally apparent across all issue areas during the 1980s partisan surge.

THE RISE OF REPUBLICAN IDENTIFICATION AND THE PARTISAN ALIGNMENT OF ISSUE ATTITUDES

The development of the Republican Party in the South since midcentury can be termed a "secular realignment"—a shift in the balance of party support occurring gradually over a series of elections (Key 1959; Campbell 1977a). Throughout the 1950s party identification among southern whites was overwhelmingly Democratic. Consistent with the party's historic defense of the regional status quo, high-status whites (i.e., those with more education and higher incomes and employed in white-collar occupations) were even more likely than low-status whites to identify with the Democratic Party. The few Republican identifiers not only tended to be of lower socioeconomic status, they also tended to reside in rural areas of the "rim South" states and not in areas with large black populations (Nadeau and Stanley 1993). Only in the mountain areas of North Carolina, Tennessee, and Virginia were there sufficient concentrations of Republicans to elect candidates to Congress and local offices on a consistent basis (Heard 1952).

By the late 1970s the Republican Party in the South had become transformed from a minor party, nonexistent in some areas, into a party of roughly equal strength to the Democratic Party among the white electorate. Initially, Republican growth in the 1950s and 1960s was attributable to upper-status northern migrants to the South, but over time in-migration accounted for an ever-decreasing proportion of Republican identification (Campbell 1977b; Stanley 1988). The changing party balance in the 1960s and 1970s was driven by the behavior of native white southerners (Beck 1977; Stanley 1988). White southerners' departure from their historic identification with the Democratic Party was contingent in part on their social status: in the new southern party system, the Republicans tend to be the party of higher-status whites and the Democrats tend to be the party of lower-status whites. By the late 1980s the Democratic advantage in party identification among whites was undermined even in the black belt of the Deep South states, which was the traditional core of conservative Democratic politics (Nadeau and Stanley 1993).

The pattern of secular realignment among southern whites contrasts sharply with the behavior of the southern black electorate. Party identification among black southerners shifted dramatically toward the Democrats between 1960 and 1964. In fact, black voting behavior in the 1964 election fits the classic definition of a "critical election" (Key 1955). The clarity of the two parties' stands on civil rights issues was associated with a sharp increase among blacks in concern with the election. The ranks of black Democrats were increased both by the mobilization of new voters and by the conversion of many voters from the Republican Party (Campbell 1977b). In succeeding years continued increases in black electoral participation were accompanied by the persistence of the new partisan alignment.

The realignment of social groups has had consequences for the balance of issue positions represented by each party. The electoral mobilization of blacks added a constituency that is solidly liberal on economic and civil rights issues to the southern Democratic Party. Subsequently, during the 1970s and 1980s, people who consider themselves conservative constituted a steadily decreasing proportion of white southern Democrats (Black and Black 1987). Southern conservatives were moving to the Republican Party: Democrats held an 11 percent advantage in party identification over Republicans among southern conservatives in 1972, but by 1984 the Republicans held a 32 percent advantage among this group. Meanwhile, the Democrats retained a 34-point advantage among southern whites who consider themselves moderate or liberal (Carmines and Stanley 1990). The movement of conservative white southerners to the Republican Party was also reflected on specific issues. In the South, as in the North, Democrats were likely to favor and Republicans were likely to oppose increased government social spending on items like welfare and education and government policies intended to increase employment and assist minorities. White southerners with conservative positions on such issues gradually defected to the Republican Party (Carmines and Stanley 1990).

As a result of the southern realignment, little difference between North and South was apparent by the late 1980s in the capacity of economic or racial attitudes to predict party choice by white voters.

Economic liberals tended to be Democrats in both the North and the South, and racial attitudes appeared to make little difference in party choice among whites in either the North or the South once the impact of economic attitudes was taken into account (Prysby 1989; Abramowitz 1994). This convergence of southern and northern patterns of party choice has been slower to occur on social issues, however. *Conservative* responses to questions on abortion, free speech, gun control, the Equal Rights Amendment, and capital punishment were still associated in the mid-1980s with *Democratic* Party identification and presidential voting among southern whites, even taking the effects of economic and racial attitudes into account. Social issues had no such association with party identification in the North (Prysby 1989).

David W. Rohde (1991a) and Richard Fleisher (1993) have both noted that because realignment has removed the most conservative voters from the constituency that supports their electoral bids, southern Democratic representatives are compelled to take more liberal issue positions. If they do not, they are likely to find their core supporters reluctant to devote time and energy to the reelection campaign, or to face liberal opposition in primaries. The latter possibility is particularly important, as conservatives are much less likely to participate in Democratic primaries where the Republican Party has developed a wide following.[1] By depriving the Democratic Party of the most conservative voters, the rise of the Republican Party in southern congressional elections has allowed the liberalization of the southern wing of the Democratic Party in Congress. It is very possibly the case, however, that the effect of Republican competition on the issue attitudes of Democratic reelection constituents depends on the specific issue area.

Have the issue positions typical of southern Democratic reelection constituents moved closer to the positions of northern Democrats and farther from those of Republicans? Does the relative movement of southern Democratic reelection constituents vary across issue areas? Have the dynamics of southern electoral realignment (confined as it is to white voters moving into the Republican column) reduced the issue differences between blacks and whites among southern Democratic reelection constituents? Answers to these questions provide a sketch of the constituency changes to which southern Democratic representatives have been exposed and serve as a guide to the parameters of change in roll call behavior that one might expect among southern Democrats in the House as a response to constituency change.

REELECTION CONSTITUENCIES IN THE
CONSERVATIVE COALITION ERA

Table 3.1 compares the mean issue positions on NES seven-point scale items of northern Democratic, southern Democratic, and Republican reelection constituents in the 1968–74 pooled sample (appendix 1 contains the text of the items used here). This period witnessed substantial coalition activity between southern Democrats and Republicans in Congress, so it is not surprising that a substantial difference occurs on each of the seven items between the typical northern and southern Democratic reelection constituent. At the same time, southerners who voted Democrat for Congress in 1968–74 were significantly more liberal than Republicans on three of the items in table 3.1—school busing, self-placement on a liberal-conservative dimension, and the role of government in providing jobs and a good standard living. In contrast, survey items regarding national health insurance, responses to urban unrest, government aid to minorities, the rights of the accused, and women's roles show no substantial difference between southern Democratic and Republican congressional voters in the early 1970s. The similarity of southern Democratic and Republican constituents on these issues and the substantial difference between southern Democratic and northern Democratic constituents across all the issue items suggest that a constituency basis existed in the early

TABLE 3.1

Issue Attitudes by Party of Congressional Vote, 1968–1974
(NES 7-point response scales)

ITEM	MEANS			
	ND	ALL SD	WHITE SD	R
School busing	5.99	6.19[b]	6.55[a]	6.51
	(812)	(340)	(277)	(849)
Government guarantee job and standard of living	4.05	4.31[a,b]	4.80[a]	4.92
	(795)	(317)	(255)	(796)
Liberal-conservative	3.76	4.29[a,b]	4.54[a]	4.56
	(703)	(260)	(217)	(719)
Women's equal role	3.15	3.45[a]	3.57[a]	3.44
	(884)	(339)	(278)	(856)
Rights of accused	3.94	4.48[a]	4.76[a]	4.44
	(1020)	(414)	(345)	(1067)
Government aid to minorities	3.97	4.57[a]	5.09[a]	4.60
	(1050)	(427)	(351)	(1087)
Government health insurance	3.33	4.48[a]	4.87[a]	4.60
	(463)	(208)	(176)	(528)
Urban unrest	3.17	3.91[a]	4.24[a]	3.72
	(1095)	(459)	(378)	(1209)

NOTES: ND = northern Democrats, SD = southern Democrats, R = Republicans.
N is in parentheses below each entry.
[a] Difference of SD – ND is significant at $p < .05$.
[b] Difference of R – SD is significant at $p < .05$.

1970s for southern Democrat-Republican roll call coalitions on a wide range of issues.

When blacks are excluded from the 1968–74 sample of southern Democratic reelection constituents, on every issue scale white southern Democrats had an average placement that was more conservative than that of northern Democrats (see table 3.1). Further, in no instance were white southern Democrats significantly less conservative than the typical congressional Republican voter. In fact, white southern Democrats were significantly more conservative than were Republicans in their response to several items: urban unrest, aid to minorities, rights of the accused, and women's roles. The appearance of the conservative coalition of Republicans and southern Democrats in Congress appears to have had a substantial basis in southern Democratic constituent attitudes on a wide range of issues. To the extent that southern black constituents continued to have a disproportionately small degree of influence on their representatives, the influence of conservative attitudes in southern Democratic electoral coalitions was reinforced.

REELECTION CONSTITUENCIES
IN THE LATE 1980s

The realignment of southern white voters in congressional elections since the early 1970s appears to have drawn southern Democratic constituents much closer to northern Democrats (and away from Republicans) on economic issues, less so on racial issues, and hardly at all on social issues. Table 3.2 shows the mean issue positions of northern Democratic, southern Democratic, and Republican reelection constituents on NES seven-point scale items in the 1984–90 pooled sample. There is no statistically significant difference between the responses of northern and southern Democrats on four of these items: national health insurance, the role of government in providing jobs, spending on government services, and busing. On each of these items except the busing question, the mean southern Democratic response differs significantly from the mean Republican response.

Four survey items reveal significant differences between the mean positions of northern and southern Democrats in the 1984–90 sample. On three of the items—the liberal-conservative scale, government aid to minorities, and defense spending—southern

TABLE 3.2

Issue Attitudes by Party of Congressional Vote, 1984–1990
(NES 7-point response scales)

	MEANS			
ITEM	ND	ALL SD	WHITE SD	R
Government guarantee job and standard of living	4.05 (1340)	4.04[b] (526)	4.43[a,b] (355)	4.99 (1327)
Government services spending	4.42 (1494)	4.42[b] (596)	4.13[a,b] (413)	3.52 (1499)
Government health insurance	3.59 (580)	3.81[b] (234)	4.03[a,b] (179)	4.48 (625)
Government aid to minorities	4.04 (1546)	4.25[a,b] (632)	4.67[a] (427)	4.72 (1519)
Liberal-conservative	3.82 (1353)	4.21[a,b] (481)	4.29[a,b] (350)	4.83 (1373)
Defense spending	3.34 (1571)	3.95[a,b] (605)	4.04[a,b] (426)	4.22 (1541)
School busing	5.67 (229)	5.95 (87)	6.38[a] (65)	6.25 (264)
Women's equal role	2.37 (1022)	2.89[a] (391)	2.86[a] (282)	2.83 (1048)

NOTES: ND = northern Democrats, SD = southern Democrats, R = Republicans.
N is in parentheses below each entry.
[a] Difference of SD – ND is significant at $p < .05$.
[b] Difference of R – SD is significant at $p < .05$.

Democratic reelection constituents fall between northern Democrats and Republicans. No statistically significant difference exists on the women's role question between southern Democratic and Republican constituents.

One can conclude that if congressional behavior is a direct response to the views of members' reelection constituencies, then the incentive of southern Democratic representatives to vote with northern Democrats is greatest on economic issues or spending on government services and least on women's issues. The aid to minorities and defense spending items appear to indicate issues on which southern Democratic representatives might be inclined either toward partisan voting on roll calls or toward voting in a conservative coalition with Republicans, depending on how the positions of northern Democrats and Republicans are framed.

The inclusion of blacks in the sample of southern Democratic constituents obscures the substantial differences between southern white Democrats and northern Democrats on several issues. The third column of data in table 3.2, which excludes blacks from the 1984–90 sample, reveals a significant difference between the issue positions of southern white and northern Democratic reelection constituents on every one of the NES seven-point issue scales. On five of these, white southern Democrats also hold positions substantially different from the positions typically held by Republicans: government role in providing jobs, spending on government services, health insurance, liberal-conservative placement, and defense spending. On questions concerning school busing, aid to minorities, and women's role in society, no substantial difference exists between white southern Democrats and Republicans. It may be instructive also that the distance between white southern Democrats and northern Democrats on defense spending according to this measure is more than three times the distance between white southern Democrats and Republicans.

The southern white realignment of the last two decades appears to have lessened the common ground between southern Democratic and Republican reelection constituents on economic questions, but considerable similarity of opinion remains between the two groups on questions concerning race and social issues, and perhaps on defense spending. Categorical response items from the NES can be used to extend and clarify the conclusion that there remains a considerable basis in constituency attitudes for the formation of southern Democratic–Republican voting coalitions in Congress on noneconomic issues. Consider the realm of social issues. Table 3.3 reflects change over the last two decades in popular attitudes on abortion rights and school prayer. A general shift in attitudes has occurred in both the North and the South and in the congressional electorate of both parties toward greater acceptance of abortion rights and less insistence on prayer in public schools. Yet change has not been of the same degree for all groups of respondents. Over the last two decades differences of opinion on abortion and school prayer have become more coincident with partisanship in congressional elections among northerners but not among southerners.

Table 3.3 shows that the percentage of southern Democratic reelection constituents in the 1984–90 sample who favor unlimited abortion rights is comparable to the proportion of Republicans who support such rights but 13 percent less than the proportion of northern Democrats who do so. Likewise, northern Democratic reelection constituents are 16 percent less likely than Republicans to support organized school prayer and 26 percent less likely than southern Democrats. On the occasions when abortion and school prayer divide Congress on partisan lines, southern Democrats will probably view their constituents as being in greater agreement with the Republican position than the northern Democratic position on these issues.

Three NES items concerning black civil rights reveal southern Democratic constituents to be more similar to Republicans than to northern Democrats in their views. Table 3.4 shows the proportion of respondents grouped by region and congressional vote who think "a lot" of progress has occurred on civil rights, the proportion who think that civil rights leaders are "pushing too fast" for change, and the proportion who respond "no" to whether the government should allow school integration. Only on the last of these three items is there an indication that realignment in congressional elections may have brought the mean southern Democratic position away from the Republican position and toward the northern

TABLE 3.3

Issue Attitudes by Party of Congressional Vote—Social Issues
(NES survey items)

ABORTION RIGHTS (FAVOR UNLIMITED RIGHTS %)

SAMPLE	ND	SD	R	R-ND	SD-ND	R-SD
1968-74	31.7	12.1	27.8	(-3.90)	(-19.60)***	(15.70)***
	(517)	(214)	(572)			
1984-90	45.9	32.7	34.7	(-11.20)***	(-13.20)***	(2.00)
	(1652)	(681)	(1608)			

PRAYER IN SCHOOLS (ALLOW %)

SAMPLE	ND	SD	R	R-ND	SD-ND	R-SD
1968-74	79.2	86.6	80.8	1.60	7.40*	-5.80
	(265)	(134)	(370)			
1984-90	52.6	78.0	68.5	15.90***	25.40***	-9.50*
	(382)	(164)	(444)			

NOTES: In the difference columns, parentheses indicate items for which lower scores represent a more "conservative" or more "Republican" response.
ND = northern Democrats, SD = southern Democrats, R = Republicans.
N is in parentheses below percentage entries.
*** *p* < .001, ** *p* < .05, * *p* < .10, difference of proportions test.

TABLE 3.4
Issue Attitudes by Party of Congressional Vote—Civil Rights
(NES survey items)

DEGREE OF CHANGE (A LOT %)

Sample	ND	SD	R	R-ND	SD-ND	R-SD
1968–74	52.6 (964)	61.5 (413)	55.4 (1154)	2.80	8.90**	-6.10*
1984–90	34.3 (1068)	42.6 (441)	43.2 (1031)	8.90***	8.30**	0.60

CIVIL RIGHTS LEADERS (PUSH TOO FAST %)

Sample	ND	SD	R	R-ND	SD-ND	R-SD
1968–74	45.8 (1257)	58.6 (532)	57.4 (1412)	11.60***	12.80***	-1.20
1984–90	22.3 (1055)	31.4 (433)	33.3 (1015)	11.00***	9.10***	1.90

ALLOW INTEGRATION (NO %)

Sample	ND	SD	R	R-ND	SD-ND	R-SD
1968–74	44.2 (799)	59.1 (364)	60.9 (951)	16.70***	14.90***	1.80
1984–90	45.9 (268)	45.5 (110)	65.0 (237)	19.10***	-0.40	19.50***

NOTES: ND = northern Democrats, SD = southern Democrats, R = Republicans.
N is in parentheses below each percentage entry.
*** $p < .001$, ** $p < .01$, * $p < .05$, difference of proportions test.

Democratic position. In either 1968–74 or 1984–90 the proportions who think that a lot of change has occurred in the conditions of blacks and that civil rights leaders are pushing too fast do not substantially differ between southern Democrats and Republicans, but the proportions for both questions differ significantly between northern and southern Democrats. The evidence here mostly supports the contention that the constituents of southern Democratic and Republican representatives are similar in their attitudes toward civil rights.

Several caveats should accompany any description of the ideological nature of the southern white congressional realignment. Most important, one must distinguish between economic and noneconomic issues in describing convergence between northern and southern Democrats (and the degree of divergence between southern Democrats and Republicans). In the late 1980s noneconomic questions continued to provide a substantial basis in constituent attitudes for the formation of a conservative coalition in Congress, but it appears that economic questions did so only to a small degree.

RACIAL DIFFERENCES AMONG SOUTHERN DEMOCRATIC REELECTION CONSTITUENTS

The southern congressional realignment has brought southern Democratic reelection constituents in closer agreement with their northern Democratic counterparts on economic matters. Because the realignment consists of white flight from Democratic electoral coalitions, it has also made black voters a larger proportion of the reelection constituency of the typical southern Democratic representative. The persistence of differences in issue attitudes following racial lines among southern Democratic voters has the potential to exert conflicting pressures on the behavior of southern Democrats in Congress. Conflicting pressures from the constituency might restrain the representative from addressing difficult issues or taking controversial positions, or the representative might instead derive from the situation a degree of discretion he would not otherwise have had.

Table 3.5 indicates differences between black and white southern Democratic reelection constituents from the 1984–90 sample on each survey item. The table includes three types of issues. The first consists of items on which substantial attitudinal differences exist between blacks and whites among southern Democrats and no differences exist between white southern Democrats and Republicans. The second consists of those items on which attitudinal differences occur not only between blacks and whites among southern Democrats but also between white southern Democrats and Republicans. The third consists of issue items on which no significant differences occur between the responses of blacks and whites among southern Democrats. These items also happen to demonstrate no significant attitudinal differences between southern Democratic and Republican reelection constituents.

Each of the three opinion patterns depicted in table 3.5 appears to correspond to a distinct issue domain. Consider first the views of white and black southern Democrats on questions that are quite explicitly racial in nature (the first five items). White southern Democrats tend to be more like Republicans than northern Democrats on such issues, and the typical position of black southern Democrats is profoundly more liberal than that of white Democrats. In tending to constituent views on issues such as school busing and government aid to minorities, the typical southern Democratic representative is likely to be pulled in two opposing directions at once. When such issues divide Congress on party lines, the behavior of the southern Democratic representative is likely to be governed by the intensity with which blacks or whites hold opinions on the specific question at issue and by the capacity of various groups

TABLE 3.5

Race and the Issue Attitudes of Southern Democrats
(NES 1984–90)

Item	BSD	WSD	R	WSD-BSD	R-WSD
Government aid to minorities (scale)	3.35 (188)	4.67 (427)	4.72 (1519)	1.32*	0.05
School busing (scale)	4.60 (20)	6.38 (65)	6.25 (264)	1.78*	-0.13
Civil rights (a lot, percent)	24.6 (130)	50.7 (302)	43.2 (1031)	26.10***	-7.50*
Civil rights (too fast %)	7.8 (128)	41.9 (296)	33.3 (1015)	34.10***	-8.60**
Integration (oppose %)	11.9 (42)	67.2 (67)	65.0 (237)	55.30***	-2.20
Liberal-conservative (scale)	3.96 (117)	4.29 (350)	4.83 (1373)	0.33*	0.54*
Defense spending (scale)	3.70 (162)	4.04 (426)	4.22 (1541)	0.34*	0.18*
Government health insurance (scale)	3.22 (50)	4.03 (179)	4.48 (625)	0.81*	0.45*
Government services spending (scale)	5.23 (166)	4.13 (413)	3.52 (1499)	(-1.10*)	(-0.61*)
Government guarantee job (scale)	3.12 (155)	4.43 (355)	4.99 (1327)	1.31*	0.56*
Women's equal role (scale)	2.95 (96)	2.86 (282)	2.83 (1048)	-0.09	-0.03
Abortion rights (favor %)	28.6 (199)	34.8 (463)	34.7 (1608)	(6.20)	(-0.10)
Prayer in schools (favor %)	84.6 (39)	75.9 (116)	68.5 (444)	-8.70	-7.40

NOTES: In the difference columns, parentheses indicate items for which lower scores represent a more "conservative" or more "Republican" response. BSD = black southern Democrats, WSD = white southern Democrats, R = Republicans.

N is in parentheses below each mean or percentage entry.

*** $p < .001$, ** $p < .01$, * $p < .05$, t-test or difference of proportions test (as appropriate).

with intense preferences to withhold their votes and other forms of electoral support in the next primary or general election.

Substantial issue differences also are associated with race among southern Democratic constituents with respect to economic items in the NES (table 3.5). Due to the defection of more economically conservative whites to the Republican party in southern congressional elections, white southern Democrats now tend to be closer to northern Democrats than to Republicans in their typical responses to economic items. Nonetheless, the typical black southern Democrat offers a more "liberal" response to each of these items than the typical white southern Democrat. The placement of white southern Democratic constituents relative to northern Democrats and Republicans might encourage alliances between southern Democratic and Republican representatives when northern Democrat–supported economic proposals in Congress are particularly "liberal" in nature. However, for those representatives with a visible and large black constituency, the temptation to defect from the northern Democrats on economic questions is likely to be muted, especially in those instances in which the issue is of distinct interest to the black community.

A third issue domain—responses to the items on women's role, abortion, and school prayer—is characterized by little difference between the positions typical of black and white southern Democrats (table 3.5). Also common to these issues is that southern Democrats tend to be much closer to Republicans than to northern Democrats. The issues on which black and white southern Democratic constituents appear to be in greatest agreement thus are also issues on which southern Democratic representatives have the greatest incentive to defect from northern Democratic positions. When these issues become subject to partisan conflict in Congress, no question should occur as to which side southern Democrats will take, if indeed constituent attitudes drive congressional behavior.

PRIMARY CONSTITUENTS

I have argued that representatives are responsive not strictly to their geographic constituency but especially to the election constituency that sent and returns them to office at election time. Not all reelection constituents have equal importance, however. Within the reelection constituency, we should expect the representative's primary constituents to have particular influence as they form the core of his or her support. The electoral support received by a candidate from her primary constituency, which consists of the individuals and groups that form her base of support in contested primary elections and provide material support (finances, volunteers, organization, endorsements) to her campaign, goes well beyond simply voting in the general election. Representatives have particular incentive to be attentive to the preferences of their primary constituents, and indeed are likely to closely share at least some of those preferences. (For the classic treatment of how representatives relate differently to their geographic, reelection, and primary constituencies, see Fenno 1978.)

Individual primary constituents are likely to be politically active members of the candidate's party. Not all of the party's identifiers or general election supporters are equally likely to be partisan activists. For instance, one might look to the membership of labor unions and teacher organizations, some types of community action groups, trial lawyers, small business persons, or local Democratic officials to find Democratic Party activists in the South. This pool of partisan political activists from which primary constituents are drawn may have preferences substantially different from those of the typical reelection constituent. Should this turn out to be the case, it further complicates the constituency cues to which representatives must respond.

ISSUE ATTITUDES OF
SOUTHERN PARTY ELITES

In the late 1980s an ideological sorting occurred among southern party elites akin to that already noted among the broader southern electorate. Attitudes on issues were found to be the best predictor of party switching in a study of delegates to southern state party conventions (Nesbit 1988). Among Republican precinct representatives, former Democrats were especially conservative (Bowman, Hulbary, and Kelley 1990). In a 1991 survey county-level party committee members who were converts to the Democratic Party were substantially more liberal than lifelong Democratic activists on several issues: support for government aid to minorities, affirmative action, abortion rights, and opposition to school prayer and to increased defense spending. Among Republican activists, party switchers were substantially more conservative than lifelong partisans on abortion and school prayer. This was especially true of activists who became Republicans after 1979 (Prysby 1992).

Among southern contributors to political action committees, those who switched to the Republican Party tended to be more conservative than those who have always been Republicans, especially on social issues. Contributors who convert to the Democratic Party are more liberal than long-standing Democrats in their attitudes toward abortion, gay rights, gun control, and federal welfare programs. Among financial contributors new members of both southern parties tend to be more conservative than their northern counterparts, but these regional differences are much smaller than the differences between new and old party members in the South (Green and Guth 1990).

The effects of party switchers on the ideological composition of party activists are matched by the effects of newer generations of party activists. Among county party committee members, younger Democratic activists were less likely than older Democrats to give conservative responses to questions on aid to minorities, affirmative action, abortion, school prayer, and defense spending. Younger Republican activists were more likely than older Republicans to give conservative responses to questions on abortion, government aid to minorities, and affirmative action, as well as on government spending, the role of government in providing jobs, and government's role in financing health care (Shaffer and Breaux 1992).

In sum, party switching and generational change increased the distance between the parties among politically active southerners much as it did among the broader southern electorate. A potentially critical difference between the mass realignment and the activist one is the greater prominence of social issues as a cue for activists to switch parties. The role of social issues in the partisanship of newer activists is potentially important for two reasons. First, we expect representatives to be especially responsive to their primary constituents, who are probably also politically active partisans. Second, there is a good possibility that the issue alignment of the mass electorate will come to reflect that of activists, if the issue in question remains politically salient for a sufficient time.

POLITICAL ACTIVISM AND "ISSUE EVOLUTION"

The theory of issue evolution hypothesizes that the reorientation of mass party alignments occurs following and in response to the partisan realignment of more politically active citizens. Political activists play this leading role in partisan change because they are the key communicators to the broader electorate of party stands on salient new issues. Edward G. Carmines and James A. Stimson (1989) first elaborated this theory as an explanation for the evolution of national party alignments since the 1960s. They present a compelling argument that the introduction of race as a partisan issue in 1964–65 reoriented the behavior of more active citizens and that the reorientation of mass party alignments followed. Greg D. Adams (1997) has provided evidence of a similar partisan issue evolution commencing in the 1970s on the matter of abortion. Partisan differences among elites on the issue of abortion (indicated by roll call votes on abortion items) emerged in the 1970s and widened with time, with Democratic elites more likely than Republicans to support abortion rights. Mass partisan differences on this issue did not emerge until well into the 1980s, however.

The implication for congressional behavior is clear: given that primary constituents are likely to be drawn from partisans who are politically active, an emerging partisan alignment on a new issue might be reflected at first only among the primary constituents. It might become evident only later among reelection constituents. In the case of a new issue or an issue on which party divisions are newly emerging, knowing the attitudes of primary constituents as well as those of reelection constituents would provide a better explanation of legislative behavior than knowing only the preferences of the latter.

POLITICAL ATTITUDES OF
PRIMARY CONSTITUENTS

The operationalization of political activism used by Carmines and Stimson provides a means of roughly defining the primary constituent pools of southern Democrats, northern Democrats, and Republicans. Among NES respondents, political activists were identified by counting the number of different acts of political participation in which respondents reported participating. The participation acts about which the NES asked were attempting to influence others' votes, attending a political rally or meeting, wearing a button or displaying a bumper sticker, working for a party or a candidate, and contributing money to a party or a candidate. NES respondents who participated in three of these five acts are considered "activists," and their responses are included in the analyses below. By dividing activists into groups according to their vote in the congressional election, we arrive at a rough characterization of the typical primary constituents of southern Democrats, northern Democrats, and Republicans.[2]

Table 3.6 presents the mean placements on the NES seven-point scale items of activist constituents of northern Democrats, southern Democrats, and Republicans in the 1968–74 samples. Typically, only about 5 to 10 percent of congressional voters (already less than half the respondents in a typical sample) meet the activist threshold, so the number of respondents in each group is fairly low. Nonetheless, we can draw some inferences from these data. First, the hypothesis that southern Democratic primary constituents are more liberal than southern Democratic reelection constituents is generally confirmed, although the difference between the two groups attains statistical significance for four items: the role of government in guaranteeing jobs, government aid to minorities, the rights of the accused, and the liberal-conservative placement. On these four items, the relative placement of southern Democratic primary constituents is closer to the northern Democrats than is the placement of southern Democratic reelection constituents in table 3.1.

The government's role in providing jobs and the liberal-conservative self-placement items provide the strongest evidence in table 3.6 for a peculiarly liberal orientation among southern Democratic primary constituents. It was on these issues that southern and northern Democratic primary constituents were most similar and the differences between southern Democratic and Republican primary constituents were largest. An issue evolution approach to realignment would lead us to expect something like this pattern. We know that the southern realignment of the 1960s to the 1980s differentiated the parties on liberal-conservative lines in the realm of economic issues. If political activists are the leading edge of issue-based realignments, then the placement of southern

TABLE 3.6

Attitudes of Political Activists by Party of Congressional Vote, 1968–1974
(NES 7-point response scales)

| | MEANS | | | DISTANCE | |
ITEM	ND	SD	R	SD-ND	R-SD
School busing	4.71	5.79	6.33	1.08**	0.54
	(80)	(24)	(82)		
Government guarantee job and standard of living	3.29	3.43[1]	5.19	0.14	1.76***
	(79)	(21)	(80)		
Liberal-conservative	3.23	3.58[1]	4.67	0.35	1.09***
	(80)	(19)	(78)		
Women's equal role	2.20	2.79	2.96	0.59	0.17
	(84)	(24)	(82)		
Rights of accused	2.96	3.55[1]	3.79	0.58	0.24
	(105)	(33)	(107)		
Government aid to minorities	3.11	3.78[2]	4.53	0.67	0.75
	(108)	(32)	(105)		
Government health insurance	2.82	4.33	5.25	1.51*	0.92
	(55)	(15)	(44)		
Urban unrest	2.47	3.51	3.80	1.04**	0.28
	(104)	(41)	(133)		

NOTES: ND = northern Democrats, SD = southern Democrats, R = Republicans.
N is in parentheses below each mean entry.
Distance between parties:
*** $p < .005$, ** $p < .05$; * $p < .10$.
Difference between activist and reelection constituent within parties:
[1] $p < .05$.
[2] $p < .10$.

Democratic activists in 1968–74 should have been most like that of northern Democratic activists on the issue of government's economic role.

The seven-point scale placements of the three groups of primary constituents in 1984–90 are shown in table 3.7. There is a statistically

TABLE 3.7

Attitudes of Political Activists by Party of Congressional Vote, 1984–1990
(NES 7-point response scales)

ITEM	MEANS			DISTANCE	
	ND	SD	R	SD-ND	R-SD
Government guarantee job and standard of living	3.66 (122)	4.16 (45)	5.12 (103)	0.49	0.96***
Government services spending	4.71 (129)	4.51 (55)	3.03 (116)	(0.20)	(-1.47***)
Government health insurance	2.98 (56)	3.69 (13)	4.62 (50)	0.71	0.93
Government aid to minorities	3.59 (132)	4.02 (60)	4.66 (110)	0.43	0.63**
Liberal-conservative	3.14 (127)	4.14 (50)	5.12 (113)	1.00***	0.98***
Defense spending	2.66 (135)	3.73 (59)	4.39 (115)	1.07***	0.66***
School busing	5.44 (25)	6.00 (4)	6.57 (21)	0.56	0.57
Women's equal role	1.80 (92)	2.18[1] (28)	2.86 (76)	0.37	0.68*

NOTES: In the distance columns, parentheses indicate items for which lower scores represent a more "conservative" or more "Republican" response. ND = northern Democrats, SD = southern Democrats, R = Republicans. N is in parentheses below each mean entry.
Distance between parties:
*** $p < .01$.
** $p < .05$.
* $p < .10$.
Difference between activist and reelection constituents within parties:
[1] $p < .05$.

significant difference between southern Democratic primary constituents and reelection constituents on only one of these items, women's role, on which the activist constituents were substantially more liberal. On this item, southern Democratic primary constituents are significantly more liberal than Republican primary constituents, while their distance from northern Democratic primary constituents does not attain statistical significance. This pattern among primary constituents is precisely the opposite of that reported in table 3.2 among reelection constituents. In the late 1980s, whereas reelection constituents would place southern Democrats in greater agreement with Republicans on the "women's role" item, primary constituents would place them in greater agreement with northern Democrats.

The movement of southern Democratic primary constituents toward the northern Democratic position on the role of women might be reflected in their attitudes on other social issues. Table 3.8 shows, however, that in the late 1980s southern Democratic primary constituents remained more similar to Republican than to northern Democratic primary constituents on both abortion and prayer in public schools. The differences between the parties on these items are greater among activist constituents than among reelection constituents, but southern Democratic primary constituents were not distinguishable from Republican primary constituents on these issues. This is especially true for the school prayer issue.

The only group of primary constituents who differ significantly from their respective group reelection constituents on these issues are northern Democrats. On abortion, the emergence of partisan differences between northern Democratic and Republican reelection constituents in the 1984–90 sample is consistent with the issue evolution model: in the early 1970s, a substantial difference between northern Democratic and Republican activists on abortion had not been matched by a similar difference among reelection constituents. By the late 1980s the northern Democrat–Republican difference on the abortion question appeared among both primary and reelec-

TABLE 3.8

Attitudes of Political Activists by Party of Congressional Vote—Social Issues
(NES survey items)

ABORTION RIGHTS (FAVOR UNLIMITED RIGHTS, PERCENT)

SAMPLE	ND	SD	R	R-ND	SD-ND	R-SD
1968–74	54.0	14.3	26.8	(-27.2)***	(-39.7)***	(12.5)
	(63)	(14)	(56)			
1984–90	56.9	39.7	31.1	(-25.8)****	(-17.2)**	(-8.6)
	(137)	(58)	(119)			

PRAYER IN SCHOOLS (ALLOW, PERCENT)

SAMPLE	ND	SD	R	R-ND	SD-ND	R-SD
1968–74	70.8	84.6	75.0	4.2	13.8	-9.6
	(24)	(13)	(44)			
1984–90	35.9	70.0	60.0	24.1*	34.1*	-10.0
	(39)	(10)	(30)			

NOTES: In the difference columns, parentheses indicate items for which lower scores represent a more "conservative" or more "Republican" response.

ND = northern Democrats, SD = southern Democrats, R = Republicans.

N is in parentheses below each percentage entry.

**** *p* < .001.

*** *p* < .01.

** *p* < .05.

* *p* < .10.

tion constituents, evidence of the impact of an issue evolution on the mass electorate.

Among southerners, the evolution of abortion as a partisan issue had not progressed sufficiently by the late 1980s to render southern Democratic primary or reelection constituents statistically distinguishable from Republicans in their level of support for abortion rights. Recall from table 3.3, however, that in the early 1970s southern Democratic reelection constituents were 15 percent *less* likely than Republican reelection constituents to support unlimited abortion rights, a difference that practically disappeared by the late 1980s. A similar movement is suggested by table 3.8, which shows that the southern Democratic primary constituents sampled in 1968–74 were 12 percent less likely to support unlimited abortion rights than were Republican primary constituents. In the 1984–90 sample, 8 percent *more* southern Democratic than Republican activists gave this response. At neither point can we have statistical confidence in the reported difference between southern Democratic and Republican activists, given their small numbers among the survey respondents.

While it is statistically insignificant, however, the observed movement among southern Democratic primary constituents parallels that observed among reelection constituents. Further, it is consistent with the more dramatic shift demonstrated by southern Democratic primary constituents on the less policy-specific "women's role" item. It turns out that this is evidence of the early stages of an issue evolution in progress.

CONTINUITY AND CHANGE IN THE 1990s

Issues and Congressional Elections

During the 1980s, social issues played a larger role in presidential voting than in partisan identification or congressional voting.

While social welfare issues are more powerful predictors of presidential voting than cultural issues, conservatism on abortion, women's role, and gay rights was associated with a greater likelihood of whites' voting for George Bush in 1988 (Abramowitz 1994: 21). In 1992 attitudes on abortion had a significant effect on voters' likelihood of supporting Bill Clinton; the effect was especially strong among voters who were both aware of party positions on abortion and concerned about the issue (Abramowitz 1995). These patterns were consistent with the evolution of substantial mass partisan differences in abortion attitudes by the late 1980s (Adams 1997).

Especially in the South, Democratic incumbents in the House were able to win reelection by insulating themselves from the liberalism of the national party, particularly on noneconomic issues. Several factors combined to reduce the degree of this insulation in 1994. Beginning in 1992, the Republican challengers competed in almost all southern Democratic districts, a sharp departure from the past. Nationally, in both 1992 and 1994 the Republicans fielded more experienced challengers than did the Democrats, a situation that had only occurred in one other election year since the late 1940s (Jacobson 1996: 215). A Democratic president who was unpopular among southern whites provided an opportunity for Republicans to gain congressional seats by making the 1994 elections a referendum on the incumbent. Republican campaigns made every effort to tie Democratic incumbents to the president and to national Democratic positions that are unpopular in the region. Nationally, district outcomes in House and presidential elections were correlated to a degree unprecedented in midterm elections since mid-century (Jacobson 1996: 211). In the South, the Pearson's r correlation between the district Republican vote for the House and that for president ranged between .61 and .72 in 1992–98, up from a range between .40 and .56 in 1976–90.

One should not overstate the degree of nationalization that occurred in the 1994 congressional elections: the national tide influenced electoral outcomes most where local electoral conditions were most favorable for Republican gains (Jacobson 1996). Nonetheless, the stronger linkage between congressional and presidential outcomes in the 1990s suggests a reduction in the ability of southern Democrats to insulate themselves from the national party. Furthermore, the coincidence of the evolution of abortion and other lifestyle matters as partisan issues with the demise of the Democratic congressional majority in the South might suggest that the issue basis of the southern mass partisan alignment in congressional elections was altered radically in 1994.

Recent research on ideological realignment in the national electorate suggests, however, that the Republican congressional gains of the 1990s were the culmination of a secular ideological realignment encompassing a broader range of issues. Since the 1978 National Election Studies, the public has become progressively more aware of party differences on economic items (government role in providing jobs, government aid to minorities, and government role in health insurance). Party identification has become more strongly associated with individual attitudes on these issues (Abramowitz and Saunders 1998). The results based on party identification in the national sample suggest that my findings from southern congressional elections in the late 1980s will not be radically different in the 1990s. Abortion and other social issues, although perhaps playing a more important role than previously in the dynamics of partisan choice, have not displaced economic issues as the dominant factor shaping the ideological composition of party identifiers.

Reelection Constituents

Table 3.9 shows the mean self-placement of northern Democratic, southern Democratic, and Republican election constituents on seven issue scale items asked of the 1990–96 NES respondents.[3] The liberalization of the southern Democratic coalition continued

TABLE 3.9

Issue Attitudes by Party of Congressional Vote, 1990–1996
(NES 7-point response scales)

	MEANS				
ITEM	ND	BLACK SD	ALL SD	WHITE SD	R
Government guarantee job and standard of living	4.10 (1338)	3.23[b,c] (162)	3.88[b] (503)	4.23[b] (326)	5.04 (1545)
Government services spending	4.33 (1323)	4.96[b,c] (146)	4.36[b] (467)	4.09[a,b] (308)	3.34 (1513)
Government health insurance	3.31 (1016)	3.24[b] (115)	3.34[b] (379)	3.42[b] (250)	4.58 (1263)
Government aid to minorities	4.38 (1367)	3.63[b,c] (171)	4.29[b] (515)	4.68[a,b] (328)	5.15 (1569)
Liberal-conservative	3.71 (1224)	3.98[a,b] (117)	3.93[a,b] (399)	3.91[a,b] (269)	4.94 (1438)
Defense spending	3.26 (1382)	3.82[a,b] (147)	3.75[a,b] (485)	3.74[a,b] (323)	4.06 (1540)
Women's equal role	2.09 (1235)	2.63[a,c] (151)	2.35[a,b] (468)	2.23[b] (317)	2.54 (1441)

NOTES: ND = northern Democrats, SD = southern Democrats, R = Republicans. N is in parentheses below each entry.
[a] Difference of SD–ND is significant at $p < .05$.
[b] Difference of R–SD is significant at $p < .05$.
[c] Difference of white–black SD is significant at $p < .05$.

in the 1990s. The marked growth of Republican contestation of seats in 1992 and the Republicans' historic gains of 1994 likely account for the continued defection of more conservative southerners from the Democratic coalition. Compared to the 1984–90 figures shown in table 3.2, differences between the mean position of all southern Democrats and that of northern Democrats disappeared on the issues of government-sponsored health insurance and government aid to minorities. The typical liberal-conservative self-placement of southern Democrats also moved somewhat closer to that of northern Democrats. Southern Democrats remained slightly closer to northern Democrats than to Republicans on the defense spending and women's role items. On the women's role item, the emergence of a difference between all southern Democrats and Republicans was a new development. It brings southern Democratic reelection constituents somewhat closer to the position of typical southern Democratic primary constituents on this issue.

The fourth column of table 3.9 reports data for white southern Democratic reelection constituents. In comparison to the 1984–90 figures in table 3.3, table 3.9 shows that the distance between the typical white southern Democrat and the typical Republican increased on every issue. In the cases of government aid to minorities and women's role, there had been no difference between Republican reelection constituents and white southern Democrats in 1984–90. White southern Democrats moved to a position somewhat closer to northern Democrats than to Republicans in the 1990–96 sample. Movement by conservative whites out of Democratic electoral coalitions in the South resulted in the remaining white southern Democratic reelection constituents being barely distinguishable from northern Democrats on government's role in the economy, health insurance, and women's role. White southern Democrats continue to state preferences closer to those of Republicans than to those of northern Democrats only on defense spending.

The movement of conservative whites out of the Democratic column should reduce some of the distance between black and white Democratic reelection constituents in the South. On six of the seven items listed in table 3.9, the white-black distance is reduced from that in 1984–90. White southern Democrats' liberal-conservative self-placement and their positions on defense spending and health insurance were not substantially different from those of black southern Democrats. Substantial differences between black and white southern Democrats persisted, however, on government's role in the economy, on government services spending, and especially on aid to minorities. Southern Democratic representatives must still bridge a gap between their black and white reelection constituents in addressing such issues.

The one scale item on which white-black differences increased in 1990–96 was women's role. The typical position of white southern Democrats on this item is somewhat to the left of black southern Democrats. In 1984–90 there had been no significant distance on this item between white and black southern Democrats or between white southern Democrats and Republicans. In the 1990s white voters, but not blacks, began to follow more activist southerners in sorting themselves on the basis of attitudes toward women's role.

Activist Constituents

Southern Democratic primary constituents also moved leftward relative to northern Democrats and Republicans. Table 3.10 lists the mean position of the three sets of primary constituents for the combined NES samples of 1990–96, identified on the basis of their engagement in three or more nonvoting acts of participation. Southern Democratic primary constituents were closer to northern Democratic activists than to Republicans on all seven items, representing a substantial leftward movement of the southern Democrats from the 1984–90 data. Especially notable is the position of southern Democratic primary constituents on defense spending and women's role. On both of these items, southern Democratic reelection constituents were placed closer to Republicans than to northern Democrats, but southern Democratic primary constituents were closer to northern Democrats than to Republicans. Southern Democratic primary constituents were significantly more liberal than reelection constituents on these two items, as well as on the health insurance item.

TABLE 3.10

Attitudes of Political Activists by Party of Congressional Vote, 1990–1996
(NES 7-point response scales)

ITEM	MEANS			DISTANCE	
	ND	SD	R	SD-ND	R-SD
Government guarantee job and standard of living	3.59[1]	3.74	5.22[2]	0.15	1.48***
	(167)	(62)	(196)		
Government services spending	4.69[1]	4.31	3.09[1]	(-0.38)	(-1.22***)
	(160)	(59)	(198)		
Government health insurance	2.91[1]	2.78[1]	4.78	-0.13	2.00***
	(124)	(41)	(158)		
Government aid to minorities	3.90[1]	4.19	5.11	0.29	0.92***
	(157)	(63)	(198)		
Liberal-conservative	3.09[1]	3.70	5.13	0.61**	1.43***
	(163)	(50)	(190)		
Defense spending	2.69[1]	3.17[1]	4.18	0.48*	1.01***
	(166)	(63)	(200)		
Women's equal role	1.79[1]	1.94[1]	2.61	0.15	0.67**
	(145)	(54)	(183)		

NOTES: In the distance columns, parentheses indicate items for which lower scores represent a more "conservative" or more "Republican" response. ND = northern Democrats, SD = southern Democrats, R = Republicans. N is in parentheses below each mean entry.
Distance between parties:
*** $p < .001$.
** $p < .01$.
* $p < .05$
Difference between activist and reelection constituents within parties:
[1] $p < .05$.
[2] $p < .10$.

On the defense spending and women's role items, representing the preferences of reelection constituents would place southern Democratic representatives closer to the position of Republicans but representing the position of primary constituents would place southern Democrats closer to northern Democrats. For the defense spending item, this is a new development. For the women's role item, it continues the 1984–90 pattern.

We have seen that southern Democratic reelection constituents moved in the direction of the subset of primary constituents on the women's role item in 1990–96. This finding is consistent with an issue evolution (Carmines and Stimson 1989), in which southern partisan activists became more differentiated on the women's role item in the late 1980s and were followed by movement among the mass electorate in the early 1990s. The more specific issue item of abortion displays a similar pattern. Table 3.11 shows the percentages supporting unlimited abortion rights among the reelection constituents and the primary constituents in each of the three party groupings. As noted earlier, the Republican–northern Democratic difference among reelection constituents on this issue emerged sometime after it was first apparent among primary constituents. Likewise, a movement of the southern Democratic position away from that of Republicans appeared to be in progress in the early 1990s, led by the more activist primary constituents.

CONCLUSION:
PREDICTING ROLL CALL VOTING PATTERNS
FROM CONSTITUENCY ATTITUDES

The findings reported in this chapter suggest that for southern Democrats, following constituency opinion on some issues is easier than on others. On government spending and government's role in providing jobs, white and black reelection constituents push southern Democratic representatives in the same direction: toward agreement with northern Democratic positions. We should be careful to note the substantial differences between blacks and whites on these issues, but these are the issues that clearly separate both white and black southern Democrats from Republican reelection constituents. It is on these issues that southern Democrats should be most likely to support northern Democratic positions in the House.

On other issues, both black and white southern Democrats are in substantial agreement with Republican reelection constituents. The attitudes of both black and white constituents push southern Democratic representatives away from partisanship and toward coalition with Republicans. This was especially true in the late 1980s. Thus we might expect lower levels of partisan roll call voting among southern Democrats on moral and cultural issues such as abortion and school prayer.

On the survey items that are explicitly concerned with race and civil rights, white southern Democrats and Republicans hold similar attitudes, but black southern Democrats take a position to the left of northern Democrats. One can conclude that southern Democratic representatives receive cross-pressures from within their own reelection constituencies on race and civil rights questions. How a member votes on such an issue may depend on the salience of a particular roll call to one or the other group and on the member's perception of how he can explain his vote if that becomes necessary.

Along with race, degrees of electoral activism distinguish different degrees of policy liberalism among southern Democratic constituents. On the women's role and abortion items, and possibly also defense and racial issues, voting realignment among activists in congressional elections has proceeded ahead of that among the mass electorate. This is consistent with a model in which activists serve as a signaling agent for issue-based realignment. In aligning their party loyalties, activists respond to the issue environment, particularly the policy proposals and actions of partisan

TABLE 3.11
Abortion Attitudes by Party of Congressional Vote, 1968–1996
(NES survey items)

REELECTION CONSTITUENTS

ABORTION RIGHTS (FAVOR UNLIMITED RIGHTS %)

SAMPLE	ND	SD	R	R-ND	SD-ND	R-SD
1968–74	31.7 (517)	12.1 (214)	27.8 (572)	(-3.90)	(-19.60)***	(15.70)***
1984–90	45.9 (1652)	32.7 (681)	34.7 (1608)	(-11.20)***	(-13.20)***	(2.00)
1990–96	55.9 (1464)	40.4 (560)	36.2 (1604)	(-19.7)***	(-15.5)***	(-4.2)*

PRIMARY CONSTITUENTS

ABORTION RIGHTS (FAVOR UNLIMITED RIGHTS %)

SAMPLE	ND	SD	R	R-ND	SD-ND	R-SD
1968–74	54.0[1] (63)	14.3 (14)	26.8 (56)	(-27.2)***	(-39.7)***	(12.5)

1984–90	56.9[1]	39.7	31.1	(-25.8)****	(-17.2)**	(-8.6)
	(137)	(58)	(119)			
1990–96	65.7[1]	53.7[1]	34.0	(-31.7)****	(-12.0)*	(-19.7)***
	(169)	(67)	(200)			

Notes: Distance between parties:
**** $p < .001$.
*** $p < .01$.
** $p < .05$.
* $p < .10$.
Difference between activist and reelection constituents within parties:
1 $p < .05$.

political leaders. The policy initiatives of presidents and presidential candidates, the contents of national party platforms, and the actions of congressional leaders all contribute to shaping party images among political activists and ultimately the public.

This issue realignment model does not clearly delineate a role for rank-and-file representatives. Are the positions taken by rank-and-file representatives more congruent with the attitudes of activist constituents than those of reelection constituents? One can make this hypothesis, on the basis of the extent to which activist constituents dominate the candidate recruitment pool and command the bulk of important electoral resources within each party. Likewise, one might expect southern Democrats' roll call votes on civil rights legislation to be especially responsive to the attitudes of blacks because of their numerical weight in primary and reelection constituencies.

Like the hypothesis of responsiveness to reelection constituents, the hypothesis of primary constituent influence is one that treats constituency as exercising influence on representation in Congress. However, rather than merely follow opinion changes among either reelection or activist constituents, members of Congress may actually play a leading role in issue realignments. Partisan theories of congressional behavior anticipate that members will react to partisan institutional imperatives as well as to their constituents.

CHAPTER FOUR

ISSUE AREAS AND
ROLL CALL VOTING

Profound changes in southern politics have been reflected on the
floors of Congress, but one must take care to note the limits of both
the change and its reflection. Roll call partisanship among southern
Democrats is greater on some issues than on others. This variation
across issues parallels the differences across issues in the association
between mass attitudes and partisanship in congressional elections.
At the same time, southern Democrats in the House have begun to
display greater partisanship in issue areas on which southern Democratic reelection constituents are no more dissimilar from Republican
constituents than was the case in the early 1970s. Variations in party
support shown by southern Democratic representatives both within
and across issue areas can be explained in part by the attitudes of
reelection and primary constituents. The increase in partisanship
during the last two decades cannot be entirely explained by constituency factors, however, suggesting that forces endogenous to the
House of Representatives are also at work in the partisan resurgence.

SOUTHERN DEMOCRATS AND THE
CONSERVATIVE COALITION

The expectation that roll call behavior depends on the issue area
should be placed in the context of historic patterns of southern

Democratic conservatism in roll call voting. When the election of 1932 sent a Democratic majority to Congress and placed Franklin Roosevelt in the White House, it signaled the emergence of a new partisan alignment with profound implications for public policy. Long the dominant group within a minority political party, southern Democrats now found themselves part of a majority party with a commitment to using government to direct the deployment of resources in the service of economic growth. Southern Democratic members of Congress agreed with their northern Democratic colleagues on the necessity for government involvement in the economy. The programs of the New Deal tended to redistribute investment toward poorer regions, of which the South had a disproportionate share, and the regulatory dimension of the New Deal placed its heaviest burden on larger industrial sectors centered outside the South. These dimensions of the northern Democratic agenda would not by themselves upset the balance of interests represented by southern Democrats, who were solid supporters of the New Deal in the early 1930s (Sinclair 1983; Brady 1988).

The emergence of a conservative voting alliance between southern Democrats and Republicans is usually traced to the late 1930s (Key 1949; Patterson 1967; Brady and Bullock 1980). The realignment in the North that transformed the Democrats from a minority party dominated by the South into a national majority party was class-based. Northern business and professional people tended to vote Republican, while working-class support was a critical element of the new northern Democratic coalition (Sundquist 1983). When the administration and northern Democrats in Congress turned their attention to the concerns expressed by labor leaders, they encountered opposition from southern Democrats. The southerners found allies in the Republican Party, and a majority of southern Democrats frequently joined the congressional Republicans in opposition to northern Democratic efforts on behalf of organized labor (Key 1949: 374–75).

The labor movement was practically nonexistent in most of the South at midcentury, a situation that the leaders of southern commerce, industry, and agriculture wanted to maintain (Marshall 1967). The southern agricultural and industrial sectors were dependent on the availability of cheap unskilled labor in a regional labor market that was relatively isolated from the national economy (Wright 1986). Efforts to organize workers, improve working conditions, and set minimum wages only served to undermine this pillar of the southern economy. As the 1940s wore on, the conservative coalition began to appear on votes concerning social welfare policy, with southern Democrats and Republicans opposing the expansion of federal assistance (Brady and Bullock 1980). Whether directed toward income maintenance or education, expanded social welfare programs could reduce the incentives for individuals to participate in the South's low-wage labor market.

Southern Democrats also opposed the northern Democratic position on civil rights for blacks. The role of blacks in the urban political coalitions of northern Democrats and in the wartime economic and military mobilization generated pressures to expand black civil rights, pressures that southern Democrats actively resisted. For example, southerners voted against allowing black soldiers to vote in primary elections and against prohibiting poll taxes for federal elections. In fact, southern members of Congress were far more unified in their opposition to black civil rights than in their opposition to organized labor. Although substantial minorities of southerners tended to support their party on labor and social welfare roll calls, race was the one issue on which virtually every southern Democrat agreed (Key 1949).

The centrality of race to the political posture of southern Democrats sets them apart from both northern Democrats and Republicans. At times, a majority of Republicans would join southern Democrats in opposition to federal involvement in racial issues or civil liberties more generally. On racial issues in particular, however, southern Democrats most frequently stood alone in their conservatism (Katznelson, Geiger, and Kryder 1993). Important roll call votes concerning black civil rights did not typically occasion a southern Democratic-Republican coalition until the mid-1960s, when Republicans began to take a conservative position on federal involvement in racial issues (Black 1979; Carmines and Stimson 1989). In the meantime, the cohesiveness of southern Democratic opposition made roll call success difficult for liberal measures on race, and the southerners typically used their positions on congressional committees to block or water down legislation designed to extend civil rights to blacks.

Two features of the race issue at midcentury are worthy of note. First, the handling of civil rights by Congress is probably the most vivid illustration of the institutional power held by southern Democrats at the time. Southern solidarity on the floors of Congress was not the most important factor shaping civil rights legislation in the 1940s and 1950s. Even more crucial was that southern Democrats, by virtue of their low rates of electoral turnover, accrued seniority advantages over northern Democrats. This enabled southern Democrats to exercise disproportionate influence over the flow and content of legislation in committee, since seniority usually dictated the chair and ranking minority member of each committee. The result was that the emergence of civil rights legislation from committee required that it be amended to satisfy the objections of southern Democrats.

The impact of southern concerns on legislative content was evident in labor and social welfare policy as well. Legislation such as the National Recovery Act, the Wagner Act, Social Security, and the Fair Labor Standards Act excluded agricultural and domestic labor from their provisions and was thus of very limited benefit to most southern blacks. Further, because of decentralized administration, programs like Aid to Families with Dependent Children (AFDC) and the various work relief programs under the New Deal could offer far less generous benefits in the southern states than elsewhere (Katznelson, Geiger, and Kryder 1993: 297).

In contrast to social welfare, civil rights, and the like, the highest levels of interregional agreement within the Democratic Party were on government management of the economy (Sinclair 1977, 1981; Brady and Bullock 1980, 1981). "Government management" generally encompasses policy proposals that to varying degrees replace private with public discretion in the deployment of productive economic resources, typically through public works spending or business regulation. Until the 1970s the degree of unity (such as it was) between northern and southern Democrats on government management votes contrasted sharply with the regional difference within the party on social welfare and civil liberties issues. This contrast was due to the combination of issue orientations that emerged among Democratic House members after the initial crisis of the early 1930s had passed. Although southern elites continued to support a government role in economic development, many were repelled by the long-term implications of New Deal policies.

Even on the issue of government management, the degree of liberalism displayed by southern Democrats declined precipitously in the late 1960s and early 1970s. Until the 1960s growth-oriented policies dominated the economic agenda, and southern support for a government role in economic development was reflected in high pro-party scores for southern Democrats on such issues. In the 1960s the policy content of economic legislation shifted toward greater emphasis on regulation and limitation of business activities in the interest of consumer and environmental protection and energy conservation. This type of regulation imposed costs on a wider range of businesses than ever before, and southern Democrats saw this as against the interests of their business supporters. Southern Democrats began to vote with the party on government management issues with declining frequency. By the early 1970s southern Democrats' liberal support scores on government management issues were not much higher than their scores on civil liberties issues (Sinclair 1981), even though government management of the economy could not be validated as an issue dimension that appeared among conservative coalition votes in that period (Brady and Bullock 1980, 1981).

In examining the issues on which northern and southern Democrats split most frequently, foreign affairs merits attention. Southern Democrats had long been noted for opposing isolationism in foreign policy, but in retrospect their internationalist approach turns out to have taken a peculiar form. In the economic sphere, southern support for free trade initiatives was tied to the dependence of the cotton industry on access to the world market. The internationalist stance in economic matters was connected to more general support for the projection of U.S. influence abroad. This southern internationalism encompassed support for the unilateral pursuit of U.S. economic and political interests. As internationalism in foreign policy became more closely associated with the multilateral pursuit of goals less directly tied to U.S. economic and political interests, southern support for activist foreign policy became less consistent (Lerche 1964). Opposition by southern Democrats to liberal foreign aid and immigration policies led to such issues emerging as a frequent subject of conservative coalition roll calls in the 1950s (Brady and Bullock 1980).

In short, from the 1950s through the 1970s the conservative coalition of southern Democrats and Republicans altered the partisan landscape in Congress on roll calls concerning labor, social welfare, civil rights, civil liberties, and foreign policy (Brady and Bullock 1980, 1981). A crucial aspect of the environment in which the conservative coalition operated was the growing numbers of northern liberals in the congressional Democratic Party between 1958 and 1964. The 1958 election brought seventeen new liberal northern Democrats to the Senate, with smaller numbers joining their ranks in succeeding elections. Liberal northern Democrats were increasing their numbers in the House as well, making their largest gains during the landslide election of 1964. Although many of these newer members were vulnerable to defeat in subsequent elections, those who remained tended to be more liberal than previous cohorts of northern Democrats and thus contributed over time to the liberalization of the Democratic Party caucus. The most immediate consequence was that, especially during the 89th Congress (1965–66), by their sheer numbers liberal Democrats were able to overwhelm the institutional advantages held by southern Democrats and pass a number of civil rights and social welfare bills (Sinclair 1989: 30–50; Rohde 1991b: 7–8). Such legislation was typically enacted over the opposition of the conservative coalition, which won a progressively smaller proportion of the votes on which it appeared (Manley 1973; Brady and Bullock 1980).

The 89th Congress also marks an increase in the frequency of conservative coalition appearances on congressional roll calls to above 21 percent, a level that had not been matched in the previous six congresses but was matched or exceeded in each subsequent year through 1978. The Democratic losses in the 1966 elections depleted the ranks of liberals somewhat, but the northern Democrats who remained were more liberal than those who had served before 1958. Hence the conservative coalition continued to form on a historically large proportion of votes, and it once again had the numbers to win on well over half its appearances (Manley 1973; Brady and Bullock 1980). After a brief period of political success that fundamentally changed civil rights and social welfare policy for a generation, liberal Democrats were once again dependent on conservative southerners for partisan control of Congress. Yet the southerners were in "revolt" against the policy direction taken by their party in the 1960s (Shannon 1972).

The southern Democratic revolt occurred despite the rapid mobilization of black voters in the late 1960s. Well into the 1970s, in fact, the most conservative Democrats in the House represented rural southern congressional districts with higher populations of blacks (Combs, Hibbing, and Welch 1984; Whitby 1985). The greater part of black voter integration into the southern electorate had occurred by the time of the 93d Congress of 1973–74, the first Congress elected from districts drawn after the 1970 census. We can also be certain that the 1970 redistricting fully reflected the implications of the "one person, one vote" decision in *Wesberry v. Sanders* for the representation of urban areas. One might have expected these factors to have produced an immediate movement to more liberal and partisan behavior among southern Democrats, but the trend to partisanship was a gradual one and it did not begin until the 96th Congress.

Both the historical patterns of roll call voting and the contemporary constituency preferences reported in chapter 3 lead one to expect differences across issue areas in the partisan behavior of southern Democratic representatives. The remainder of this chapter tests this proposition for roll call votes during the 93d through 104th Congresses.

PARTISAN ROLL CALLS

Our focus is on issue differences in the level of partisanship displayed by southern Democrats in roll call voting. We must first isolate those roll calls that are partisan. To do so, we take advantage of the essentially partisan basis of both the party unity and the conservative coalition roll calls: all of the conservative coalition votes and the vast majority of party unity votes occur when a majority of northern Democrats oppose a majority of Republicans. The conservative coalition appears when a majority of southern Democrats side with the Republicans when such a northern Democrat–Republican split occurs, and party unity votes occur when southern Democrats side with northern Democrats in such a split.[1] If a majority of northern Democrats oppose a majority of Republicans on a given roll call, whether the roll call falls into the party unity or the conservative coalition category depends on the proportion of southern Democrats favoring or opposing the northern Democrats' position. A party agreement score based on both sets of roll calls is the most appropriate indicator of the

TABLE 4.1
Partisan Voting

Rate of Agreement with Majority of Northern Democrats
When Opposed by Majority of Republicans

Congress	Northern Democrats	Southern Democrats	Republicans
93d	81	49	26
94th	82	49	23
95th	79	51	23
96th	81	56	20
97th	82	53	22
98th	88	64	22
99th	89	73	22
100th	91	77	21
101st	89	74	23
102d	88	75	19
103d	90	81	13
104th	87	74	09

relative attraction of partisanship and conservatism for southern Democrats in their roll call voting.[2]

For the set of partisan roll calls in each Congress from 1973 to 1996, I have computed partisan voting scores for each member. The score indicates the member's rate of agreement with the position taken by a majority of northern Democrats on partisan roll calls. Partisan scores were computed for both the overall set of partisan roll calls and within issue areas. Table 4.1 displays the mean overall partisan score of northern Democrats, southern Democrats, and Republicans in each Congress. The pattern is broadly similar to that reported in chapter 1 with respect to party unity scores. Southern Democrats are closer to Republicans than to northern Democrats during the 93d and 94th Congresses. The movement to more partisan voting occurs during the 95th through 100th Congresses. The high levels of support among southern Democrats for President Ronald Reagan's tax cut package probably accounts for the interruption of this trend in the 97th Congress (1981–82).

Southern Democrats' overall rate of agreement with the northern Democratic position on partisan votes increased from 75 in the 102d Congress to 81 in the 103d. It dropped back to 74 in the 104th Congress, after the Republican victory in the 1994 elections. The 1992 congressional redistricting resulted in a marked increase in the number of black southern Democratic representatives, from five to seventeen. Black Democrats display higher levels of party support on roll calls, but the increased partisanship of southern Democrats after 1992 was not attributable solely to the increased number of black representatives. The partisan agreement rate of white southern Democrats increased to 78 percent in the 103d Congress and fell to 67 in the 104th. Only forty-two white southern Democrats remained in the House following the electoral losses of 1994 and the subsequent switches to the Republican Party by five white southerners who won in 1994 as Democrats. The response of these forty-two members to their party's minority status was typically reflected in less partisan roll call voting.

Issue Categories

It is hypothesized here that southern Democrats are more partisan on some issues than on others. To examine this question, a scheme for classifying roll calls into issue areas is necessary. The conceptual foundation for such a scheme was established by Aage R. Clausen. Clausen's policy dimension theory is based on the assumption that the pattern of voting alignments on a set of roll calls will depend on their policy content. Following this assumption, one can classify roll calls by policy area to examine the impact of issue content on roll call voting. If issue content affects roll call voting decisions of individual legislators, then the voting alignments that characterize different issue areas will be distinguishable, even taking into account likely intercorrelation across issue areas (Clausen 1973).

Using cluster analysis of Yule's Q correlations among roll call votes, Clausen validated issue dimensions in the 83d to 88th Congresses. Most roll call votes could be classified as being concerned with one of the following: government management of the economy, social welfare, agricultural assistance, civil liberties, and international involvement (Clausen 1973). A study of the 91st to 95th Congress validated six dimensions, with the international dimension being split into two, one dimension concerning involvement in international affairs and the other concerning defense policy (Wilcox and Clausen 1991).

In the roll call analysis presented below, the categories labor, civil rights, and budget were added to those validated by Clausen.[3] (Table 4.2 provides a summary listing of the issue areas into which roll calls have been classified for analysis.) Separating labor votes from other economic votes is suggested by David W. Brady and Charles S. Bullock's finding that labor issues presented a unique issue alignment when the conservative coalition was just beginning to form. Given the relatively weak position of organized labor in much of the South, we might expect southern Democrats to be less supportive of national party positions on labor issues than on other economic issues. Separating civil rights votes from civil liberties votes is suggested by the different constituency pressures to which southern Democratic representatives must respond on these two types of issues. In chapter 3, I noted that southern Democratic reelection constituents appear to be uniformly conservative on issues such as abortion and prayer in schools, but on issues related to black civil rights a substantial group in many reelection constituencies is very supportive of national Democratic positions.

The emergence of the congressional budget process in the context of interbranch conflict during the 1970s and the importance of the budget deficit as an issue unto itself in the 1980s suggest treating votes on matters such as overall budget levels, supplemental

TABLE 4.2
Issue Categories for Roll Call Analysis

CATEGORY	TYPICAL ISSUES
Budget	Overall budget levels, debt ceiling
Civil liberties	Crime, defendant's rights, abortion, family planning
Civil rights	Voting rights, affirmative action provisions, fair housing, civil rights act renewals
Defense	Defense funding levels, overall and specific programs; nuclear weapons and arms control
Foreign affairs	Foreign aid, international institutions, foreign intervention, sanctions
Economic management	Banking, energy and environmental regulation, consumer protection, treasury and interior programs, price controls, tax reform
Labor	Minimum wage, prevailing wage, plant closing, striker replacements
Social welfare	Housing programs, welfare reform, Head Start, children's services

appropriations, and the debt ceiling as a separate category from other economic issues. The potential for budget bills to unite southern Democratic fiscal conservatives with liberals seeking to protect social programs from encroachment by defense spending or other priorities makes it prudent to treat budget votes separately from issues such as economic regulation or social welfare (see Rohde 1991b; Palazollo and Rich 1992).

On the basis of the attitudes of reelection and primary constituents, the trend to partisanship among southern Democratic representatives should have progressed farther in some issue areas than others by the end of the 1980s. Constituency attitudes lead one to expect the following patterns in different issue areas.

1. On the economic management and social welfare dimensions, southern Democrats have clearly moved farther from the typical Republican position and closer to the position of northern Democrats, so that by the late 1980s the distance between southern Democrats and northern Democrats is less than that between southern Democrats and Republicans.

2. On defense matters, in the late 1980s southern Democrats are closer to Republicans than to northern Democrats, although their position is distinct from that of both of the other partisan groups. We may surmise from earlier roll call studies that this would represent a leftward movement in the placement of southern Democrats on defense issues.

3. On the civil liberties dimension, attitudes of reelection constituents place southern Democrats and Republicans together at a similar distance from northern Democrats. Southern Democratic roll call voting should display a similar tendency. (An alternative hypothesis is that southern Democrats have moved slightly leftward in the late 1980s, a phenomenon associated with the beginnings of a leftward movement of their primary constituents on abortion.)

It is not clear from the review of constituent attitudes in chapter 3 what pattern of partisanship we should expect on civil rights votes. Responsiveness to white constituents would place southern Democrats with Republicans in opposition to northern Democrats. Responsiveness to black constituents would place southern Democrats in agreement with northern Democrats. Responsiveness to primary constituents would place southern Democrats closer to northern Democrats than to Republicans (on the question of government aid to minorities). These patterns occur both at the beginning and at the end of the period. Any increase in southern

Democratic partisanship on civil rights would be indicative of increasing responsiveness to black voters.

The constituent attitude data do not include items that specifically refer to foreign affairs, labor, or budget issues. Still, one can engage in some informed speculation about southern Democrats' roll call votes on such issues. Studies of the conservative coalition revealed southern Democrats to be closer to Republicans than to northern Democrats on foreign affairs votes, and we have no constituency-based reason to expect that a major partisan shift has occurred (for evidence of increasing partisanship on foreign policy, however, see Rohde 1994a, 1994b). Labor issues were an important catalyst in the early development of the conservative coalition. The liberalization of southern Democratic constituents on economic issues might be mirrored in a leftward movement on labor votes. Finally, to the extent that budget votes are primarily about partisan control of the appropriations process, we can expect high levels of agreement with northern Democrats. Fiscal conservatism could pull southern Democrats away from that agreement, however.

Constructing Issue Scales from Roll-Call Votes

My method of analyzing roll call votes is based on that developed by Duncan MacRae (1958, 1970). Others have used similar scaling methods (Clausen 1967, 1973; Shannon 1968; Clausen and Cheney 1970; Sinclair 1977; Brady and Bullock 1980, 1981; Brady 1988). The approach identifies sets of roll call votes in each Congress that can be combined into scales that are interpretable as measuring support for a single policy object (e.g., government involvement in the economy). It is designed to address those changes in roll call voting that are caused by changes in legislators' attitudes toward relatively fixed policy ideas, and to leave aside temporary issues.

The first step was to classify the partisan votes (party unity votes and conservative coalition votes) for each Congress into issue areas. The next step was to perform hierarchical cluster analyses of the roll calls in each issue area for each Congress. The cluster analyses were based on matrixes of Yule's Q coefficients computed for each pair of votes included in a given issue area.

I used the results of the cluster analysis to select the roll calls that would form the basis for issue scale scores. Among the clusters with a minimum Yule's Q of .6, those that included three or more votes were used to compute issue scale scores for each member of the House. A member's scale score on a given cluster is the proportion of votes cast in agreement with the position taken by a majority of northern Democrats.

One cluster of votes was selected as the primary scale of partisan support for each issue area in each Congress. For Congresses in which there was more than one cluster from which to choose for a given issue, the cluster selected to measure the issue alignment was determined by examining the correlations (Pearson's r) between Congresses of the scales computed for that issue area. For each pair of Congresses, the scales with the highest inter-Congress correlation were selected within each issue area. On three occasions this procedure resulted in two scales being selected for the same issue in the same Congress, one having the highest correlation with a scale in the preceding Congress and the other having the highest correlation with the succeeding Congress. In these cases the set of scales selected was that having the highest mean correlation for the three Congresses.

After the primary issue scale was determined, it was possible to use the same procedure to identify secondary dimensions within an issue area. Secondary issue scales were identified if their inter-congress correlations exceeded their within-Congress correlations with clusters in the same issue area already included in the primary set of scales. In some instances the identification of secondary issue scales assists in understanding shifting roll call patterns among southern Democrats.

Results: Issue Differences in Southern Democratic Partisanship

Table 4.3 reports the mean scale scores of southern Democrats in eight issue areas.[4] During the period of the partisan surge, the 96th through 101st Congresses, the pattern is as expected. Southern Democrats were more supportive of the typical northern Democratic position on budgeting, social welfare, and economic management than on civil liberties, foreign affairs, and defense. The pattern is broadly consistent with my hypotheses of cross-issue differences in southern Democratic partisanship.

During the 102d and especially the 103d Congresses, issue differences in partisanship decreased markedly. In the 104th Congress, southern Democratic partisanship was again substantially lower on civil liberties, foreign affairs, and defense than on budget, welfare, and economic management. The average difference between the issue areas in the two groups was smaller in the 104th Congress than it had been in the 1980s, however.

It is also revealing to know the relative placement of southern Democrats compared to northern Democrats and Republicans on these issues. Table 4.4 reports southern Democrats' mean difference from the partisan scale scores of Republicans for each issue area, expressed as a percentage of the difference between northern Democrats and Republicans. Because of the scaling technique used, these differences can be interpreted as distances between the typical member of each partisan group on distinct (though intercorrelated) policy dimensions. In Table 4.4, the distance measure takes the value of zero if southern Democrats voted for the northern Democratic position at the same rate as the Republicans did, and 100 if southern and northern Democrats had the same rate of partisan agreement. A score of 50 is the midpoint between the typical northern Democratic and Republican positions on a given issue scale. Except for a few instances in the early 1970s, southern Democrats are always located somewhere between northern Democrats and Republicans.

TABLE 4.3

Partisan Scale Scores by Issue Area—Southern Democrats

Congress	Budget	Economic Management		Social Welfare	Labor	Civil Rights	Civil Liberties			Foreign Affairs	Defense	
							Crime	Abortion				
93d	84	38		57	49	19	32			33	22	
94th	65	45		57	52	35	31*	41		35	16	
		Regulation	General									
95th	68	39*	63	55	50	31	34	53*		32	29	
96th	76	41*	68	51	45	41		37		38	23	
97th	62	31	72*	63	55	42	29			44	23	
98th	76	48	78*	84			53			45	39	
99th	85	63	76*	81	58	91	48			60	35	
											Policy	Partisan/ Procedural
100th	85	89		82	68	90	43			52	58*	97
101st	77	86		72	64	75	45			65	53*	87
							Crime	Abortion/ Procedural				
102d	78	89		82	68	74	36	70*		85	45	92*
								Proce- dural	Abortion			
103d	88	90		85	87	95	45	81*	72	88	53	96*
104th	94	90		85	82	88	66*		68	77	70	

*Primary issue scale within the economic, civil liberties, or defense issue area.

TABLE 4.4

Partisan Scale Distances by Issue Area—Southern Democrats

Congress	Budget	Economic Management		Social Welfare	Labor	Civil Rights	Civil Liberties			Foreign Affairs	Defense	
		Regulation	General				Crime	Abortion	Procedural		Policy	Partisan/Procedural
93d	85		28	55	38	-16	17			-47	00	
94th	66		40	54	45	10	12*	47		-18	-06	
95th	71	36*	66	56	44	25	21	78*		08	21	
96th	84	41*	79	51	35	38		41		32	08	
97th	64	27	72*	65	49	35		24		28	05	
98th	79	38	79*	83				51		45	31	
99th	90	61	79*	81	51	91		53		59	32	
100th	91		89	86	63	91		47		53	59*	100
101st	82		86	75	64	74		46		64	52*	89
102d	86		94	85	67	78	42	77*		94	45	96*
103d	93		94	89	87	96	56	79	87*	95	55	102*
104th	96		95	91	83	88	79*	85		88	78	

*Primary issue scale within the economic, civil liberties, or defense issue area.

Economic Issues

The economic management, social welfare, and budget dimensions have typically displayed the greatest agreement between northern and southern Democrats, particularly since the 97th Congress. On the economic management dimension, southern Democrats were clearly closer to Republicans than to northern Democrats through the 96th Congress (column 2 of table 4.4). Beginning with the 97th Congress, however, southern Democrats were positioned closer to northern Democrats than to Republicans. By the 102d Congress, the southern Democrat–Republican difference was fifteen times that between southern and northern Democrats. The movement of southern Democrats is in the expected direction, and their relative placement is about what one should expect given the attitudes of reelection constituents.

Southern Democratic partisanship in the early Congresses in the series is perhaps even lower than one would have expected on the basis of constituency attitudes on economic questions. As reported by Sinclair (1981), southern Democratic conservatism in the early 1970s appears to be linked to the prominence of regulatory issues on the economic management dimension. Between the 96th and 97th Congresses, a shift occurred in the major emphasis of the primary economic management scale. The primary roll call scale for the 96th Congress was dominated by regulatory issues. Of thirty-two roll calls, nineteen concerned consumer, environmental, or energy regulation and five concerned the windfall profits tax on oil. Such issues did not dominate the primary issue scale in the 97th Congress: it contained thirty-five roll calls, eighteen of which concerned authorization and spending levels for National Science Foundation (NSF), National Bureau of Standards, and energy, water, and transportation programs, the National Oceanic and Atmospheric Administration (NOAA), and the Corporation for Public Broadcasting (CPB). Six more votes concerned the establishment

of national park or historic sites, and three concerned Indian land
or legal claims. Only two roll calls on the primary economic scale
in the 97th concerned consumer or environmental regulation, and
both concerned funding levels. In the 98th Congress, the primary
economic scale included only two environmental items among 54
roll calls. Transportation and interior appropriations, worker training
and trade adjustment assistance, communications regulation, and
energy research were the prominent issues.

Regulation did persist as a distinct but secondary issue within
the economic domain in the 97th through 99th Congresses. In the
97th Congress, a cluster of fourteen roll calls included four votes on
tax cuts proposed by President Reagan and a total of 8 votes concerning regulatory approaches to vehicle emissions, solid waste
disposal, nuclear licensing and waste storage, and insecticide regu-
lations. A similar cluster of nineteen votes occurred in the 98th
Congress, including nine votes on environmental regulation, four
on energy conservation, and two on the Consumer Product Safety
Commission (CPSC). An eleven-vote cluster in the 99th Congress
included eight votes concerning consumer and environmental protection. In each of these Congresses, southern Democrats were less
partisan on this regulatory dimension than on the primary economic
dimension, scoring respectively 31, 48, and 63 in the 97th through
99th Congresses. Even in the regulatory area, however, southern
Democratic partisanship was increasing. Of course, with the dominance of deregulation as a policy approach in the 1980s, partisan
roll calls on the subject were likely to cast the northern Democratic
position as one of defending existing programs rather than establishing new ones. By the 100th Congress, the primary economic
management scale again encompassed a mixture of spending and
regulatory issues, and the inter-Congress correlation indicates the
merging of the regulatory and spending dimensions.

Southern Democratic movement on the social welfare dimension was not so dramatic, but the pattern is consistent with my
expectations (column 3 of table 4.4). Southern Democrats were

only marginally closer to the typical northern Democrat during the 93d through 96th Congresses, but they became substantially more partisan on this dimension in the 97th Congress and again in the 98th, so that their distance from Republicans was typically four to five times that from northern Democrats after the 98th Congress.

On budget issues, southern Democrats were substantially closer to northern Democrats than to Republicans in each Congress (column 1 of table 4.4). The most salient in the series of Congresses is the 97th, in which southern Democrats demonstrated their lowest level of partisanship. This coincides with the first budgets under Ronald Reagan, which garnered some southern Democratic support, particularly in their tax and deficit provisions. It is also notable that southern Democrats averaged higher partisan scores after the 99th Congress than before.

On labor issues, southern Democrats moved from a position closer to Republicans during the 93d through 96th Congresses to a position about midway between the Republican and northern Democratic positions in the 97th and 99th Congresses and then to a position nearer the northern Democrats after the 99th Congress. This movement is what one might have expected on the basis of the movement of southern Democratic reelection constituents to the left on economic questions, but southern Democratic partisanship on labor issues reached levels comparable to that on the other economic issues only during the 103d and 104th Congresses.

Defense and Foreign Affairs Issues

On defense issues, southern Democrats typically occupied about the same position as the Republicans through the 97th Congress. During the 98th and 99th Congresses, they moved away from the Republican position, but their distance from Republicans was still a bit less than half their distance from northern Democrats. In the 100th and 101st Congresses, southern Democrats were more nearly midway between the northern Democratic and Republican positions on partisan defense roll calls. In the Congresses following the 101st, southern Democrats displayed very high levels of party support on the roll call votes composing the primary defense scale. This was especially the case during the 102d and 103d Congresses, when southern Democrats had party support scores in the 90s. During the 104th Congress, their partisanship on the defense scale fell to 70.

Except for the 102d and 103d Congresses, southern Democratic partisanship is lower on defense issues than on economic and social welfare issues. Yet their movement toward greater partisanship on defense issues is similar to that on economics and welfare. The trend of defense scores could be said to lag behind that of the economic and social welfare scores by two to three Congresses.

Secondary dimensions in the defense issue area provide clues to the forces that generate southern Democratic partisanship. In the 102d Congress two scales actually tied for the highest correlation with scales in the 101st Congress. These represented two persistent dimensions in defense voting. In addition to the primary policy dimension that characterized defense roll calls through the 101st Congress, a second, more partisan alignment emerged in the 100th Congress. These two dimensions persisted in the defense voting patterns through the 103d Congress, with the partisan dimension becoming the primary voting pattern in the 102d and 103d Congresses.

Of the eighty-six votes included in the defense policy scale in the 100th through 103d Congresses, thirty were associated with funding or deployment of ballistic missile defense systems (including the Strategic Defense Initiative, or SDI) and compliance with the Anti-Ballistic Missile Treaty. Votes concerning deployment of the MX missile, production of the B-1 ("Stealth") bomber and the D-5 submarine missile, and nuclear weapons testing were also prominent. Over the four Congresses, southern Democrats agreed with the northern Democratic position an average of 52 percent of the time. Southern Democrats were less inclined than northern Democrats to restrict SDI and nuclear testing and were more favorable to the B-1 bomber and the MX and D-5 missiles.

Southern Democrats' support for northern Democratic positions on the partisan defense dimension averaged 93 percent over the four Congresses, compared to 52 percent on the policy dimension. What inspired more partisan voting among southern Democrats on defense matters?

The 101st Congress is exceptional in that the partisan defense dimension encompassed primarily substantive, rather than procedural, matters. The fifteen votes on the partisan scale in this Congress included five on militarily sensitive exports and five on defense production, procurement, and economic adjustment. In the other Congresses the partisan defense scale was dominated by procedural votes.

Of the thirty-one partisan defense scale votes in the 100th Congress, eighteen occurred in late 1988 and involved southern Democrats joining northern Democrats to prevent a vote on whether to override President Reagan's veto of the 1989 defense authorization bill. (A conference committee report of a compromise defense authorization bill was later passed by the House with bipartisan majorities.) Seven other votes were on rules governing consideration of defense authorization, intelligence authorization, and military construction appropriations bills. Three were votes to pass the 1988 and 1989 defense authorization bills.

Of thirteen votes on the partisan defense scale in the 102d Congress, eight were on rules and final passage of bills and the others were on amendments concerning veterans' benefits, hiring preferences for defense contractors, and economic aid to areas affected by defense cuts. The partisan dimension in the 102d Congress was thus dominated by procedural and final passage votes but also included substantive issues similar to some of those eliciting more partisan behavior by southern Democrats in the 101st Congress. In the 103d Congress, eight of the twelve votes in the partisan

cluster were on rules for considering authorization and appropriations bills and two were party line votes on final passage of defense
authorization bills. This contrasts with the policy scale, which continued the spending and weapons program emphasis characteristic of the dominant defense dimension through the 101st Congress.
Of eleven votes included in the latter scale, five were concerned
with elimination of or cuts in the D-5 submarine missile program
and five were concerned with spending for ballistic missile defense;
the remaining vote was on a proposal to make cuts in a supplemental appropriations bill.

Dimensional analysis of roll call votes thus reveals clearly the
emergence of partisan/procedural and policy dimensions in defense
voting beginning with the 100th Congress. A policy area in which
constituency forces were not pushing southern Democrats toward
greater partisanship nonetheless demonstrated strong partisan
tendencies among southern Democrats on rules and final passage
of major bills. On votes denoting their level of commitment to
specific weapons programs, however, as a group southern Democrats remained about midway between northern Democrats and
Republicans in their preferences. This pattern is noted by Rohde
(1991b) in his explanation of the role of majority party leadership
in structuring policy choices. Southern Democrats were able to
express their preferences regarding spending levels and authorization of specific defense programs and weapons systems while
supporting partisan control of institutional outcomes through their
votes on rules and final passage. The pattern is also consistent with
Gary W. Cox and Mathew D. McCubbins's (1993) view of the
majority party as a "legislative cartel," the maintenance of which
is of value to all the party's members.

The partisan dimension was clearly the dominant defense dimension in the 103d Congress, when Democratic control of the House
was coupled with the leadership of a Democrat in the White House.
After the Democrats lost their House majority, they could no longer
use the Rules Committee to structure roll call votes to allow con-

servative Democrats to both express their dissent and support partisan outcomes. In the 104th Congress, southern Democrats' typical rate of partisan voting on the primary defense scale declined to 70 percent.

Foreign affairs votes demonstrate a pattern similar to defense. Southern Democrats displayed high levels of partisanship on the dominant foreign affairs dimension in the 102d and 103d Congresses (85 and 87 percent party support, respectively) and a somewhat lower party support rate in the 104th Congress (77 percent). southern Democratic partisanship in both foreign affairs and defense was higher in the 104th Congress than in any Congress before the 102d but still somewhat lower than their party support scores on budget, economic management, and social welfare issues.

Foreign affairs is also characterized by the existence of a less partisan secondary dimension in the 102d Congress, when two vote clusters actually tied for the highest correlation with the foreign affairs scale for the 101st Congress. On the more partisan primary dimension, southern Democrats voted with the northern Democrats 85 percent of the time. Six of the twelve votes in the partisan cluster in the 102d Congress were on rules for the consideration of foreign operations and foreign trade bills, and three were on amendments regarding security at the U.S. embassy in Moscow. The very first vote to occur in this cluster was a January 1991 resolution concerning the authorization to use force in the conflict with Iraq over its occupation of Kuwait. The resolution asserted that the Constitution vests in Congress the power to declare war.

The less partisan secondary cluster in the 102d Congress included eight votes on which southern Democrats' average party support score was only 52 percent. Two of these votes, concerning the Iraq conflict, occurred in January 1991 immediately after the vote on the resolution on war powers. In consecutive votes southern Democrats split with the northern Democratic positions in favor of a sense of the Congress resolution in favor of continued sanctions and diplomacy as the best course and against authorizing military action. (The northern Democratic position was not unanimous on these votes.) Other votes concerned ending presidential certification as a condition for aid to Pakistan, prohibiting aid to the South African Communist Party, suspending the repatriation of Haitian refugees, and provisions of the Export Administration Act. These issues represent substantive disagreements within the Democratic caucus on foreign policy issues, while the primary cluster represented support for partisan advantages in the distribution of policy-making power. Again, southern Democrats' support for partisan rules reflects placement of some value in maintaining their own party's control of the legislative apparatus even on issues with relatively low intraparty agreement on policy preferences.

Civil Liberties Issues

On the civil liberties scale southern Democrats were closer to the Republican position than to northern Democrats in every one of the Congresses from the 93d through the 97th, except for the 95th. In fact, southern Democrats were only 8 points less partisan on civil liberties in the 95th Congress than northern Democrats and 28 points away from the Republican position. (The total northern Democrat–Republican distance was itself the smallest on this or any other dimension, except for foreign affairs in the 93d Congress.) An important factor in the 95th Congress might be the emergence of abortion as the dominant civil liberties issue. All sixteen primary civil liberties roll calls in the 95th Congress concerned abortion, as did ten of the seventeen votes on the primary civil liberties scale in the 96th Congress. The newness of the abortion issue perhaps rendered southern Democrats more susceptible to partisan cues. The primary civil liberties scale in the 93d and 94th Congresses included issues such as access to legal services, parole, rules of criminal procedure, and use of federal funds to promote gender integration and secular humanism. Such issues persisted as a secondary dimension during the 95th Congress before becoming subsumed in the primary civil liberties scale in later Congresses. The typical southern Democrat's relative partisan distance on this secondary civil liberties dimension was 21.

Southern Democrats moved somewhat left on the civil liberties scale in the 98th through 101st Congresses, to a position squarely between northern Democrats and Republicans. In the 100th and 101st Congresses they were slightly closer to the Republicans. During these Congresses, the primary issue scale in this domain typically consisted of a variety of issues, including abortion funding, criminal procedures and sentencing, the death penalty, obscenity in art and communications, and drug policy.

In the 102d Congress, two clusters of votes tied for the highest correlation with the primary scale for the 101st Congress. One cluster contained thirteen items in the 102d Congress, including six votes concerning restrictions on the National Endowment for the Arts (NEA) and six concerning criminal procedures and sentencing (five of the six crime-related votes were on amendments to an omnibus crime bill). The northern Democrats were opposed to restrictions on the NEA, the death penalty, mandatory minimum sentences, and limits on habeas corpus and search and seizure appeals. This policy dimension continued in the 103d Congress as a cluster of twenty-three votes, nine of which concerned provisions of the omnibus crime bill (seven on the death penalty). Thirteen of the twenty-three were related to the politics of sexual morality: four votes concerned the administration's new policy on homosexuals in the military, three on domestic partner benefits in the District of Columbia, and three on local discretion over sex education instruction. Southern Democrats' level of party support on this civil liberties policy dimension averaged 36 and 45 percent in the 102d and 103d Congresses, respectively.

On a second voting cluster in the 102d Congress, southern Democrats supported the northern Democratic position 70 percent of the time. Thirty roll call votes were included in this group. Of these, twelve concerned abortion restrictions or family planning programs; six concerned requiring drug tests for new employees of the Coast Guard, the State and Defense Departments, and intelligence agncies; and six were procedural votes on the omnibus crime bill. This partisan dimension of civil liberties issues persisted in the 103d Congress, and southern Democratic party support increased to 81 percent. Procedural votes (mostly on rules) constituted almost half the roll calls included on the scale (23) in the 103d while the share of abortion-related votes declined to six of the fifty votes, all of them procedural.

A distinct dimension dominated by abortion-related votes occurred in the 103d and 104th Congresses. Of seventy-seven votes included in this dimension in the two Congresses, fifty-two concerned abortion or family planning. Southern Democratic party support scores on this new abortion scale averaged 72 and 68 percent in the 103d and 104th Congresses, respectively.

This divergent clustering of votes in the civil liberties domain shows some similarity to the foreign affairs and defense areas, both of which are characterized by distinct voting patterns on party-procedural and issue preference scales. In civil liberties, however, partisan-procedural concerns were at first part of a dimension dominated by abortion and family planning votes. The party support score of 70 on this dimension is far greater than we would expect on the basis of the abortion issue preferences of the reelection constituents of southern Democrats. The rate of partisan agreement is associated with the movement of southern Democratic activists away from the Republican position and in the direction of greater support for abortion rights (chap. 3).

In the 104th Congress a single roll call scale was most strongly associated with both the partisan and policy scales of the 103d Congress. Votes related to criminal procedure dominated this single dimension in the 104th Congress, continuing the substantive emphasis of the civil liberties policy dimension from the 102d and

103d Congresses. Of thirty-three votes, twenty-one concerned criminal procedure and sentencing (including ten on the death penalty), and six more concerned stipulations attached to anti-crime block grants. As occurred on defense votes, a distinct partisan procedural dimension was no longer apparent on civil liberties votes after the Republicans won control of the House. Southern Democrats' party support averaged 66 percent on this policy dimension, making it the issue on which southern Democrats displayed the lowest level of partisanship in the 104th Congress.

THE CASE OF CIVIL RIGHTS

The most dramatic behavioral shift among southern Democrats occurred with respect to civil rights issues (table 4.4). As late as the 97th Congress, southern Democratic representatives were substantially closer to Republicans than to northern Democrats. In Congresses after the 98th, however, southern Democrats moved to a position of frequent agreement with northern Democrats. In the 99th and 100th Congresses, northern–southern Democrat difference in scores was only a tenth of the difference between southern Democrats and Republicans. In the 101st and 102d Congresses, the northern–southern Democrat difference grew again to one third the southern Democrat–Republican difference, but this still represented a profound shift from the relative distances in the earlier Congresses. This movement from a conservative to a partisan voting pattern does not reflect substantial movement in the relative placement of southern Democratic reelection or primary constituents. It does bring southern Democratic representatives into greater conformity with the relative placement of black southern Democrats—and, to a lesser extent, southern Democratic primary constituents—on this dimension.

This is not to say that southern Democrats, particularly white southern Democrats, articulate a uniformly liberal position on civil rights issues. On the five most divisive votes scored by the Leadership Conference on Civil Rights (LCCR) in the 100th, 101st, 102d, and 103d Congresses, there was frequently substantial difference between white southern and northern Democrats. In fact, white southern Democratic support for the LCCR position was less than 50 percent on all but four of these twenty roll calls. Northern Democratic support was more than 60 percent on each of these votes (and more than 80 percent on thirteen of the twenty). Black representatives voted with the LCCR at a rate of 92 percent or higher on each one of these divisive votes (Whitby 1997: 97–103). Nevertheless, white southern Democrats moved toward a more partisan stance on civil rights votes. This movement reflects the influence of blacks and activists in southern Democratic constituencies.

CONCLUSION: ISSUE AREAS, CONSTITUENCIES, AND ROLL CALL VOTES

In broad outline, the roll call voting by southern Democrats in the House exhibited substantial variation across issue areas and across time within issue areas. Southern Democratic representatives were closer to northern Democratic positions on budget, economic management, and social welfare than on defense, foreign affairs, or civil liberties. The position of southern Democrats on labor issues tended to fall between these two broad groups of issues.

These patterns of roll call voting provide some support for asserting that the conditions for southern Democratic partisanship varied across issue areas and that the roots of this variation were in constituency attitudes. Issues on which southern and northern Democratic reelection constituents were relatively far apart according to survey data—defense and social issues—were among those most likely to see the formation of a conservative southern Democrat–Republican coalition. Issues on which southern and northern Democratic reelection constituents were closest—the role of government in the economy and the level of domestic spending—were those on which southern Democratic representatives were most partisan.

The dramatic leftward movement of southern Democrats on civil rights issues after the 98th Congress and on the abortion civil liberties scale in the 102d suggests a responsiveness to two important subsets of the reelection constituency. Partisan positions on civil rights are much more reflective of the position of black than white southerners on this dimension. Liberal votes on abortion and other issues in the civil liberties realm are more responsive to partisan activists than to the typical southern Democratic reelection constituent.

The rise of partisan dimensions in the foreign affairs and defense areas also indicates that perhaps constituency forces did not alone drive the rise of partisanship. Party-centered approaches hold that legislative party members in substantial agreement on a salient policy dimension (and facing opposition from outside the party) are likely to empower their party leaders to enforce the collective interests of the party (Aldrich 1995b, Rohde 1991b). Members may find it in their electoral or policy interests to support partisan outcomes on some occasions when constituency attitudes alone would not support such a result. Party leaders may have the ability to structure alternatives so that the costs of supporting partisan outcomes are reduced and the benefits are enhanced. This was certainly the case in the House in the 1980s (Rohde 1991b). The behavior of southern Democrats on many foreign affairs, defense, and civil liberties votes may have reflected such calculations: members supported party control of procedures and voted their own preferences on legislative amendments.

It is an open question, in fact, whether the liberalization of southern Democratic activists is a cause or an effect of the change in southern Democratic roll call voting. A significant divergence between southern Democratic activist and reelection constituents on defense spending emerged in the 1990s, following the development of partisan voting patterns in the House during the late 1980s.

The liberalization of activist attitudes on abortion occurred at roughly the same time as the evolution of abortion as a peculiarly partisan social issue in roll call voting. This partisan evolution was preceded by a movement of southern Democratic activists in the 1980s toward a more liberal position on women's role in society.

Finally, even in the context of empowered majority party leadership and the issue-based realignment of partisan activists, southern Democratic roll call voting in the House reflected the variation across issues in the relative placement of reelection constituents. In the next chapter I pursue the question of whether variation across districts also affected rates of southern Democratic partisanship in the postreform House.

DISTRICT CHARACTERISTICS AND SOUTHERN DEMOCRATIC PARTISANSHIP

During the partisan surge of the 1980s, the degree of southern Democratic partisanship in the House depended on the issue area involved. In most cases, the issues on which southern Democratic representatives were more partisan were those on which southern Democratic reelection constituents were most like northern Democratic reelection constituents. Were the constituency characteristics associated with issue attitudes during this period also associated with roll call voting? A critical condition for partisan behavior is the similarity of the individual representative's reelection or primary constituency to the constituencies typical of other party members in the legislature. If employed carefully, constituency demographic characteristics can serve as surrogate indicators of district attitudinal configurations.

This chapter reports results of a multivariate model of partisanship among southern Democrats. The regression model constitutes a direct test of a constituency-influence model of roll call partisanship. Indicators of partisan voting were regressed on a combination of variables including race of representative, racial and urban composition of the district, Republican vote percentage in the previous congressional election, and liberalism among whites in the district. During the partisan surge of the 1980s, the association between district characteristics and the rate of party support on all partisan roll calls was consistent with expectations drawn from a pure constituency-influence model. After 1992 these patterns of association changed in ways that reflect the impact of majority-minority redistricting and expanded Republican electoral competition and success.

When party support is disaggregated by issue area and regressed on the same variables, the observed differences across issues are not consistent with the predictions of a pure constituency-influence model. Instead they suggest that roll call voting on certain party-defining issues structures that on other issue dimensions.

RACE AND ROLL CALL VOTING

In any analysis of the constituency basis of southern Democratic behavior, an assessment of the degree of responsiveness to black constituents must play a central role. Black and white attitudes differ substantially on a range of public policy questions, and these differences place black constituents in the South closer to the preferences typical of national Democrats. Most scholars conclude that this pattern should influence legislative behavior in at least one of two ways. The first hypothesis is that representation by a black Democrat will be more liberal than that by a white Democrat, owing to differences in both the attitudinal dispositions and the core constituencies of black and white Democrats. The second, known as the black influence hypothesis (Cameron, Epstein, and O'Halloran 1996), is that responsiveness to black constituents is demonstrated by a positive association between liberal roll call voting by southern Democratic representatives, white or black, and the size of the black population in their districts.

In the South before the civil rights era, precisely the opposite of the black influence hypothesis held. Southerners representing areas with larger black populations had more conservative roll call records. With black electoral participation held to very low levels by legal and extralegal means, white liberalism was presumably the key factor in southern Democratic roll call voting. From the pattern of roll call voting, as well as from the geographic pattern of support for racially conservative candidacies, Key (1949) concluded that areas with larger black populations were also those with the most conservative white electorates.

As the mobilization of black voters proceeded during the 1960s, William R. Keech (1968) hypothesized that the association between black population and representation would be curvilinear. At lower levels of black population, issues associated with race have little salience for whites and representatives can be responsive to black preferences without negative consequences from white constituents. At relatively high levels of black population, perhaps 20 percent and higher, the salience of racial issues for white constituents is such that responsiveness to black constituents is problematic. Under such circumstances, one could expect no relationship or a negative relationship between black population and liberalism in roll call voting, at higher levels of black population short of a black majority.[1] Such a curvilinear relationship emerged by the early 1970s in roll call voting on civil rights legislation and conservative coalition votes (Black 1978; Bullock 1981).

It is important to recall that in the early stages of the black voting rights revolution, areas of high black population were not only characterized by the most conservative racial attitudes among whites; they were also the areas in which black electoral participation was most severely restricted (Matthews and Prothro 1963; 1966: chap. 5). It makes sense, then, that the initial findings of research into the impact of black mobilization would find greatest roll call responsiveness at lower levels of black population. White conservatism and the impediments to black participation loomed greatest as obstacles to black influence in the very places where black participation had the greatest potential for altering historical political patterns.[2]

The urbanization of the South introduces a further complication to the pattern of black influence one should expect. In less urbanized districts, greater black population is associated with more conservative attitudes among whites on economic and civil rights questions, but the association between black population and white liberalism tends to be positive in urban areas. In the late 1980s self-reported turnout in congressional elections among blacks was by far highest in urban districts with a large black population and lowest in rural black belt districts.

Michael W. Combs, John R. Hibbing, and Susan Welch (1984) analyzed the relationship between the size of the black electorate and the behavior of southern representatives from districts of varying levels of urbanization and found a positive relationship between percent black of the population and conservative coalition support scores in rural districts. In urban districts they found a negative relationship between percent black and conservative coalition scores, and it was most strongly negative in districts with the highest proportions of residents living in center cities. This pattern of interaction between urbanization and black population also influences LCCR scores and several other measures of issue positions expressed in roll call voting (Whitby 1985, 1987).[3]

Based on these findings and on our knowledge of the distribution of white attitudes, it is appropriate to accommodate the interaction of black population and urbanization in modeling the influence of black constituents on roll call voting, at least among southern Democrats. As a start in this direction, table 5.1 lists average conservative coalition scores of white southern Democrats for each year from 1983 to 1998. Averages for each of four demographic types of district are listed in addition to the overall average. The table also includes a similar breakdown of scores on the partisan voting scale developed in chapter 4 from party unity and conservative coalition roll calls. The district categories are the same as those used in chapter 2 in discussing geographic variation in southern white attitudes. The most conservative southern Democrats are

TABLE 5.1

Conservative Coalition and Partisan Voting Scores of White Southern Democrats by District Type and Year

| Congress/ | Year | Conservative Coalition Support | | | | | Score on Partisan Votes | | | | |
| | | Rural | | Urban | | | Rural | | Urban | | |
		Low Black	High Black	Low Black	High Black	Total	Low Black	High Black	Low Black	High Black	Total
98th	1983	70	75	69	57	69	62	60	61	73	63
	1984	71	77	67	58	70					
99th	1985	66	81	63	58	69	70	69	76	79	73
	1986	70	79	66	63	71					
100th	1987	70	83	67	69	74	75	72	82	81	76
	1988	67	80	61	63	69					
101st	1989	70	81	57	62	69	69	70	79	78	74
	1990	73	83	60	61	71					
102d	1991	76	82	56	66	72	74	73	73	78	74
	1992	72	76	61	67	70					
103d	1993	74	82	62	74	73	76	73	82	78	78
	1994	80	82	67	72	76					
104th	1995	83	82	59	72	73	59	64	76	85	67
	1996	83	87	64	85	77					
105th	1997	77	83	62	72	72	71	67	82	75	74
	1998	81	84	54	77	72					

consistently those representing districts of above average black population and below-average urban population. In every year the representatives of more urban districts voted less conservatively than did those from more rural districts. These patterns are especially apparent with respect to conservative coalition scores, which represent members' rate of party defection on that portion of the partisan roll call agenda receiving the least support from southern Democrats.

A CROSS-SECTIONAL MODEL OF ROLL CALL PARTISANSHIP

The interactive effect of racial and urban context on southern Democrats' roll call voting is estimated here using a linear regression model, with partisan voting scores as the dependent variable. The interactive effect of black and urban population is represented in the model by an interaction term that is the product of percent black and percent urban. In the estimated model, the coefficient for each of the interacting variables percent urban and percent black represents the association of that variable with partisan voting *when the other interacting variable is equal to zero.* The association between black population and southern Democratic agreement with northern Democrats should be negative at low values of percent urban and positive at high values of percent urban. If so, the coefficient for percent black in the model will be negative and the coefficient for the interaction term will be positive. Also included in the model is an indicator of whether the representative is black (set to 0 if no, 1 if yes), which will be associated with greater roll call partisanship.

In addition to the effects of black and urban population, the model includes the Republican vote (in percent) in the previous congressional election as an indicator of the size of the Republican election constituency in the district. If defections to the Republicans leave the Democratic reelection constituency in a given district more liberal, and if representatives are particularly responsive to reelection constituents, then Republican congressional vote should have a positive relationship with liberal roll call voting by southern Democrats (Fleisher 1993).

Temporal Change in a Cross-Sectional Model

Having outlined the elements necessary to explain cross-sectional variation in southern Democratic partisanship, we are left with the question of explaining the overall increase in party voting by southern Democrats over time. Increases over time in the independent variables cannot explain the partisan surge that occurred roughly between the 96th and the 100th Congresses. For the most part, the independent variables did not themselves change over this period (Hood and Morris 1998; Hood, Kidd, and Morris 1999). The black proportion of congressional district populations did not increase, having averaged 19 percent in the 1970s and 18 percent in the 1980s. As reported in table 5.2, the proportion of eligible blacks registered to vote in the South did not increase substantially after 1972. Moreover, the average Republican vote against southern Democratic representatives barely increased in the early 1980s, a trend that was not sustained over the entire period. If black constituents and Republican competition are responsible for the liberalization of southern Democrats' roll call voting, it must be that the responsiveness to these two variables has increased over time. If this is the case, we can detect it by assessing the district-level correlates of party support at different times using multiple cross sections.

Cohort Effects and Change

M. V. Hood III and Irwin L. Morris (1998) argue that the behavior of new cohorts of members accounted for a much larger share of

TABLE 5.2

Time Series of Black Voter Registration and Republican Congressional Vote in the South, 1972–1986

ELECTION YEAR	BLACK VOTER REGISTRATION RATE, ELEVEN-STATE SOUTH[1]	AVERAGE REPUBLICAN CONGRESSIONAL VOTE IN DISTRICTS WON BY SOUTHERN DEMOCRATS
1972	62.9	19.7
1974	62.9	18.7
1976	61.8	21.5
1978	62.3	21.6
1980	58.9	23.3
1982	53.3	23.4
1984	65.7	19.9
1986	60.8	19.5

NOTES: [1] From Timpone 1995: 437.

the increase in southern Democratic liberalism in 1983–92 than did adjustment over time by older cohorts. As we discussed above, in Rohde's (1989) analysis of the critical 1977–86 period, cohort change appears to explain a portion of the partisan shift in southern Democrats' behavior, but that change within member cohorts also accounts for partisan change.

Table 5.3 shows the pattern of cohort and period change in southern Democrats' party support scores for the 93d through 100th Congresses. The table includes the party support scores of those members who served in the 100th Congress, broken down by entering cohort. In the 96th Congress and again in the 98th through 100th Congresses, every cohort displayed an increase in partisan roll call voting. Beginning with the 94th Congress, the 1972 and earlier cohorts were consistently the most partisan group. Only the 1982–86 cohorts were consistently more partisan than previous cohorts. Thus their behavior contributed to the dramatic rise in southern Democratic partisanship after the 97th Congress. Yet their 100th Congress average partisan support score of 79 was only three

TABLE 5.3

Mean Party Support on Partisan Roll Calls among Southern Democrats Serving in the 100th Congress

COHORT	93D	94TH	95TH	96TH	97TH	98TH	99TH	100TH	N
1972 and earlier	57	55	58	61	60	71	79	82	25
1974		53	52	58	57	64	70	75	7
1976			38	43	44	55	66	67	5
1978				57	57	63	71	76	10
1980					39	47	56	59	5
1982						69	75	79	18
1984							76	80	3
1986								79	10
Total (members of) 100th Congress)	57 (25)	54 (32)	54 (37)	58 (47)	56 (52)	66 (70)	73 (73)	77 (83)	
Total (all members)	49 (84)	49 (92)	50 (90)	56 (86)	53 (78)	64 (90)	73 (81)	77 (83)	

points higher than the combined pre–1982 cohorts' average. The fifty-two pre-1982 cohort members who served in the 100th Congress had had an average party support score of 56 in the 97th Congress. Adjustment by returning members, then, was a critical factor in the post-1980 partisan surge among southern Democrats.

CORRELATES OF PARTISAN VOTING IN THE 93D THROUGH 102D CONGRESSES

Table 5.4 reports unstandardized coefficients from an ordinary least squares model estimated for each Congress from the 93d through the 102d. It is most important to consider the effect of the interaction between percent black and percent urban. Although

TABLE 5.4

District Composition and Republican Congressional Vote as Predictors of Party Support among Southern Democrats, House

Congress	Intercept	% Urban	% Black	% Urban* % Black	Member Race	Republican Congress %	R^2
93rd (73–74)	48.66***	.0371	-.3893	.0027	39.17*	.1275	.21**
94th (75–76)	42.15***	.1741	-.0838	-.0028	44.00**	.0649	.20**
95th (77–78)	40.48***	.3565**	.1331	-.0094	50.45**	-.0879	.19**
96th (79–80)	41.38***	.2616**	.1693	-.0026	29.22	.0560	.22**
97th (81–82)	41.76***	.0894	.0101	.0029	26.27	.1630	.25***
98th (83–84)	55.68***	-.0269	-.1375	.0053	17.16	.2751*	.17**
99th (85–86)	69.14***	.0378	-.1198	.0020	16.47	.1106	.13
100th (87–88)	74.79***	.0477	-.2815	.0018	22.80**	.1649	.21*

101st (89–90)	71.03***	.0899	-.2094	.0007	24.53**	.0497	.20**
102d (91–92)	72.53***	.0064	-.1421	.0014	20.53*	.1119	.11
93rd-96th	37.34***	.2085**	-.0011	-.0020	36.81***	.0869	.24***
97th-102nd	56.78***	-.0088	-.2380**	.0031*	26.97***	.1734***	.47***

Dummy variables for each cohort and year except first

NOTES: Entries are unstandardized regression coefficients.

* $p < .05$.
** $p < .01$.
*** $p < .001$.

the coefficients for the interactive term are very small, they are potentially the most important substantive element of the model. A change of several percent urban could produce a substantial change in the relationship between percent black and roll call voting. Focusing especially on the interactive term, one notes a qualitative shift in the model estimates between the 96th and 97th Congresses. The interactive term changes sign from negative in the 94th through 96th to positive in the 97th and later.

The table also includes estimates for two equations using data pooled across several Congresses, the 93d through 96th and the 97th through 102d. Pooling data from several years offers the advantage of a larger set of cases from which to draw inferences. Separate dummy variables for each Congress were added to the model, and dummy variables denoting membership in entering cohorts were also included. For the 97th through 102d Congresses, the data confirm expectations. The partial coefficient for percent black ranges from -.24 with percent urban set at zero to .07 at 100 percent urban. The most conservative southern Democratic representatives were clearly those from rural districts with larger black constituencies. Republican congressional vote also had a positive association with roll call liberalism.

Comparing the estimates from the two periods using pooled data makes easier the task of assessing the hypotheses of change over time. Before 1981 the magnitude of the effect of urban population on party support varied from .20 to .10 across the range of 0 to 50 percent black population. In the post-1980 period the urbanization effect was in the range of 0 to .16 across this same range. At higher levels of black population, the fairly small impact of urbanization on party support in the 1980s was comparable to that in the 1970s. At lower levels of black population, a substantial association between urbanization and party support in the 1970s was reduced to practically zero in the 1980s. Overall, urbanization was a less important predictor of southern Democratic partisanship in the 97th through 102d Congress than before.

Black population became a more important predictor of roll call voting in the 1980s, but not because of a uniformly liberalizing effect. The most important shift, in fact, was the emergence of a substantial relationship between higher black population and greater conservatism in rural districts. In the most urban districts, the association between black population and partisan roll call voting shifted in a positive direction, from -.20 in the 93d through 96th Congresses to .07 after the 96th.

One might attribute the changes after 1980 to the circumstances surrounding the election of Ronald Reagan to the presidency. The themes of economic and social conservatism championed by Reagan, and the geographic connection among white southerners between conservatism and racial context, appear to have sharply divided the South on racial lines. First, in the 97th Congress when Reagan's economic agenda accounted for several conservative coalition appearances and victories, black population was more closely associated with more partisan voting among urban southern Democrats than in any other year. Then in 1983 and afterward members representing large black populations became a distinctively conservative group among rural Democratic representatives, as they had clearly been before the 94th Congress. The result is that the anticipated pattern asserts itself strongly in the 1980s: greater black population was associated with more partisan scores among urban districts but with less partisan scores among rural districts.

A DISTRICT-LEVEL ESTIMATE
OF WHITE LIBERALISM

The interactive effect of black and urban population occurring in the 1980s is what one would expect on the basis of the distribution of white attitudes across congressional districts. On most issues, more conservative attitudes among whites are associated with greater black population in rural districts and with smaller black population in urban districts. Given the apparently lower rates of black voting participation in rural districts, one might expect representatives in more urban areas to be more responsive to increases in the percentage black in the district even when white attitudes are taken into account. A district-level indicator of white preferences is desirable for this purpose. Fleisher (1993) has used residual values from the regression of 1984 Democratic presidential vote on district percent black as an indicator of the level of white liberalism in southern congressional districts. I have computed this measure for the 1972–88 presidential elections and employ it below, using the residual Democratic support from the previous presidential election as the indicator of white liberalism for each case.

Table 5.5 lists regression estimates with the indicator of white Democratic presidential vote added to the other independent variables. For the 93d through 96th Congresses, the additional variable did not substantially affect the coefficients for percent urban or for the interactive effect of percent urban and percent black. The coefficient for percent black changed, indicating that when white liberalism was controlled the size of the black constituency exerted a slight positive influence on roll call liberalism in the most rural districts. In the 97th through 102d Congresses, the control for white liberalism removed urbanization and black population from having a significant impact on southern Democratic roll call voting. Overall, roll call partisanship was responsive to the liberalism of white voters and not to the size of black constituencies.

Comparison of the two pooled models confirms the hypothesis that the relative size of party election constituencies became more important in later years. District Republican vote for Congress had a larger unstandardized regression coefficient in the 1980s than in the 1970s. This finding is consistent with the notion that as party election constituencies became more differentiated on policy grounds, a larger Republican vote became associated with greater defection by conservatives from the Democratic coalition. The strength (in vote share) of the typical Republican challenge to a southern Democratic

TABLE 5.5

White Liberalism Indicator with District Composition and
Republican Congressional Vote as Predictors of Party Support
among Southern Democrats, House

	93D–96TH CONGRESS		97TH–102D CONGRESS	
% Urban	.2085**	.1843**	-.0088	.0391
	(.3571)	(.3156)	(.0172)	(.0758)
% Black	-.0011	.1777	-.2380***	.0178
	(-.0007)	(.1069)	(-.1861)	(.0139)
% Urban* % Black	-.0020	-.0023	.0031*	-.0009
	(-.0957)	(-.1086)	(.2179)	(-.0604)
Member Race	36.81***	17.05*	26.97***	15.97***
	(.2911)	(.1348)	(.2942)	(.1742)
Republican Congress %	.0869	.1765**	.1734***	.2351***
	(.0772)	(.1569)	(.1732)	(.2348)
White Liberalism		1.003***		.6653***
		(.4179)		(.3030)
Intercept (multiple dummies not shown)	37.34***	32.77***	56.78***	47.91***
R^2	.24***	.37***	.47***	52***

NOTES: Entries are unstandardized regression coefficients. Standardized
coefficients are in parentheses.
* $p < .05$.
** $p < .01$.
*** $p < .001$.

member did not increase appreciably over the period. However,
the implications of a larger Republican vote share for the composition of southern Democrats' reelection constituencies became
greater as Republican congressional voters became more disproportionately conservative.

THE NEW ELECTORAL ERA:
MAJORITY-MINORITY DISTRICTS
AND THE REPUBLICAN MAJORITY

Two dramatic changes differentiate the electoral conditions of 1992 and later from those before 1992.One is that the redistricting that followed the 1990 census produced thirteen new black-majority districts in the South. Observers typically identify three notable implications of majority-minority districts for southern Democrats. First, majority-minority districts dramatically increase the likelihood of electing minority representatives, especially blacks. The importance of race in representation is reflected in a fairly clear differentiation between white and black southern Democrats in their levels of partisan and liberal roll call voting.

Second, the drawing of majority-black districts concentrates a group with relatively liberal preferences into a smaller number of districts. In most of the white-majority districts that remain, blacks necessarily have less numerical weight in primary or general elections. More conservative primary, election, and geographic constituencies will compel white Democrats to provide more conservative representation. In this scenario, it is possible that the responsiveness of white southern Democrats to black preferences could actually decline.

Third, majority-minority districting has an impact on Republican electoral fortunes: Republicans have a better chance of winning elections in districts with lower black populations. Democrats typically win large majorities of the black vote in general elections, on the order of 85 to 90 percent in most cases. The larger the black proportion of the electorate, the more difficult it is for a Republican candidate to win a majority in the district. By reducing the black percentage in the typical white-majority district, the 1992 redistricting can be said to have increased the odds of electing Republicans in many districts.

The second dramatic change of the 1990s was the Republican victory of 1994. While majority-minority districting certainly enhanced the prospects for Republican victory in several instances, the rise of a Republican majority was an electoral event distinct from the redistricting phenomenon. It is notable, for instance, that the largest Republican gains did not come in 1992, the election in which the new majority-minority districts first took effect. The redistricting was perhaps a contributing factor in the 1994 congressional elections, but one can consider the outcome to be the culmination of the gradual realignment of white voters on liberal-conservative lines. The ideological realignment is an underlying long-term factor pushing southern congressional election dynamics away from Democratic dominance toward two-party competitiveness.

If the ideological realignment was the underlying cause, several proximate influences converged in the early 1990s to produce the Republican congressional majority. Majority-minority districting was only one, and perhaps the least important, of these. Two other proximate influences on the 1994 outcome were the emergence of Republican congressional candidates and the nationalization of the 1994 congressional elections. Beginning in 1992, Republican competition extended to virtually all southern congressional districts held by Democrats, including rural districts where southern Democrats typically represent fairly conservative electorates. Redistricting is normally associated with an increase in the number and quality of challengers who emerge, and in 1992 Republican-allied interest groups were aggressively pushing congressional candidates to challenge as many Democrats as possible across the nation.

The 1994 election was nationalized to the degree that national issues and ideology played an unprecedented role in influencing congressional election outcomes, displacing to a degree the importance of local conditions. The Republicans could not have been so successful in the South with their nationalized and ideological congressional campaign of 1994 in the absence of either the gradual

ideological realignment of the 1980s or the increased success in
Republican candidate recruitment since the late 1980s. Together,
these factors resulted in the Republican majority of 1994.

Arguably, the 1994 election was also a watershed in defining
core southern Democratic constituencies. With southern congressional electorates more ideologically aligned than ever before,
southern Democrats are more likely than ever to represent an
election constituency that is definably liberal relative to the median
voter of the geographic constituency. The geographic association
of white conservatism with black population is less relevant with
the advent of universal Republican contestation of congressional
elections; sustained two-party competition will induce Democrats
to represent relatively liberal election and primary constituencies
even in the most conservative geographic areas. In the new electoral era, southern Democratic partisanship in the House is likely
to be even more strongly associated with the liberalism of the
geographic constituency and the relative sizes of Democratic and
Republican election constituencies. At the same time, the degree
of variation among Democrats on these two variables is likely to
be lower because of the wider extent of Republican competition
and the loss of several of the most conservative districts to the
Republicans.

THE NEW ELECTORAL ERA AND
ROLL CALL VOTING

A review of the data in table 5.1 reveals that white southern
Democrats from the rural high-black districts were less distinctive
after 1994 than before in their conservative coalition and party
support scores. This outcome is primarily the result of more conservative and less partisan voting by other southern Democrats.
The average level of party support declined in the 104th Congress
among white southern Democrats from all four district types, but

the decline was most pronounced among those from urban high-black and rural low-black districts. We have already speculated that loss of the Democratic majority reduced the incentives and opportunities for southern Democrats to support party positions on roll call votes. One can also surmise that southern Democrats reacted to the regional conservative tide reflected in the 1994 election outcome. Even as Democrats represent more liberal primary and election constituencies than in the past, they are also compelled to be responsive to the median of the geographic constituency.

Estimates of the cross-sectional model for the 103d through 105th Congresses reveal both continuity and change in the correlates of southern Democratic partisanship in the new electoral era. Table 5.6 reports estimates of regression models of southern Democratic party support scores excluding and including the white liberalism indicator as an independent variable. With the white liberalism variable excluded, the representative's race and the size of the Republican election constituency persisted as significant predictors of roll call partisanship: black representatives were more supportive of northern Democratic positions than were whites, and a larger Republican congressional vote was associated with a higher rate of party support.

What is markedly different about the model for the 103d through 105th Congresses is that the black and urban population of the district no longer had the same interactive effect on roll call partisanship as during the 1980s. White southern Democrats from districts with high black populations were no longer uniquely conservative in their voting patterns. The effect of black and urban population during the 103d Congress was practically zero. During the 104th and 105th, higher urban population predicted higher party support among southern Democrats representing few blacks, but the association tapered off with increases in black population.

In the model including the residual indicator of white liberalism, the important predictors of southern Democratic party support were black population, Republican congressional vote, and

TABLE 5.6

District Composition, White Liberalism, and Republican Congressional Vote as Predictors of Party Unity Scores among Southern Democrats, House

	103RD CONGRESS		104TH CONGRESS		105TH CONGRESS (1997 PARTY UNITY)	
% Urban	.0794 (.1954)	.0320 (.0787)	.3359*** (.5876)	.2698*** (.4722)	.1706* (.4028)	.1401[a] (.3308)
% Black	.0432 (.0589)	.6435** (.8778)	.1119 (.1254)	.8220** (.9217)	-.0046 (-.0068)	.4142[a] (.6131)
% Urban* % Black	-.0011 (-.1255)	-.0010 (-.1205)	-.0043 (-.3915)	-.0042[a] (-.3865)	-.0019 (-.2537)	-.0017 (-.2345)
Member Race	19.78*** (.5564)	-4.40 (-.1238)	35.47*** (.8214)	7.17 (.1660)	19.937* (.6543)	7.172 (.2354)
Republican Congress %	.3916[a] (.2278)	.6114*** (.3556)	.8053** (.3092)	.9959*** (.3824)	.1006 (.0823)	.3797* (.3106)
White liberalism		1.070*** (.5977)		1.316*** (.5590)		.9818*** (.5386)
Intercept	59.81***	42.88***	17.58	-1.91	62.815***	43.353***
R²	.31***	.37***	.55***	.73***	.34***	.52***

NOTES: Entries are unstandardized regression coefficients. Standardized coefficients are in parentheses.
  * p < .05.
  ** p < .01.
  *** p < .001.
  [a] p < .10

white liberalism. During the 104th Congress, district urbanization was also an important predictor. The effect of the race of the representative on Democratic Party support was accounted for by other variables when white liberalism was inserted into the model. Black representatives are elected by relatively liberal constituencies, especially as indicated by black population. Statistically, white-black differences in party support after the 1992 redistricting could be explained almost entirely by differences in constituency characteristics, but before 1992 race accounted for differences in roll call voting even when constituency variables were controlled. Assuming policy liberalism and Democratic Party support to be the manifestation of black influence on roll call voting, one might conclude that the level of congruence between southern Democratic constituency preferences and roll call voting increased in the 1990s.

ISSUE AREA VARIATION IN THE CORRELATES OF PARTY SUPPORT

According to the observations in chapters 2 and 3, the constituency correlates of attitudes in the South exhibit three types of variation across issues: varying degrees of difference between whites and blacks; differences in the geographic distribution of white conservatism; and differences in the degree of party polarization of opinion. If variation in constituency attitudes maps directly onto roll call voting patterns in the legislature, one would expect issue differences to be reflected when the cross-sectional model is used to predict party support in different issue areas.

Issue Variation and Constituency Influence: Some Hypotheses

Let us hypothesize for the moment that variation across issues in the constituency correlates of mass attitudes will be reflected directly in roll call voting. Race is most strongly related to attitudes on questions of race and civil rights, and it also has a strong association with attitudes toward economic policy. Racial differences are so pronounced on these issues that the typical white southern Democratic constituent is closer to the average Republican election constituent than to the positions taken by black southern Democrats. Race should make the largest difference in representation on civil rights issues, and it should also have a substantial effect on economic issues. One might expect the impact of race to be evident in different levels of party support by white and black representatives on economic and racial matters, as well as in the impact of racial composition on roll call voting on such issues when liberalism among whites is controlled. On other issues, however, blacks and whites in the South exhibit similar attitudes. These include social or cultural questions such as abortion, the role of women, and school prayer. A direct mapping of constituents' preferences onto their representatives would not produce a substantial relationship between race and representation on these issues, which generally fall within the civil liberties roll call domain.

The geographic variation of white attitudes is such that in rural areas black population is associated with white conservatism and in urban districts black population is associated with white liberalism. This pattern is apparent across all types of issues. Only on social issues, however, are rural whites clearly more conservative than are those from urban whites. In the model of party support in civil liberties, the coefficient for urbanization of district should be positive across all values of percent black. In the models for civil rights and economic issues, this coefficient should be zero or negative at lower levels of percent black and positive only at higher levels of black population.

One might also expect the impact of Republican congressional vote to vary by issue area. In an electorate realigning on the basis of issue attitudes, the relative sizes of the parties' election constituencies will induce changes in the aggregate issue positions of each.

A larger Republican election constituency, reflected in the Republican share of the congressional vote, results in a smaller and more liberal Democratic election constituency. This relationship will be true for those issues on which election constituencies are differentiated. In the South during the late 1980s, southern Democratic election constituents were on average most like northern Democrats on economic issues, less similar to northern Democrats on defense and civil rights questions, and least similar to northern Democrats on social issues. The issue-based congressional realignment was related primarily to economic issues. If electoral competition affected southern Democrats' roll call voting through the liberalization of their election constituencies, then Republican congressional voting should have been most important for predicting party support scores on economic issues and least important for predicting party support on civil liberties.

The role of activist constituents in closely competitive campaigns may confound such expectations, however. One likely reason that high levels of competition induce greater responsiveness to more ideologically oriented groups is that the representative is sympathetic or at least sensitive to the issue demands of groups that are likely to make a great difference in his or her prospects for reelection. Candidates are more likely than not to have emerged from and share the issue positions of politically active partisans, and the activists' contributions of campaign efforts and resources give them more direct influence on the elected representative than the influence exerted by the larger election constituency. Differences between activist and election constituencies have potential implications for the content of representation. On questions concerning women's role, abortion, and defense spending, southern Democratic activist constituents were closer to northern Democrats than to Republicans during the 1990s. On the women's role item, this placement of primary constituents was first evident in the late 1980s. If greater responsiveness to primary constituents is responsible for the impact of electoral competition on representation, the result could be that Republican congressional vote has its largest impact on southern Democrats' party support scores on civil liberties and defense votes and its smallest impact on economic issues.

Issue Area Variation, 1981–1992

Table 5.7 presents regression estimates computed for the 97th through 102d Congresses with the eight issue scales as dependent variables. For every issue scale, black population carries a negative association with party support at low levels of urbanization. In more urban districts, the relationship with percent black is reduced to zero or becomes slightly positive. Conversely, the relationship between urban population and partisan voting is near zero at low levels of percent black and positive at higher levels. Thus these equations depict a peculiarly conservative pattern of voting among representatives from districts with low urban and high black populations.

Where the conservatism of southern Democrats from rural black belt districts stands out most is on those issues on which southern Democratic party support is generally lowest: civil liberties, defense, foreign affairs, and labor. For these dependent variables, the coefficient for percent black is between -.52 and -.65 at zero percent urban and between .02 and .15 at 100 percent urban. The coefficient for percent urban in these equations is between -.03 and .04 at zero percent black and .31 to .38 at 50 percent black. From 1981 to 1992, then, the most distinctly conservative roll call behavior was displayed by southern Democrats from rural black belt districts on civil liberties, defense, foreign affairs, and labor issues. Race of representative and Republican congressional vote are also important predictors of more liberal roll call voting. Race of representative has an especially strong impact on levels of party support on civil liberties and defense votes. Similarly, Republican competition

TABLE 5.7

Demographic Predictors of Party Support among Southern Democrats, 97th-102d Congresses, by Issue Area

	Economic Management	Social Welfare	Budget	Civil Liberties	Defense	Foreign Affairs	Labor	Civil Rights
% Urban	-.0027	-.0138	-.0163	.0148	-.0089	-.0332	.0441	.0705
	(-.0049)	(-.0227)	(-.0258)	(.0165)	(-.0102)	(-.0376)	(.0538)	(.0882)
% Black	-.2118*	-.2041	-.2094*	-.5210***	-.5399***	-.5353***	-.6470***	-.3551**
	(-.1539)	(-.1358)	(-.1343)	(-.2350)	(-.2482)	(-.2447)	(-.3193)	(-.1695)
% Urban* % Black	.0033*	.0034*	.0025	.0059*	.0067**	.0068**	.0067**	.0029
	(.2133)	(.2020)	(.1445)	(.2376)	(.2752)	(.2758)	(.2942)	(.1304)
Member Race	16.81***	20.23***	26.80***	52.10***	56.17***	40.02***	43.15***	29.05***
	(.1703)	(.1876)	(.2396)	(.3278)	(.3601)	(.2552)	(.2999)	(.2069)
Republican Congress %	.2133***	.1990***	.2062***	.2522***	.2548***	.2467***	.1939**	.1904***
	(.1979)	(.1690)	(.1689)	(.1453)	(.1496)	(.1440)	(.1221)	(.1229)
Intercept	75.51***	66.52***	68.07***	34.20***	29.66***	53.77***	69.77***	45.44***
R^2	.28***	.28***	.33***	.37***	.39***	.41***	.40***	.54***

NOTES: Entries are unstandardized regression coefficients. Standardized coefficients are in parentheses.

* $p < .05$.
** $p < .01$.
*** $p < .001$.
[a] $p < .10$.

is a stronger predictor of partisan voting on civil liberties, defense, and foreign affairs than of partisanship on other issues.

In most respects issue area differences in the correlates of partisan roll call voting are the exact opposite of the expectations derived from a constituency-influence approach. The introduction of white liberalism into the models produces results that highlight two points (see table 5.8). First, urban and black population are associated with roll call voting through the geographic distribution of white liberalism. When the white liberalism indicator is introduced into the model, the interaction between black and urban population fades in importance as a predictor of roll call voting. Second, the models accounting for the impact of white liberalism sharpen the appearance of variation across issues in the difference race makes in representation. Member's race is the strongest predictor of party support on defense issues. It is second only to white liberalism in its strength as a predictor of civil liberties scores. In all the other issue areas, white liberalism and Republican congressional vote are the two most important predictors of party support. Race is a stronger predictor of defense and civil liberties scores than of scores in any other issue area. On these very issues, differences between black and white southern Democrats in the mass electorate are smallest.

Issue Area Variation in the New Electoral Era

The 1992 redistricting, which brought a substantial increase in the number of majority-minority districts, was associated with a fundamental change in the district correlates of Democratic Party support. The important predictors of southern Democrats' party support in the 103d through 105th Congresses were black population, Republican congressional vote, and white liberalism. The election of more blacks to the 103d Congress and the rise of the Republican majority in the 104th were watershed events in representation

TABLE 5.8

White Liberalism and Demographic Predictors of Party Support among Southern Democrats, 97th–102d Congresses, by Issue Area

	Economic Management	Social Welfare	Budget	Civil Liberties	Defense	Foreign Affairs	Labor	Civil Rights
Urban %	.0267	.0282	.0189	.0620	.0335	.0071	.0912	.0941
	(.0480)	(.0465)	(.0300)	(.0693)	(.0382)	(.0080)	(.1113)	(.1176)
Black %	.0362	.1498	.0872	-.1229	-.1820	-.1954	-.0902	-.0571
	(.0263)	(.0996)	(.0558)	(-.0554)	(-.0836)	(-.0893)	(-.0445)	(-.0289)
Urban*Black	.0011	.0003	-.0001	.0024	.0036	.0038	.0019	.0005
	(.0714)	(.0166)	(-.0052)	(.0962)	(.1456)	(.1534)	(.0840)	(.0228)
Member Race	6.14	5.00	14.04*	34.97***	40.76***	25.40***	20.24***	17.62***
	(.0622)	(.0463)	(.1255)	(.2200)	(.2613)	(.1619)	(.1407)	(.1255)
Republican Congress %	.2731***	.2843***	.2777***	.3482***	.3411***	.3286***	.3100**	.2484***
	(.2534)	(.2415)	(.2274)	(.2006)	(.2002)	(.1919)	(.1952)	(.1603)
White Liberalism	.6451***	.9205***	.7713***	1.035***	.9310***	.8839***	1.377***	.6873***
	(.2729)	(.3565)	(.2879)	(.2879)	(.2492)	(.2353)	(.3981)	(.2037)
Intercept	66.91***	54.24***	57.80***	20.41***	17.25***	42.00***	51.51***	36.32***
R^2	.33***	.37***	.38***	.42***	.43***	.44***	.49***	.56***

NOTES: Entries are unstandardized regression coefficients. Standardized coefficients are in parentheses.

* $p < .05$.
** $p < .01$.
*** $p < .001$.
[a] $p < .10$.

in the South. Does the new pattern hold across issue areas? Are expectations of issue divergence outlined above, as suggested by the congruence model of representation, more likely to be met in the new electoral era? Alternatively, perhaps the distinctiveness of civil liberties and defense issues observed in the 1980s persists in the 1990s.

The important predictors of roll call partisanship among southern Democrats in the new era are for the most part consistent across issue areas, with the major exception of the civil liberties issue scale. Table 5.9 reports the estimates of the regression model for issue scales for the 103d Congress. For all the issues where it is statistically significant, black population predicts more partisan roll call voting regardless of the level of urbanization in the district. Black population and white liberalism are the two strongest predictors of partisanship in all the issue areas except defense and civil liberties. White liberalism is the only statistically significant predictor of partisan variation in defense votes (as well as in civil rights votes). The most striking issue area is civil liberties, the only one for which race of representative is a significant predictor of roll call partisanship. These patterns also hold true for the 104th Congress, which differs from the 103d only in that urbanization of district is also a significant predictor of southern Democratic partisanship in most issue areas.

Issue Areas and Constituency Influence

Southern Democrats in the electorate are in closest agreement with national Democrats on economic issues, and such issues are the ones on which southern Democratic representatives are most likely to support partisan positions in roll call voting. Southern Democratic representatives display less partisan behavior on those issues that show greater distance between the typical positions of southern and northern Democratic reelection constituents. The

TABLE 5.9

Demographic Predictors of Party Support among Southern Democrats, with White Liberalism Indicator, 103d Congress, by Issue Area

	Economic Management	Social Welfare	Budget	Civil Liberties (Crime)	Defense (Policy)	Foreign Affairs	Labor	Civil Rights
Urban %	.0429	.0414	.0500	.2917*	-.1116	.0857	.0036	.0717
	(.1087)	(.0808)	(.1439)	(.3010)	(-.1297)	(.1853)	(.0063)	(.2151)
Black %	.7205***	.9839***	.3978*	.4346	.4187	.7119*	.4518	.3535
	(1.012)	(1.065)	(.6348)	(.2486)	(.2699)	(.8536)	(.4388)	(.5878)
Urban* Black	-.0017	-.0020	-.0013	-.0045	.0006	-.0026	.0019	-.0017
	(-.2086)	(-.1889)	(-.1713)	(-.2227)	(.0317)	(-.2662)	(.1564)	(-.2414)
Member Race	-9.00	-14.73	.2372	51.74**	28.41	-7.55	-5.30	-4.31
	(-.2086)	(-.3289)	(.0078)	(.6105)	(.3775)	(-.1868)	(-.1062)	(-.1479)
Republican Congress %	.7136***	.8285***	.3641*	.4200	.5541	.4955*	.7960**	.1218
	(.4273)	(.3824)	(.2478)	(.1024)	(.1522)	(.2534)	(.3297)	(.0863)
White liberalism	1.011***	1.521***	.7411***	1.303***	1.748***	.6464***	1.466***	.6362**
	(.5812)	(.6741)	(.4844)	(.3053)	(.4612)	(.3174)	(.5829)	(.4332)
Intercept	47.20***	32.72***	63.25***	-1.87	19.70	52.85***	43.31***	80.27***
R^2	.45**	.50***	.37***	.66***	.49***	.24**	.42***	.21**

NOTES: Entries are unstandardized regression coefficients. Standardized coefficients are in parentheses.

* $p < .05$.
** $p < .01$.
*** $p < .001$.
[a] $p < .10$.

degree to which southern Democratic representatives follow the party line on issues such as civil liberties and defense, on which their constituents are most dissimilar to those of northern Democrats, is influenced by those factors that we expect to be most influential in predicting southern Democratic partisanship on economic issues. That is, constituent characteristics that are more closely associated with liberal or partisan attitudes on economic issues are more effective in predicting variation in southern Democrats' roll call partisanship on civil liberties and defense issues than on economic issues.

In this respect, members' roll call voting on noneconomic issue dimensions is to a considerable degree subordinated to their districts' orientation to economic issues. This subordination of minor issue dimensions to major ones is characteristic of the description by John Aldrich and others of the role of parties in structuring multidimensional issue preferences. Economic issues are the major party-defining issues in electoral politics. Reelection constituencies are most clearly differentiated along economic lines, and Democrats' reelection constituents tend to hold relatively liberal positions across districts of varying characteristics. District characteristics associated with economic liberalism among constituents are associated with roll call partisanship on economic issues, but they are far more closely associated with roll call partisanship on noneconomic issues. The willingness of southern Democrats to support party positions on minor dimensions like civil liberties and defense issues is associated with the presence of district characteristics that predict constituent liberalism on the party-defining economic issues. Stated differently, representatives' willingness to support a united party position on minor issues is associated with their stake in partisan outcomes on the major party-defining issues.

This approach can also explain why, in the new electoral era, race of representative has the strongest association with roll call voting on the same issues for which race has the smallest association with constituent attitudes. Blacks have the greatest stake in achieving party-supported outcomes on economic and civil rights issues, and

this is faithfully reflected in the voting patterns of black representatives. On abortion and other social issues, the faithful representation of black preferences would apparently result in lower roll call
support for party positions by black southern Democrats. Black
representatives judge their stake in partisan outcomes on economic,
social welfare, and civil rights issues to be such that they are willing
to contribute to a united party effort even in many situations in
which their constituents would not support party-favored outcomes.

CONCLUSION: CONSTITUENCIES AND ROLL CALL PARTISANSHIP

The findings reported thus far are inconsistent with models of
congressional partisanship that rely solely on constituencies to
explain roll call voting, but constituency attitudes and change remain
central explanatory elements. Constituency influence on member
behavior is most clearly reflected in the aggregate roll call indicator
of party support. Roll-call partisanship among southern Democrats
was associated with the extent of white liberalism and with Republican congressional vote percentage in the 1970s, 1980s, and 1990s.
The effect of the Republican congressional vote increased when
the ideological realignment in southern congressional elections
became more marked in the 1980s. The redistricting of the 1990s
altered the impact of race on roll call partisanship. During the 1980s,
race was associated with party support scores only through its
association with the distribution of white conservatism and through
the association of representative's race with party support. In the
electoral environment of the 1990s, the black population of the
district was directly associated with partisan roll call voting by
southern Democrats.

Disaggregating partisan roll calls by issue area revealed that
southern Democrats tend to be less partisan on those issues on
which their reelection constituencies are in less agreement with

partisan positions, such as civil liberties or defense spending. This is consistent with the proposition that roll call partisanship depends on the partisan distribution of attitudes in the constituency. The analysis also revealed, however, that members' roll call voting on noneconomic issue dimensions was to a considerable degree subordinated to their districts' orientation to economic issues. As a result, southern Democrats in the aggregate had more partisan roll call records on issues such as civil liberties than would have been expected on the basis of their constituents' proximity to national party positions.

Over time, and especially on more salient issues, congressional behavior can serve as a cue for partisan realignment among more activist constituents and to some degree among the mass public. For instance, more partisan voting by southern Democrats on abortion and other civil liberties roll calls was accompanied by a degree of partisan sorting among the congressional electorate, particularly the more activist voters, according to abortion attitudes. Such dynamics apparently contributed to the culmination of the southern congressional realignment during the 1990s, in which social conservatives were a substantial portion of the new Republican electoral majorities of 1994 and after.

CHAPTER SIX

SOUTHERN DEMOCRATS, SOUTHERN ELECTORATES, AND THE HOUSE OF REPRESENTATIVES

Across a wide range of public policy issues, southern Democratic representatives have tended since the early 1980s to take roll call voting positions more similar than before to the positions taken by northern Democrats. It is difficult to imagine this new relationship between southern Democratic representatives and their party having occurred in the absence of constituency change in the South. The coalitions that elect southern Democrats to Congress have become more similar to those that elect northern Democrats.

The "northernization" of southern Democratic politics is commonly attributed to three processes that altered the mass composition of southern Democratic electoral coalitions: urbanization, the mobilization of black voters, and the rise of Republican electoral competition. Urbanization and the enforcement of the voting rights of blacks are seen to have made southern congressional electorates more liberal, whereas Republican competition is seen to have drawn the most conservative southerners out of Democratic electoral coalitions—further liberalizing southern Democratic congressional politics (Carmines and Stanley 1990; Rohde 1991a; Rohde 1991b: 45–48).

Yet the "northernized electorate" model of southern congressional politics cannot provide the sole explanation for the level of
partisanship southern Democrats now exhibit in roll call voting.
For Democratic coalitions in the South, the liberalizing impetus of
urbanization, black voting, and Republican competition is not
consistent across different issue areas or across different types of
congressional districts. Furthermore, the northernization of southern
Democratic roll call voting is matched in only some of its dimensions by the liberalization of attitudes among Democratic congressional voters in the South. Thus one finds both that the description
of southern Democratic electorates as having become "northernized"
must be qualified in several respects and that southern Democratic
partisanship in roll call voting has in some respects increased in
spite of the limited nature of northernization. To be complete,
explanations of partisan behavior must include reference to the
influence of partisan activists in the constituency and to the institutional or situational incentives to partisanship in Congress.

SOUTHERN DEMOCRATS AND
REPRESENTATION

The Progress of Northernization through the 1980s

Probably the least ambiguous change in the environment of
southern congressional elections over the last three decades has
been the incorporation of blacks into southern electorates. Yet the
impact of even so massive an extension of voting rights is not
without limits. The mobilization of black voters has had a profoundly liberal influence on the typical attitudes of the electorate
on questions of economics and race; however, such is not the case
for social questions. Also, the impact of black citizens on politics
is still not likely to be a simple function of their numerical strength
in a given place. Consistent with historical patterns, whites are

most conservative in those rural areas with the largest concentrations of black population, and these same areas are the sites of the lowest rates of black voting participation in congressional elections (chap. 2; Key 1949: 378–82, 670; Matthews and Prothro 1963; Mathews and Prothro 1966: chap. 5; Glaser 1994).

A second northernizing influence, urbanization, is associated with several deviations from traditional southern political patterns. The marked conservatism of whites in the black belt has no equal in urban areas. The liberal economic attitudes that are traditionally associated with upland rural areas also are not equalled in urban areas. In addition, urbanization has been accompanied by the concentration of pockets of economic and racial conservatism in suburban areas where few blacks live.

The geographic distribution of attitudes in southern urban areas is similar to that in northern urban areas. Yet one should not assume that urbanization in the South is always associated with more liberal politics. Only on questions such as women's role in society and prayer in schools is urban residence unambiguously associated with more liberal attitudes. Whites who were most conservative in their responses to questions on economics and race reside in rural areas where many blacks live, but the most liberal whites reside in rural areas where few blacks live. On economic matters, at least, the balance of opinion among whites in the southern mass public is more conservative in urban than in rural areas.

By the late 1980s the rise of Republican competition in the South had an observable impact on the character of southern Democratic electoral coalitions. The movement of white southerners toward the Republican Party in congressional elections occurred primarily among those with more conservative attitudes on economic issues. The apparent eclipse of the conservative coalition in Congress roughly corresponded in time to the liberalization of the typical economic attitudes of southern Democrats resulting from the defection of the most conservative southerners from Democratic electoral coalitions.

Two critical caveats to this statement should be noted. First, the liberalization of the southern Democratic electorate caused by white defection was confined to economic issues. On the question of tolerating social behavior that deviates from traditional norms and values, or of taking action to reinforce such norms and values, the typical voter who supported Democratic congressional candidates in the South was not dissimilar in his attitudes from the typical voter who supported Republican candidates in the South and elsewhere.

Second, even on economic issues electoral defection by whites was not the entire cause of more liberal roll call voting by southern Democratic representatives. Although one could clearly distinguish white southern Democrats from Republicans by their attitudes on economic issues, significant differences also persisted on such issues between white southern Democrats and northern Democrats. Furthermore, civil rights issues virtually disappeared from the list of conservative coalition roll call votes, even though white southern Democrats' attitudes on civil rights questions were hardly more distinctive from the attitudes of Republican voters in the late 1980s than they had been in the early 1970s.

Such observations point to the conclusion that the importance of conservative defections from southern Democratic electoral coalitions lies in the way they magnified the importance of more liberal constituencies—blacks most visibly—to the electoral success of Democratic congressional candidates. In the face of persistent and credible Republican competition that already attracts much of the conservative white vote, the votes mobilized in support of a Democratic candidate moving leftward from the position of the "median voter" can easily exceed the votes lost to the candidate because of such movement. Given the substantial difference between the attitudes of black and white southern Democratic voters on economic and civil rights questions (see chap. 3), the degree of leftward movement that is optimal for the Democratic candidate is a delicate calculation that depends heavily on the size of the potential black electorate and on the degree of mobilization of black voters.

Political Activism and Partisan Representation

Changes in roll call voting that cannot be explained as a response to change in mass alignments in congressional elections *can* be explained with reference to the issue alignments of party activists and campaign contributors. Especially on social issues, the aggregate position of southern Democratic activists is moving closer to that of Northern Democratic activists and farther from that of Republican activists (chap. 3; Bowman, Hulbary, and Kelley 1990; Green and Guth 1990; Prysby 1992). Differences between southern and northern Democratic primary constituents have likewise narrowed on the abortion and women's role items in the National Election Studies. Particular attentiveness to primary constituents by southern Democrats could have resulted in the increased partisanship they displayed on the abortion-dominated civil liberties scale in the 102d Congress. (Southern Democratic partisanship remained low on a set of civil liberties votes dominated by issues other than abortion; see chap. 4.)

The observation that southern Democrats' roll call voting varies in a liberal direction from the attitudes of their reelection constituents on some issues is contrary to the traditional pattern of representation in the South. Before two-party competition became widespread, there was a conservative bias in representation compared to the distribution of attitudes in the electorate. This bias was a consequence of a conservative bias in political activism. The organizations and individuals engaged in political activity in the South were disproportionately conservative, even for an electorate from which blacks were effectively excluded and in which working-class whites were underrepresented (Boynton 1965).

The conservative bias in representation persisted long after the rise of black voting and Republican competition. A study by Darrell M. West (1988) revealed the peculiar effects of conservative communications on southern Democrats' behavior with respect to Reagan's 1981 economic package. The degree of conservative bias in constituent communications to southern Democratic representatives is reflected in the mail and telephone calls they received in the weeks before the roll call votes on elements of the plan. The level of support for tax and spending cuts among random samples of constituents differed little between constituents represented by Democratic opponents of the economic plan, Republican supporters of the package, or "Boll Weevil" Democrats who supported the plan. To a substantial degree, the probability that a representative voted in favor of the Reagan economic package increased with the degree of conservative bias in the constituent mail and had no relationship to survey measures of constituency opinion. The Boll Weevil Democrats received the most strongly supportive mail for the president's economic package; they were also the representatives most likely to say that they felt bound by district opinion to vote as they did and most likely to use constituent mail and telephone calls as an indicator of constituency opinion.

If all representatives were equally responsive to their mail in deciding how to vote on Reaganomics, many more Democrats would have voted in favor of the tax cuts. Even Democratic opponents of the plan were receiving more letters and calls supporting than opposing the plan. These representatives were conspicuous in citing "to go with the party" more often than any other motive for voting, except "to help the middle class," which they cited about as often as partisanship (West 1988).

One can argue that for the Democratic opponents of the plan supporting the party position was a form of responsiveness to their primary and reelection constituencies. Through their affinity for and familiarity with the groups that form their partisan constituencies, representatives develop general dispositions toward public policy that serve them in decision making even if they have no information regarding constituency preferences on specific roll calls. Northern Democrats were able to discount the district opinion that was communicated to them through the mail because they could project the effects of tax and spending cuts on their primary and reelection constituents. While Republican supporters of the cuts could be comforted knowing they had voted in agreement with most of the mail they received, Democratic opponents placed themselves in the position of responding to a constituency that had not effectively expressed its opinion on the specific votes at hand.

One might go so far as to argue that southern Democrats were being responsive to their primary constituencies in supporting the Reagan tax plan in opposition to the national Democratic position. Several white southern Democrats in Congress in the 1980s defined their differences with the Republicans less in terms of working-class interests than in terms of the interests of small versus big business (e.g., Rae 1994). With labor unions less effective in much of the South, and with Republican competition sporadic in many areas, business leaders had a prominent role in southern Democratic primary constituencies.

We have seen that the realignment of partisan activists moved the position of likely southern Democratic primary constituents leftward from the early 1970s to the late 1980s and again from the late 1980s to the early 1990s. The changing ideological characteristics of southern Democratic party activists not only may alter the composition of primary constituencies; they can ultimately be reflected by changes in the characteristics of the party's congressional candidates and representatives (Kazee and Thornberry 1990).

We should place this observation in the context of the role of parties in the election of candidates to office. One can easily argue that the contemporary activities of party organizations are of little electoral importance compared to the classic role of the urban political machine in election campaigns (e.g., Keefe 1994: 28–29).[1] Yet party organizations have adapted to the rise of "candidate-centered politics" (Wattenberg 1991) by serving a clearinghouse function for the services of campaign consultants and the financial contributions of political action committees. Candidate-oriented activities are thus increasingly channeled by the partisan affiliations of consultants and contributors (Herrnson 1988, 1990; Sorauf and Wilson 1990).

At the same time that candidate-centered political activities have become organized along partisan lines, the campaign consulting and fund-raising capacities of party organizations have been strengthened at the national, state, and local levels. The parties seek not only to assist candidates to win particular elections but also to maintain an organizational infrastructure that will serve as a ready source of candidates and activists to take advantage of electoral opportunities as they arise. These "party-building" activities were first pursued by the Republicans in the 1970s, and state Republican parties in the South made great strides as a result. While the advance of local Republican organization has proceeded more slowly, Democrats in the South have intensified their own party organizational activities at both the state and the local levels in response to Republican successes in presidential elections and statewide contests (Gibson et al. 1983, 1985; Gibson, Frendreis, and Vertz 1989; Bibby 1990; Aistrup 1996).

The future pattern of development of local party organizations in the South will be critical to the issue incentives that partisan activists present to congressional candidates. In any region, the minority party is more likely to contest local elections (such as congressional or state legislative elections) in areas where it has strong local party organizations, and the presence of candidates in lower-level elections enhances the party's vote totals in higher-level elections. In the South, the presence of a strong local Republican organization is associated with a greater likelihood that Republicans will contest state House and congressional elections, and the presence of Republican state House candidates on the ballot is associated with higher Republican vote totals in congressional races (Frendreis,

Gibson, and Vertz 1990).[2] If past patterns hold, Democratic Party organizations will emerge as important elements of Democratic congressional campaigns in the South in response to the effects of Republican Party building efforts (Gibson et al. 1985; Gibson, Frendreis, and Vertz 1989).

It is important to note that the scope of activities of political parties and their influence on electoral outcomes today are far greater than they were in the one-party South. No longer is the Republican Party an organization dedicated solely to distributing federal patronage under Republican presidents. No longer is the Democratic Party the relatively neutral arbiter of the "real election," the Democratic primary.[3] In its contemporary role partisan activism is more important to the outcome of southern elections than it has been in over a century. The realignment of partisan activism is thus a critical component of change in southern congressional politics in the 1990s.

Parties, Leaders, and Roll Call Voting

Decision-making mechanisms within the Democratic Party in the House influenced how the composition of southern Democratic electoral coalitions was reflected in the roll call voting of southern Democratic representatives in the late 1980s. House party reforms during the 1970s had empowered party leaders in ways that had consequences for southern Democratic behavior. Democratic leaders took pains to structure votes on amendments so that on some bills southern Democrats could take positions favored by some constituents back home without jeopardizing the final content of party-endorsed legislation. This enabled members to act in the interest of party policy goals and their own reelection interests in cases in which there might be some conflict between the two. At the same time, defections from partisanship on issues important to the party caucus became an invitation to be denied transfers to desirable committees, election to committee chairmanships, and advancement in the party hierarchy. Thus the party attempted to use resources relevant to various member goals and motivations— influence within the party or chamber and opportunities to pursue personal policy interests and constituency benefits in committee— to gain member support in pursuing partisan policy goals (Rohde 1991b).[4] Increasing roll call partisanship by southern Democrats on issues such as abortion and defense spending may reflect in part their response to the new incentives to partisanship.

The interplay between potentially competing member goals highlights the existence of different domains of legislative activity. Rohde describes three domains of legislative activity corresponding to the three varieties of legislative theory: distributive, informational, and partisan. Issues can be characterized as involving one or a combination of these domains. The distributive domain is characterized by policies whose benefits may be widely distributed across congressional districts or narrowly focused on particular districts but which in either case involve inconsequential costs and low uncertainty over implementation. Issues on which there is general agreement concerning policy goals but which involve greater cost or complexity are more likely to involve the informational domain. Issues on which there is more conflict, and on which that conflict is divided on partisan lines, involve the partisan domain (Rohde 1995a, 1995b).

The multiple domains of legislative activity have implications for the role of the legislative parties in structuring member-constituency relations. Consider the potential interaction between two domains: the distributive domain, involving matters on which conflict often is low and that typically involve either or both low cost and wide distribution of policy benefits among districts; and the partisan domain, involving matters in which philosophical or programmatic differences are at issue and follow partisan lines. In the member's pursuit of reelection, acceptable performance in the distributive domain can leave some room for maneuver in the partisan domain, and deficiencies in the distributive domain can render one's entire legislative record suspect. As an example, first-term Republican senators in the 1980s who placed a heavy emphasis on ideological position taking were penalized in their reelection attempts for neglecting more local concerns of their districts (Overby 1993). Southern Democrats' party support must be seen in this light when we consider that party loyalty and support for party leadership positions influenced Democratic committee assignments, especially to prestige committees like Appropriations or Ways and Means (Smith and Ray 1983; Smith and Deering 1984: 242; Rohde 1991b; Cox and McCubbins 1993: chap. 7).

Although they were an important variable, institutional incentives probably were not the central impetus to partisan behavior among southern Democrats. In the absence of major change in partisan incentives in the Senate, southern Democrats in that body displayed more partisan behavior in the 1980s than previously, a pattern similar to the behavior of southern Democrats in the House. Yet institutional differences between the House and the Senate may have caused their members to respond differently to changes in the composition of their electoral constituencies at home. In the House, party leadership was empowered to give southern Democrats some incentive to reach accommodation with northern Democrats on issues such as abortion or defense spending, on which southern Democratic reelection constituents had substantial differences with northern Democrats. Excessive party defections by southern Democratic representatives might have resulted in a loss of influence within the party on economics and welfare, for example, on which important segments of their reelection constituencies were relatively close to the party majority.

The lack of change in the institutional incentives to partisanship in the Senate probably means that constituency change was even more important for the Senate than for the House as a factor that can explain the increased partisanship in roll call voting. On those issues for which the attitudes of southern and northern Democratic reelection constituents became more similar, one should expect that southern Democrats in both the Senate and the House moved to more partisan positions. On issues for which constituency incentives to support party positions are weaker, partisan voting by southern Democrats should have been more likely in the House than in the Senate because the institutional incentives for partisan behavior are greater in the House than in the Senate. The resulting hypothesis is that by the late 1980s increases in party support among southern Democrats in the Senate were similar to the increases in the House on economic and social welfare issues but substantially less than in the House on issues like abortion, foreign policy, and defense policy.

However, incentives to partisanship that are inherent in the legislative context are not entirely the product of particular institutional arrangements. Partisan theories of legislative behavior hinge on the willing acceptance by legislative party members of party discipline. Members accept party leadership to the degree that they are interested in enforcing partisan outcomes related to some overriding principle. Such enforcement may necessitate discouraging defections in pursuit of individually favored outcomes on secondary dimensions (Aldrich 1995b). Institutional arrangements in the Senate furnish party leaders in that chamber with fewer avenues for enforcing party discipline than in the House. If the basic assumption of partisan approaches is correct, however, Senate members do have incentives to subordinate their preferences on secondary dimensions to the pursuit of favored outcomes on the overriding party-defining issues.

A partisan calculus might lead some members to routinely vote against what would be their constituents' preferences on secondary issues. If such issues become salient over a considerable time among at least the activist constituents in such members' districts, the members' roll call behavior could well induce some realignment of voter loyalties on the basis of these secondary issues. The description in chapter 4 of the abortion issue in the late 1980s and 1990s is not inconsistent with such a scenario.

In sum, the major impetus for the partisan surge of the 1980s was the realignment of southern congressional votiong and partisan activism along economic issue lines. In turn, partisan behavior by southern Democratic representatives on issues such as civil liberties may well have induced a further issue differentiation between the southern parties, at least among political activists. The scenario implies that the relationship between legislative and mass partisanship is best described as a reciprocal one.

CONGRESSIONAL BEHAVIOR AND THE FUTURE OF SOUTHERN POLITICS

The 1990s in Historical Context

The three-election sequence of 1992–96, together with party switches and special elections during the period, produced a net gain of thirty-eight seats for the Republicans in the southern House delegation. This shift was of historic proportions, bringing to the South its first Republican majority in the House since Reconstruction. It is typically viewed as part of a long-term realignment of southern politics that is progressing inexorably from the presidential level to lower electoral levels. Projecting this trend to future elections, it is difficult to avoid the conclusion that the outcome will be the development of overwhelming Republican electoral majorities at all electoral levels everywhere, from presidential to statehouse elections, from Texas to Virginia. In assessing the current and future state of congressional politics in the South, however, we should place these results in historical context.

In the early 1960s the Republican Party embarked on a "southern strategy" for gaining a national electoral majority. In reaction to the party's loss in the 1960 presidential election, Barry Goldwater and other Republican conservatives advanced the theory that a presidential majority could be built by conceding northern black votes to the Democrats and pursuing the votes of southern whites more aggressively. The effect of the issue appeals at the core of the southern strategy was arguably to create a political dichotomy between the Democrats as the party of blacks and the Republicans as the party of whites (Aistrup 1996: 18–55).

The southern strategy eclipsed a national party approach that had aimed to take advantage of the indigenous rise of Republicanism in southern urban areas (Klinkner 1992). Especially in Rim South states such as North Carolina, Texas, and Florida, the emergence of a professional and managerial class coupled with an influx of transplanted northern Republicans had provided a base for challenging the Democrats as a middle- and upper-class party (Strong 1956, 1960; Seagull 1975; Black and Black 1987: 264–77).

In 1964 Goldwater aimed to gain support in the South not only from progressive conservatives, who were likely to favor racial moderation at least as a necessary condition for economic development, but also from other southerners who desired stricter limits on the federal government's role in their society. Southern political leaders promoted his candidacy as the best opportunity to avoid national interference in racial matters. The stridency of Goldwater conservatism compared to the social and economic activism espoused by the Democrats produced a class polarization in the 1964 election that was rare in southern elections to that time (Nadeau and Stanley 1993), and the Republican vote for president generally declined in urban areas and in the rural mountains. At the same time, the Goldwater candidacy was most successful in the conservative traditionally Democratic strongholds—the black belt regions (Cosman 1966; Seagull 1975).

The 1968 presidential elections would find black belt and working-class whites supporting the candidacy of segregationist George Wallace and white-collar voters supporting Richard M.

Nixon. Ultimately, the Nixon landslide of 1972 was effected in the South by the combination of precincts that had supported Wallace and Nixon in 1968 (Seagull 1975; Wright 1977). Black belt conservatism and urban Republicanism were successfully fused behind the Republican presidential candidate in 1972, and Republican presidential candidates have won the majority of the white vote in the South ever since.

In the era of the southern strategy in presidential politics, Republican growth at the congressional level was driven by two different catalysts. The first was urbanization: Republican growth resulted from the exploitation of beneficial demographic changes and party organizational strengths in urban areas (Strong 1956, 1960; Seagull 1975; Black and Black 1987: 264–77). Urban Republicanism was the sole source of Republican growth at the congressional level before the advent of the national party's southern strategy, and it continued to be the most important source of Republican gains through the 1980s.

The second catalyst for Republican congressional growth is referred to by Joseph A. Aistrup (1996) as top-down advancement: the successful translation of support for Republican presidential candidates into electoral success at lower levels. In the rural South top-down advancement faced considerable obstacles. Republican congressional growth turned out to be least sustainable in the most conservative areas, the black belt counties. Even as the whites of the black belt contributed substantially to the emergence of a Republican presidential majority, their continued participation in Democratic primaries for Congress and other offices assured continued success for Democratic conservatives. As long as Democratic candidates could distance themselves from the liberalism attributed to their national party, there was little incentive for voters, candidates, or activists to concern themselves with supporting or building the Republican Party. (On the ability of southern Democratic candidates to place distance between themselves and the national party, see Bartley and Graham 1975: 111–35, Glaser 1996.)

As an additional disincentive to the emergence of Republican candidates, the mobilization of black voters changed the composition of the electorate in black belt districts to the disadvantage of Republican candidates. Typically (although not always), black voters have supported Democratic candidates for Congress and the presidency at rates of about 90 percent. In deciding whether to run for office, potential Republican candidates must assess the prospects of winning a supermajority of the white vote in traditionally Democratic districts (Aistrup 1996).

During the 1980s, conditions became more favorable to the emergence of Republican congressional candidates outside of urban areas. Party identification of native southern whites became polarized along class lines well before the 1980s. Since 1976 higher-status whites in the South have tended to identify as Republicans and lower-status whites have tended to be Democrats (Nadeau and Stanley 1993). In estimating a multivariate model of the dynamics of southern whites' party identification, however, Richard Nadeau and Harold W. Stanley reveal that residence in a county of over 15 percent black population was a predictor of Democratic Party identification through 1982. The Republican disadvantage in party identification in the black belt practically disappeared after 1984. Republicans considering House candidacies in these congressional districts would have discovered a more receptive environment among the electorate in the mid-1980s than previously.

Not only did the Democratic advantage in party identification among black belt whites disappear, but Republican candidacies for state senate seats became more common in rural areas of the South in the 1980s (Aistrup 1990). With the exception of some recruitment of state legislative candidates by Republican organizations during the early 1980s in Rim South states such as Tennessee and North Carolina, the extension of Republican legislative candidacies to less urban contexts occurred in the absence of an overall candidate recruitment strategy. Instead, the emergence of Republican state senate candidates in rural areas reflects the outcome of individual decisions by potential candidates across the region. It is suggestive of the response of potential Republican candidates to the rising acceptability of Republican identification among whites in the black belt. This role for party in the calculus of candidacy is consistent with that suggested by Joseph A. Schlesinger (1985) in his ambition-based theory of the role of political parties.

The geographic variation in the emergence of Republican congressional candidacies exhibited a similar shift in the late 1980s (table 6.1). Before 1986 Republican challengers of Democratic incumbents were least likely to emerge in rural districts with higher than average black populations. The relatively high likelihood of Republican candidacies in the rural low black district category is due in part to the fact that the traditional "mountain Republican" districts of Tennessee and North Carolina are in this category. The greatest likelihood of Republican candidate emergence before 1986 was in suburban-type (urban low black) districts, the areas in which electoral success was probably most likely. After 1986 Republican congressional challenges were as likely in the black belt districts as in the other types. Overall, the number of Republican candidacies did not rise substantially until 1992. However, the shift in Republican prospects for victory in the black belt districts (at least as estimated by potential candidates) was in retrospect a necessary precondition for the Republican congressional gains of the 1990s.

In this regard, one should note that in the 1980s many Republican House gains in the South proved to be reversible. For instance, in only three of the southern states did the landmark 1994 election mark a peak in the share of seats won by Republicans. In the other states, Republicans had achieved at some time before 1994 a share of congressional seats at least as great as their 1994 share (Rohde 1996). The regionwide Republican seat share, which had reached 31 percent by 1973, peaked at 37 percent in 1985 and settled at 34 percent in the elections of 1986–90. The reversibility of Republican gains, coupled with the aggregate stability in the Republicans' share of southern House seats, leads to the conclusion that

TABLE 6.1
Democrat-controlled House Seats with Republican Candidates, by Type of District
(% of Democrat-held seats)

District Type	1976	1978	1980	1982	1984	1986	1988	1990	1992	1994	1996
Rural, low black	71	67	65	60	74	62	68	68	100	94	100
Rural, high black	52	52	54	56	39	59	67	69	95	87	92
Urban, low black	89	80	90	79	71	67	53	75	90	100	100
Urban, high black	53	67	72	77	53	63	56	56	85	83	90
Total	67	66	70	66	58	62	62	67	93	91	95

competition in those areas being regularly contested by Republicans was within range of an equilibrium point. Only the expansion of Republican competition would result in long-term additions to the Republicans' aggregate seat total.

The Interdependence of Party Attractiveness

The case has been put forward elsewhere that, in the wake of the Republican seat gains of 1992–96, partisan competition for House seats in the South has reached the point at which in future elections Republican seat losses are about as likely as Republican seat gains. In other words, the distribution of southern House seats between the two parties is within range of a long-term equilibrium (around which factors specific to particular election years or districts will cause fluctuation). (See Rohde 1996; Berard and Rohde 1998.)

Table 6.2 shows that Republican seat gains in the 1980s were confined to the suburban-type districts. This continued the pattern of urban Republican growth of previous decades. After 1990, however, Republican seat gains were disproportionately in rural districts. Of the thirty-eight seats gained by Republicans in 1992–96, thirty-two were in rural districts. Finally, congressional election results exhibited the results of Republican "top-down advancement," the effort to tie local Republican candidates to the good fortunes of the national party by linking local Democrats to national Democratic policies (Aistrup 1996).

What had occurred gradually in urban districts through the 1980s occurred rapidly in rural ones in the 1990s: the achievement by the Republicans of the bulk of their potential seat gains. The results of the 1996 elections are consistent with this conclusion. Democrats were able to retain a relatively large number of open seats (12 of 19) and to reverse previous Republican gains in four races. Among these sixteen Democratic victories were three majority-minority seats, five

TABLE 6.2

Partisan Division of House Seats, by District Type,
after the Elections of 1980, 1992, and 1996
(% Democratic in parentheses)

DISTRICT TYPE	1980		1990		1996		
	DEMS.	REPS.	DEMS.	REPS.	WHITE DEMS.	BLACK DEMS.	REPS.
Low urban, low black	20 (61%)	13	22 (67%)	11	11	0 (28%)	29
Low urban, high black	26 (87%)	4	27 (87%)	4	9	4 (42%)	18
High urban, low black	19 (61%)	12	17 (45%)	21	12	0 (28%)	32
High urban, high black	14 (52%)	13	19 (70%)	8	7	12 (86%)	3
Total	79 (65%)	42	85 (66%)	44	39	16 (40%)	82

SOURCE: Adapted from Berard and Rohde 1998.

suburban seats, and eight black belt seats. Thus Democratic candidates were victorious in a variety of district contexts (Berard 1997).

The fluctuation of congressional outcomes around their long-term equilibrium will be influenced by a variety of short-term factors: the impact of national political conditions on the emergence of candidates in each party (Jacobson and Kernell 1983), the exposure of weak freshman incumbents of the president's party at midterm (Oppenheimer, Stimson, and Waterman 1986), and the pool of experienced candidates available in each party. Another short-term factor, of particular interest here because of its implications for the character of partisan representation, is a product of the interdependence of the two party nominees' attractiveness to the voters in any congressional district. Nationally, partisan activists are consistent across states and regions in their deviation from the local typical voter (Erikson, Wright, and McIver 1989; Aldrich 1995b). This is also the case in the South: Democrats are consistently to the left of the typical voter and Republicans are consistently to the right. Within each party, however, the potential exists to nominate candidates who are at varying distances from the typical voter. The Democratic nominee in a given district might be anywhere in a range from extremely liberal to moderate, and the Republican nominee might be anything from moderate to extremely conservative. In any congressional district the attractiveness of the two parties' candidates is interdependent because the candidates are evaluated in relation to each another. Candidates seen as more moderate relative to their district have an advantage in the general election over those perceived as more extreme (Berard and Rohde 1998).

The interdependence of candidate attractiveness affected outcomes throughout the 1980s and 1990s (Rohde 1996; Berard and Rohde 1998). Not only are Republicans sometimes able to portray Democrats as "too liberal" for the district, but Democrats are also sometimes able to portray Republicans as "extremist." Democratic incumbents as well as nonincumbent candidates have a history of success in positioning themselves closer than their Republican opponents to their district's typical constituent. They do so by balancing liberal positions on some issues with conservative positions on others—for instance, supporting a balanced budget amendment or taking a tough stand on crime. Another approach is to establish visible links with other conservative Democrats, such as through the Conservative Democratic Forum in the 1980s or the "blue dog" coalition of conservative Democrats and moderate Republicans in the 1990s (Rohde 1991a; Glaser 1996: 80–141).

Heterogeneity of preferences within a party is the source of potential variation in the distance of its nominees from the typical constituent. As the preferences within a given party become more heterogeneous, variation in the closeness to the median voter of its candidates for nomination becomes more likely. Primary outcomes in a heterogeneous party will vary depending on the size and level of mobilization of various groups within the party. Over time, a more heterogeneous primary electorate has greater potential to produce party nominees who vary in their proximity to the district median than does a more homogeneous primary electorate.

Several factors introduce preference heterogeneity into southern primary electorates. Within the Democratic Party, race is the most obvious correlate of issue preferences, at least on economic and civil rights issues. Not only did the mobilization of blacks render the general electorate more heterogeneous, it also had the same effect on Democratic primary electorates. As conservative whites defected from the Democratic Party, the role of blacks in Democratic primary and election constituencies and the issue differences between black and white Democrats became more central to election outcomes. The balance that Democratic incumbents and candidates try to achieve between conservative and liberal issue themes is most typically an effort to balance their attractiveness to white and black constituents. A Democrat viewed by whites as too closely tied to black concerns will lose white votes, while being viewed by blacks as unsympathetic to black concerns will also be detrimental to the Democrat's electoral chances.

Other sources of issue diversity are sometimes important to Democratic nomination politics as well. In some districts labor unions have enough organizational strength to make a difference in mobilizing voters, as do teachers' organizations and local Democratic officials. Adherence to the agendas of these groups among the Democratic electorate is not universal, but they are frequently important building blocks of a winning coalition. National interest groups representing pro-choice, environmental, and labor concerns also are potential influences on primary politics. Here it is important to recall the preference heterogeneity among party activists: among Democrats, newer activists are typically more liberal than longtime activists, especially on noneconomic issues. The interaction of these various issue concerns and preferences in Democratic primaries can produce a variety of results in terms of the nominee's placement relative to the median voter in the geographic constituency.

In Republican nomination politics, the most important source of issue heterogeneity is the potential for conflict between elements of the Christian right and party regulars who emphasize economic over social conservatism. The level of intraparty conflict between old guard Republicans and the Christian conservatives varies across states. Judging from recent relations within state party organizations, accommodation has been easiest in Mississippi, Kentucky, and perhaps Tennessee, while open differences occur between the regulars and the newer conservative activists in most of the other southern states. Christian conservatives have varying levels of influence in the state party organizations. Where the religious right holds more party positions, they do not necessarily control primary outcomes. The result is that Christian right party activists and party-regular elected officials have been at odds with one another in some states, such as Texas, Virginia, South Carolina, and Louisiana (Wyman 1997).

In some states, for example, Mississippi and Alabama, the organizational advantage gained from the support of Christian right organizations can offset the potential impact of such endorsements on a Republican nominee's attractiveness in the general election. In states such as Florida, Texas, and Virginia, in contrast, candidates of the "New Right" lose some support that Republicans have come to count on in suburban middle- to upper-class areas (Aistrup 1996: 143–66). How the outcome of intraparty nomination politics influences the dynamics of choice between the parties depends in part on the district context.

OLD ISSUES, NEW ISSUES,
AND SOUTHERN DEMOCRATS

Continued Republican Party success in the South is likely to depend somewhat on popular receptiveness to the issues emphasized by the party's candidates. In any electoral setting, several issues are available around which durable mass coalitions might conceivably be organized. Whether one issue displaces another as the basis for partisan alignments is likely to depend both on the characteristics of the issue and on its use by political elites to mobilize voters (Schattschneider 1960; Sundquist 1983). Carmines and Stimson (1989: 9–12) note that two characteristics determine the likelihood of a new issue displacing an old one as the basis for party alignments: whether the new issue can be easily conceptualized by most voters without much information and whether the new issue has salience for voters. Even when these conditions occur, the new issue might simply be an extension of the old, leaving existing electoral alignments intact.

Another central insight of Carmines and Stimson is that political elites play a key role in the evolution of partisan issues. Candidates use issues as a means of mobilizing supporters and building electoral coalitions. Political activists become involved in politics in response to the issues that concern them. It is from the politically involved strata, particularly grassroots activists, that mass electorates learn party positions on various issues. Although it is the mass response to elite activity that determines the success or failure of particular issues in reorganizing electoral politics, the competing issues are framed and injected into politics by elites (Carmines and Stimson 1989: 89–114). The candidates who win elections are the ones who make the best use of the most potent issues. In the process, election campaigns orient the behavior of political activists and ultimately the public toward parties.

It is reasonable to hypothesize a linkage between two developments in the 1980s: (1) the growth of differences between Republican and Democratic Party activists in the South on social issues and (2) the emergence of Republican electoral activity in rural congressional races. The emergence of social issue activism in the Republican Party has made it more likely that Republican candidates will make electoral appeals based on social conservatism. The absence of an existing Republican organization in much of the rural South and the relatively greater appeal in rural areas of conservatism on the new social issues make it likely that social issue activism would emerge in less urban areas as an important force within the party. The mobilization of political activists in turn generates both the potential candidates and the perceptions of electoral opportunity necessary for Republicans to emerge as contestants for congressional seats in rural Democratic strongholds.

In concluding that social issues were peculiarly important to the spread of Republican success into less urban congressional districts, one should not infer that conservatism on social issues lacks appeal among suburban Republicans or that economic conservatism has no appeal in rural areas. The rural black belt has always been a bastion of economic conservatism in the South, and social issue activism reflects the social conservatism of white southerners living in all sorts of political environments. One can infer from our knowledge of the geographic distribution of attitudes in the South, however, that recent Republican growth in the rural areas has been more dependent on an appeal to social issue conservatism than was the party's initial growth in urban areas. In fact, a desire to emphasize economic conservatism and to deemphasize social conservatism in Republican campaigns continues to characterize the orientation of old guard Republican activists, and their position has been reflected at times in open conflict between themselves and social conservatives.

Further Republican gains in less urbanized districts will likely be associated with the primacy of social issues in the recruitment of new Republican candidates and voters. If social issues do not replace economic issues as central to the organization of partisan attitudes for a substantial part of the mass electorate, however, then Republican gains in many rural districts could prove to be reversible. Using social conservatism to alter the partisan balance in rural districts could lead to gains in suburban districts being hindered or reversed, as the proportion of urban constituencies that favor such causes is smaller than that of rural constituencies. With social issues playing a major role in future elections, the dynamics of party activism could continue to push the position of urban and suburban southern Democrats leftward on these issues.

More than in other types of districts, emphasis on either economic or social conservatism can bring the Republicans lasting electoral gains among whites in the rural black belt. By contesting rural black belt seats and extending their organizational efforts to these areas, Republicans in 1994 were able to capitalize on political opportunities created by the reduced core of black Democrats in several of these districts and by the dissatisfaction of many southern whites with the national Democratic Party. The creation of black-majority districts has reduced the weight of black voters in some white-majority districts. Despite such reductions, substantial numbers of blacks remain in many of these districts, and they can provide an electoral base for continued Democratic competition even where the Republicans have won the seat. The likely outcome of two-party politics in the black belt will be consistent with the trends of the previous two decades in the urban South: the most conservative Democratic representatives will be replaced by Republicans, and Democratic candidates in the future will be somewhat more liberal than their predecessors.

Democratic success in black belt districts in which blacks are a minority depends on the creation of black-white electoral coalitions. Maintaining such coalitions requires Democrats to engage in the balancing act described earlier: blacks must be motivated to turn out and vote Democratic, and at the same time sufficient numbers of white voters must be convinced that the Democratic congressional candidate is not "too liberal."

At least through the early 1990s southern Democrats in Congress had regularly achieved this balance by firmly supporting civil rights measures, maintaining a conservative voting record on social issues, and attempting to bridge the gap between black and white southerners concerning the role of government in the economy. The debate over economic issues, particularly in the black belt, revolves around Republican attempts to pry whites away from the black-white Democratic coalition and Democratic attempts to emphasize the common economic interests of blacks and working-class whites. Republican successes in the black belt may move the Democratic Party to the left by denying Democrats access to the votes of the most conservative whites, but the fundamental arithmetic for Democratic victory remains unchanged.

Against the backdrop of the continuing racial divide in southern politics, the future prospects for southern Democrats in Congress depend on what issues will motivate voters and partisan activists in future congressional elections. The persistence of economics as the central issue dividing whites in congressional elections would likely result in the continuation of the trends of the 1980s in roll call voting and other patterns of policy making by southern Democrats. However, if social issues play an increasingly important role in congressional elections, then the movement toward more partisan congressional behavior on such matters will intensify, and the policy domain of the conservative coalition will become even smaller. At the same time, the prominence of social issues appears to be the most reliable route to Republican success in rural areas, particularly outside the black belt.

Social issue activism thus could render the Democrats a permanent minority in southern congressional delegations while making them a group with a more liberal bent than previously. Yet Democrats continue to nominate candidates who are moderate relative to the typical voter across the full variety of southern congressional districts. Even in some of the most conservative southern districts, Democratic candidates emerge who are viewed by the district electorate as closer to district preferences than their Republican opponents (Berard and Rohde 1998). This phenomenon will be extended into the foreseeable future by the continued availability of Democrats in lower offices (state legislators, etc.) to offer themselves as experienced candidates with records of pragmatic accomplishment.

One result of these dynamics is that Democrats will retain a substantial share of southern House seats beyond the core of minority-majority and urban minority-influence districts that are often seen as the party's only long-term base in the region. The consequences for congressional politics are twofold. First, the South will not be nearly as large a liability as many expect for the Democrats in their efforts to elect a House majority. Second, Democratic representatives from the South will continue to represent a range of ideological positions and to be a source of preference heterogeneity within the House Democratic caucus.

APPENDIX

NATIONAL ELECTION STUDIES ATTITUDINAL ITEMS FOR CHAPTERS 2 AND 3

The attitudinal data analyzed in chapters 2 and 3 are from the National Election Studies Cumulative Data File, 1956–90, and the American National Election Studies data files for 1992, 1994, and 1996 (Miller and the National Election Studies 1991; Miller et al. 1993; Rosenstone et al. 1995, 1997). For the analyses in chapter 2, data were pooled from the 1984–90 NES surveys to compare the attitudes of southern whites and blacks and to compare attitudes among southern whites across the categories of education, income, and religion.

The educational level of NES respondents is classified in the Cumulative Data File in three categories: grade school or less, high school or noncollege training, and college. NES income classifications were collapsed for the analyses here into three categories corresponding to the lower, middle, and upper third of the national sample. Respondents who were members of fundamentalist Christian denominations (according to the NES classification in place through 1988) were compared to respondents who were not members of these denominations. Through 1988 the "Protestant, neo-fundamentalist" category of responses included United Missionary, Protestant Missionary, Church of God, Holiness, Nazarene, Free Methodist, Church of God in Christ, Plymouth Brethren,

204 APPENDIX

Pentecostal, Assembly of God, Church of Christ, Salvation Army, Primitive Baptist, Free Will Baptist, Missionary Fundamentalist Baptist, Gospel Baptist, Seventh-Day Adventist, Southern Baptist, Missouri Lutheran Synod, and "other fundamentalists."

Chapter 2 also examines the association between the attitudes of white southerners and population characteristics of the congressional districts in which they reside. Since NES data contain insufficient samples from any congressional district to produce reliable estimates of district population parameters, respondents are assigned to larger groups according to the characteristics of their congressional districts. Hence, groups of similar congressional districts, rather than individual districts, were the units of analysis. Table A.1 lists those southern congressional districts included in at least one NES sample in 1984–90, grouped according to urban and racial composition of their populations. Districts above the mean percent urban for the entire South (51.8 percent according to the 1980 census) are classified as "urban," and those below the mean are classified as "rural." Likewise, sampled districts are classified according to whether they are above or below the mean percent black for all southern districts (18.3 percent).

Chapter 3 is concerned with changes from about 1970 to 1990 in the attitudes of southern voters who support Democratic congressional candidates in relation to the attitudes of northern Democrats and Republicans. For this analysis, three criteria guided the selection of survey items and years: the existence of items of comparable content at both ends of the period 1970–90; the availability of items in consecutive surveys for the purposes of pooling subsamples of respondents; and the representation of a variety of issue concerns in the analysis. These purposes are best fulfilled by comparing two pooled samples of NES respondents, one from the surveys of 1968–74 and one from 1984–90. The periods in which these samples were drawn represent, respectively, the heyday of the conservative coalition in Congress and the late 1980s period of resurgent congressional partisanship. A comparison of the 1980s with the new electoral era of the 1990s is facilitated by a pooled sample from the NES surveys of 1990–96.

The comparison of southern Democrats with northern Democrats and Republicans requires comparing subsamples of respondents who voted for different parties in congressional elections. In any one election year survey, the number of respondents on which conclusions can be based becomes quite small when congressional voters are divided by the party for which they voted, their region, and their race. For instance, white southerners who vote Democratic for the U.S. House number as few as 146 in one election year sample. Pooling data from several consecutive surveys will not allow us to detect changes occurring between consecutive elections, but we are most concerned with broad changes in congressional election constituencies occurring over a period of more than a decade. For instance, if indeed the most durable issue basis for the shift of white voters to the Republican Party in southern congressional elections is economic in nature, then this conclusion should be clear even through data pooled across four elections.

Table A.2 lists the survey items used in chapters 2 and 3. They include items in which respondents were asked to place themselves on a seven-point scale and items with two to four response categories. The items generally ask for opinions on specific issues of public policy. The most notable exception is the item in which respondents are asked to place themselves on a seven-point ideological continuum. Comparing pooled samples from 1984–90 and 1968–74 maximizes the number of issue items fitting the criteria of having been asked in both periods and of having been asked in more than one survey in each period. However, some items used were asked in either only one of the two periods or in only one survey in each period. Such items were included to maximize the number of comparisons that could be made across issue areas and across time.

TABLE A.1

Southern Congressional Districts Included in the NES, 1984–1990

Districts Classified by Levels of Urban and Black Population

LOW URBAN, LOW BLACK	LOW URBAN, HIGH BLACK	HIGH URBAN, LOW BLACK	HIGH URBAN HIGH BLACK
Alabama 4 (4)	Alabama 3 (43)	Florida 4 (11)	Alabama 6 (122)
Tennessee 3 (33)	Alabama 7 (38)	Florida 10 (183)	Florida 3 (30)
Tennessee 4 (247)	Arkansas 1 (190)	Florida 16 (7)	Florida 17 (10)
Texas 6 (6)	Georgia 1 (239)	Florida 18 (30)	Georgia 5 (9)
Texas 15 (178)	Georgia 3 (121)	Florida 19 (23)	Georgia 10 (5)
Virginia 9 (43)	Louisiana 4 (32)	Georgia 4 (4)	North Carolina 7 (247)
		Georgia 7 (4)	Texas 5 (4)
		Tennessee 2 (141)	Texas 18 (52)
		Texas 3 (6)	Texas 24 (14)
		Texas 8 (35)	Texas 25 (36)
		Texas 11 (27)	Virginia 3 (164)
		Texas 12 (3)	Virginia 4 (29)
		Texas 19 (191)	
		Texas 22 (39)	
		Virginia 8 (4)	
		Virginia 10 (6)	

NOTES: The number of respondents sampled by NES in each district in 1984–90 is in parentheses. Percent urban and percent black of the district population are designated "high" or "low" relative to the means for all southern congressional districts: 51.8 percent urban and 18.3 percent black.

TABLE A.2
National Election Studies Items Used in Chapters 2 and 3

ITEM/YEARS USED	WORDING	SCALE
Government guarantees job and standard of living (1972–74; 1984–96)	Some people feel that the government in Washington should see to it that every person has a job and a good standard of living. Others think the government should just let each person get ahead on his own. Where would you place yourself on this scale, or haven't you thought much about this?	7-point scale increases with greater proximity to "let each person get ahead on his own" (conservatism)
Liberal-Conservative (1972–74; 1984–96)	We hear a lot of talk these days about liberals and conservatives. Here is a 7-point scale on which the political views that people might hold are arranged from extremely liberal to extremely conservative. Where would you place yourself on this scale, or haven't you thought much about this?	7-point scale (conservatism)
Government health insurance (1970–72; 1984; 1988; 1992–96)	There is much concern about the rapid rise in medical and hospital costs. Some feel there should be a government insurance plan which would cover all medical and hospital expenses. Others feel that medical expenses should be paid by individuals, and through private insurance like Blue Cross. Where would you place yourself on this scale, or haven't you thought much about this?	7-point scale increases with greater proximity to "private insurance plan" (conservatism)

TABLE A.2 (continued)

Item/Years Used	Wording	Scale
Government aid to minorities (1970–74; 1984–96)	Some people feel that the government in Washington should make every possible effort to improve the social and economic position of blacks (1970: Negroes) and other minority groups. Others feel that the government should not make any special effort to help minorities because they should help themselves (1970: but they should be expected to help themselves). Where would you place yourself on this scale, or haven't you thought much about it?	7-point scale increases with greater proximity to "blacks should help themselves" (conservatism)
Women's equal role (1972–74; 1984; 1988–96)	Recently there has been a lot of talk about women's rights. Some people feel that women should have an equal role with men in running business, industry and government. Others feel that women's place is in the home. Where would you place yourself on this scale, or haven't you thought much about this?	7-point scale increases with greater proximity to "women's place is in the home" (conservatism)
School busing (1972–74; 1984)	There is much discussion about the best way to deal with racial problems. Some people think achieving racial integration of schools is so important that it justifies busing children to schools out of their own neighborhoods. Others think letting children go to their neighborhood schools is so important that they oppose busing. Where would you place yourself on this scale, or haven't you thought much about this?	7-point scale increases with greater proximity to "keep children in neighborhood schools" (conservatism)

Variable	Question	Coding
Urban unrest (1968–74)	There is much discussion about the best way to deal with the problem of urban unrest and rioting. Some say it is more important to use all available force to maintain law and order—no matter what results. Others say it is more important to correct the problems of poverty and unemployment that give rise to the disturbances. Where would you place yourself on this scale, or haven't you thought much about this?	7-point scale increases with greater proximity to "use all available force" (conservatism)
Rights of accused (1970–74)	Some people are primarily concerned with doing everything possible to protect the legal rights of those accused of committing crimes. Others feel that it is more important to stop criminal activity even at the risk of reducing the rights of the accused. Where would you place yourself on this scale, or haven't you thought much about this?	7-point scale increases with greater proximity to "stop crime regardless of rights of accused" (conservatism)
Civil rights—degree of change (1968–72; 1984–90)	In the past few years we have heard a lot about civil rights groups working to improve the position of black people (1964–70: the Negro) in this country. How much real change do you think there has been in the position of black people (1964–70: the Negro) in the past few years: a lot, some, or not much at all?	percent responding "a lot" (conservatism)
Civil rights leaders (1968–72; 1984–90)	Some say that the civil rights people have been trying to push too fast. Others feel they haven't pushed fast enough. How about you: Do you think that civil rights leaders are trying to push too fast, are going too slowly, or are they moving about the right speed?	percent responding "too fast" (conservatism)

TABLE A.2 (continued)

ITEM/YEARS USED	WORDING	SCALE
Allow integration (1968–72; 1986; 1990)	Some people say that the government in Washington should see to it that white and black (before 1972: Negro) children go (before 1972: are allowed to go) to the same schools. Others claim this is not the government's business. Have you been concerned (1986, 1990: interested) enough about [in] this question to favor one side over the other? (IF YES:) Do you think the government in Washington should?	precent responding they oppose government action (conservatism)
Power of federal government (1968–72; 1984; 1988)	Some people are afraid the government in Washington is getting too powerful for the good of the country and the individual person. Others feel that the government in Washington has not gotten (1968: is not getting) too strong for the good of the country. Have you been interested enough in this to favor one side over the other? (IF YES:) What is your feeling?	percent responding government is too powerful (conservatism)
Abortion (1972; 1984–96)	There has been some discussion about abortion in recent years. Which one of the opinions on this page best agrees with your view? You can just tell me the number of the opinion you choose. 1. By law, abortion should never be permitted. 2. The law should permit abortion only in case of rape, incest, or when the woman's life is in danger. 3. The law should permit abortion for reasons other than rape, incest, or danger to the woman's life, but only after the need for the abortion has been clearly established.	percent responding abortion should always be available (liberalism)

4. By law, a woman should always be able to obtain an abortion as a matter of personal choice.

Prayer in schools (1968; 1984)	Some people think it is all right for the public schools to start each day with a prayer. Others feel that religion does not belong in the public schools but should be taken care of by the family and the church. Have you been interested enough in this to favor one side over the other? (IF YES) Which do you think—schools should be allowed to start each day with a prayer or religion does not belong in the schools?	percent responding "schools should be allowed to start with prayer" (conservatism)
Government services spending (1984–96)	Some people think the government should provide fewer services, even in areas such as health and education, in order to reduce spending. Other people feel that it is important for the government to provide many more services even if it means an increase in spending. Where would you place yourself on this scale, or haven't you thought about it much?	7-point scale increases with greater proximity go "government should provide many more services" (liberalism)
Defense (1984–96)	Some people believe that we should spend much less money for defense. Others feel that defense spending should be greatly increased. Where would you place yourself on this scale, or haven't you thought much about it?	7-point scale, from "greatly decrease defense spending" to "greatly increase defense spending" (conservatism)

Source: National Election Study, Cumulative Data File (Miller and NES 1991).

NOTES

CHAPTER 1.
SOUTHERN DEMOCRATS AND
PARTY GOVERNMENT IN THE HOUSE

1. *Congressional Quarterly* is the source of the definition of "party unity" used in this study. A party unity vote occurs when the majority of voting Democrats oppose the majority of voting Republicans on a roll call vote. A member's party unity score is the proportion of party unity votes on which he or she supported the position of the majority of his or her own party.

2. The editors of *Congressional Quarterly* define an appearance of the conservative coalition as a roll call vote on which a majority of voting Republicans and a majority of voting southern Democrats are both opposed to the position taken by a majority of voting northern Democrats. The conservative coalition is the alliance of southern Democrats and Republicans that occurs in such situations. A member's conservative coalition score is the proportion of conservative coalition appearances on which he or she voted for the position favored by the coalition. For the purpose of determining when the conservative coalition appears, the South is defined by *Congressional Quarterly* as comprising the following states: Alabama, Arkansas, Florida, Georgia, Kentucky, Louisiana, Mississippi, North Carolina, Oklahoma, South Carolina, Tennessee, Texas, and Virginia. States not in the South are considered "northern." Unless otherwise noted, these will be the working definitions of the conservative coalition and of the South throughout this study.

3. Cox and McCubbins (1993) present a similar statement of the role of parties in the organization of the House, but they assert that the empowerment of party leaders is a fixed feature of House structure, not a conditional phenomenon. Party leaders work toward providing a positive reputation for the party. A positive party reputation is always in the electoral best interest of all the party members, regardless of the degree of heterogeneity or homogeneity of policy preferences within the party. The role and power of party leaders in delegating authority to committees and structuring rules is thus a fairly constant feature of the House, used for the purpose of enhancing partisans' electoral prospects. What varies over time and across issues is the range of votes on which party leaders will attempt to lead members. This latter variation is a function of the heterogeneity of preferences within the party.

CHAPTER 2.
SOUTHERN GEOGRAPHIC CONSTITUENCIES

1. Relevant literature documenting variation among blacks as well as interracial differences in political attitudes and behavior includes Jaynes and Williams 1989; Schuman, Steeh, and Bobo 1985; Sigelman and Welch 1991; Tate 1993; and Dawson 1994.
2. The next three paragraphs are based heavily on Black and Black 1987: 24–30.
3. In using this label, Black and Black refer to Barrington Moore's (1966) description of tradition-maintaining patterns of late industrialization.
4. See Jennings 1977, however, for evidence of some policy consequences of the populist-influenced Long administrations in Louisiana.
5. See Wald 1997: 210–15 for a discussion of research findings regarding the role of social integration in the link between religion and political attitudes.
6. The measure of urbanization used here is the proportion of the congressional district population residing in an "urbanized area," which "consists of a central city or cities and surrounding closely settled territory ('urban fringe') that together have a minimum population of 50,000" (U.S. Census 1982). By this measure, the mean percent urban for congressional districts in place in the South in 1984–90 was 51.8.
7. For the purposes of the analyses in this chapter, fundamentalist denominations have been defined as they were in the National Election

Studies through 1988. By this grouping, responses that were placed in the "Protestant, neo-fundamentalist" category are: United Missionary, Protestant Missionary, Church of God, Holiness, Nazarene, Free Methodist, Church of God in Christ, Plymouth Brethren, Pentecostal, Assembly of God, Church of Christ, Salvation Army, Primitive Baptist, Free Will Baptist, Missionary Fundamentalist Baptist, Gospel Baptist, Seventh-Day Adventist, Southern Baptist, Missouri Synod Lutheran, and "other fundamentalists."

8. Here one might also refer to correlation coefficients computed for a dummy version of each of the three variables with the percent urban of each respondent's congressional district. Percent urban is positively associated with the respondent having a college education ($r = .14$) and having an income in the upper third of the national sample ($r = .13$); urbanization has a negative association with the respondent belonging to a fundamentalist congregation ($r = -.10$). All three correlations are statistically significant ($p = .001$).

9. Relatively high and low levels of percent black population were determined with reference to the mean percent black for all southern congressional districts, which was 18.3.

CHAPTER 3.
CHANGE IN REELECTION AND
ACTIVIST CONSTITUENCIES

1. The liberalization of the Democratic presidential primary electorate in the South is documented by Black and Black (1992: 268–71).

2. Carmines and Stimson include a sixth act of participation, voting in the presidential election, and operationalize political "activists" as those who engaged in four of the resulting six participation acts. The operationalization of primary constituents used here is similar: all the respondents included in the following tables reported voting in the congressional election in addition to participating in three of five nonvoting acts of participation.

3. The analyses reported in tables 3.9 and 3.10 were also conducted separately for 1990–92 and 1994–96. The results were substantially the same as those reported here for both pairs of elections, indicating that the 1994 election alone had negligible impact on mass and activist issue alignments.

CHAPTER 4.
ISSUE AREAS AND ROLL CALL VOTING

1. Only rarely does a southern Democratic majority opposing a Republican majority produce a party unity vote without a majority of northern Democrats also voting against the Republicans. A little more often a conservative coalition vote is also a party unity vote, when either a particularly large majority of northern Democrats oppose the southern Democrats and Republicans or a particularly small majority of southern Democrats agree with the Republicans.

2. We are thus observing the choices made by southern Democrats when a roll call vote is squarely in what Rohde (1995a) calls the "partisan domain" of congressional activity, if we define that domain as a set of issues on which partisan conflict exists between northern Democrats and Republicans. What is left out are issues for which distributive or informational approaches are more appropriate for analysis.

3. In addition, following Shelley (1983), some roll call votes were classified as dealing with executive-legislative relations or internal legislative branch business.

4. Only a very few partisan roll calls were classified as agriculture votes, mostly in the 93d, 94th, and 95th Congresses. These are dropped from the analysis here, as are roll calls whose primary concern was executive branch relations or procedural issues.

CHAPTER 5.
DISTRICT CHARACTERISTICS AND
SOUTHERN DEMOCRATIC PARTISANSHIP

1. In the wake of the Voting Rights Act of 1965, southern legislatures accelerated efforts to reduce or eliminate opportunities for local black majorities to exercise influence. The most blatant effort to dilute the black vote in congressional districting in the late 1960s was probably Mississippi's. Shortly after passage of the act, redistricting dismembered a black-majority congressional district in the Delta region and apportioned majority-black counties into three white-majority districts. Davidson 1984, Grofman and Davidson 1992, and Davidson and Grofman 1994 are useful sources on practices designed to dilute minority influence and on Voting Rights Act implementation more generally.

2. It should be added that the participation revolution of the 1960s and 1970s among blacks was matched by similar expansions in the voting participation of whites. Some (e.g., Kernell 1973; McDonald 1992) have characterized this as a conservative countermobilization. In his work on the dual mobilizations of the southern electorate since the 1960s, Harold Stanley (1987) concludes that the increase in white voting was due to increased levels of education among whites rather than to a racial backlash.

3. Few studies reveal support for the black influence hypothesis among Southern Democrats. Using Poole-Rosenthal scores (Poole and Rosenthal 1991) calculated for the years 1972–92, David Lublin (1997: 78–86) reports that southern Democratic conservatism in roll call voting declined as percent black in the district increased. He models a step-decrease in white conservatism at 40 percent black, a threshold at which the association between black population and roll call liberalism becomes stronger. The threshold effect might be created by the greater likelihood of electing black representatives from urban than from rural districts, or even by the interaction of urban and black population. His model includes neither the race of representative nor an interaction effect.

CHAPTER 6.
SOUTHERN DEMOCRATS, SOUTHERN
ELECTORATES, AND THE
HOUSE OF REPRESENTATIVES

1. Although party contacting of voters does not occur with the frequency it once did, there is evidence that contact with party workers during congressional campaigns makes a significant difference in the voting behavior of the individuals contacted. See Wielhower and Lockerbie 1994.

2. The link between the strength of party organizational activity and the level of party competition is also noted by Patterson and Caldeira (1984) and Barrilleaux (1986).

3. V.O. Key (1949) and Alexander Heard (1952) describe the role of party organizations in southern politics in the days when Republican congressional candidates won practically no congressional elections outside their traditional mountain strongholds.

4. Sarah Brandes Crook and John R. Hibbing (1985) make a strong case that congressional reforms led to increased party discipline in the

House. In the 1980s southern Democratic committee chairs routinely admitted to assisting the Democratic caucus on some legislation in recognition of the caucus's role in assigning chairmanships (Ehrenhalt 1987; Rae 1994). At the same time, the party leadership took actions to facilitate party members' support of party positions in cases where such support could be electorally costly otherwise. Southern Democrats clearly were influenced by the ability of party leaders to provide both cover and rewards for supporting the party (Rohde 1991b).

REFERENCES

Abramowitz, Alan I. 1980. "Is the Revolt Fading? A Note on Party Loyalty among Southern Democratic Congressmen." *Journal of Politics* 42: 568–76.

———. 1994. "Issue Evolution Reconsidered: Racial Attitudes and Partisanship in the U.S. Electorate." *American Journal of Political Science* 38: 1–24.

———. 1995. "It's Abortion, Stupid: Policy Voting in the 1992 Presidential Election." *Journal of Politics* 57: 176–86.

Abramowitz, Alan, John McGlennon, and Ronald Rapoport. 1982. "Presidential Activists and the Nationalization of Party Politics in Virginia." In Laurence W. Moreland, Tod A. Baker, and Robert P. Steed, eds., *Contemporary Southern Political Attitudes and Behavior*. New York: Praeger.

Abramowitz, Alan I., and Kyle L. Saunders. 1998. "Ideological Realignment in the U.S. Electorate." *Journal of Politics* 60: 634–54.

Adams, Greg D. 1997. "Abortion: Evidence of an Issue Evolution." *American Journal of Political Science* 41: 718–37.

Aistrup, Joseph A. 1990. "Republican Contestation of U.S. State Senate Elections in the South." *Legislative Studies Quarterly* 15: 227–45.

———. 1996. *The Southern Strategy Revisited*. Lexington: University Press of Kentucky.

Aldrich, John. 1995a. "A Model of a Legislature with Two Parties and a Committee System." In Kenneth A. Shepsle and Barry R. Weingast, eds., *Positive Theories of Congressional Institutions*. Ann Arbor: University of Michigan Press.

———. 1995b. *Why Parties? The Origin and Transformation of Political Parties in America*. Chicago: University of Chicago Press.

Aldrich, John, and David W. Rohde. 1995. "Theories of Party in the Legislature and the Transition to Republican Rule in the House." Paper presented at the Annual Meeting of the American Political Science Association, Chicago.

———. 1996a. "The Republican Revolution and the House Appropriations Committee." Paper presented at the Annual Meeting of the Southern Political Science Association, Atlanta.

———. 1996b. "A Tale of Two Speakers: A Comparison of Policy Making in the 100th and 104th Congresses." Paper presented at the Annual Meeting of the American Political Science Association, San Francisco.

Arrow, Kenneth. 1951. *Social Choice and Individual Values*. New Haven: Yale University Press.

Asher, Herbert B., and Weisberg, Herbert F. 1978. "Voting Change in Congress: Some Dynamic Perspectives on an Evolutionary Process." *American Journal of Political Science* 22: 391–425.

Ayres, B. Drummond, Jr. 1993. "Christian Right Splits GOP in South." *New York Times*, June 7, A7.

Bach, Stanley, and Steven S. Smith. 1988. *Managing Uncertainty in the House of Representatives*. Washington, D.C.: Brookings Institution.

Baker, Ross K. 1985. "Party and Institutional Sanctions in the U.S. House: The Case of Congressman Graham." *Legislative Studies Quarterly* 10: 315–38.

Baker, Tod A., Robert P. Steed, and Laurence W. Moreland. 1982. "Southern Distinctiveness and the Emergence of Party Competition: The Case of a Deep South State." In Laurence W. Moreland, Tod A. Baker, and Robert P. Steed, eds., *Contemporary Southern Political Attitudes and Behavior*. New York: Praeger.

Barone, Michael, and Grant Ujifsa. 1994. *The Almanac of American Politics*. Washington, D.C.: National Journal.

Barrilleaux, Charles. 1986. "A Dynamic Model of Partisan Competition in the American States." *American Journal of Political Science* 30: 882–40.

Bartley, Numan V. 1969. *The Rise of Massive Resistance: Race and Politics in the South in the 1950s*. Baton Rouge: Louisiana State University Press.

Bartley, Numan V., and Hugh D. Graham. 1975. *Southern Politics and the Second Reconstruction*. Baltimore: Johns Hopkins University Press.

Bass, Jack, and Walter DeVries. 1976. *The Transformation of Southern Politics*. New York: BasicBooks.

Beck, Paul Allen. 1977. "Partisan Dealignment in the Postwar South." *American Political Science Review* 71: 477–97.

Berard, Stanley P. 1997. "The 1996 House Elections in Regional Perspective." Paper presented at the annual meeting of the Pennsylvania Political Science Association, Elizabethtown, Pa.

Berard, Stanley P., and David W. Rohde. 1998. "What You See Is . . . Essentially . . . What You Get: House Elections in the Contemporary South." Paper presented at the annual meeting of the Midwest Political Science Association, Chicago.

Berry, William D., and Stanley Feldman. 1985. "Multiple Regression in Practice." Sage University Paper series on Quantitative Applications in the Social Sciences, 07-050. Beverly Hills, Calif.: Sage.

Bianco, William T. 1994. *Trust: Representatives and Constituents*. Ann Arbor: University of Michigan Press.

Bibby, John F. 1990. "Party Organization at the State Level." In L. Sandy Maisel, ed., *The Parties Respond: Changes in the American Party System*. Boulder, Colo.: Westview Press.

Billings, Dwight B., Jr. 1979. *Planters and the Making of a "New South."* Chapel Hill: University of North Carolina Press.

Black, Earl. 1976. *Southern Governors and Civil Rights: Racial Segregation as a Campaign Issue in the Second Reconstruction*. Cambridge, Mass.: Harvard University Press.

———. 1998. "The Newest Southern Politics." *Journal of Politics* 60: 591–612.

Black, Earl, and Merle Black. 1987. *Politics and Society in the South*. Cambridge, Mass.: Harvard University Press.

———. 1992. *The Vital South: How Presidents Are Elected*. Cambridge, Mass.: Harvard University Press.

Black, Merle. 1978. "Racial Composition of Congressional Districts and Support for Federal Voting Rights in the American South." *Social Science Quarterly* 59: 435–50.

———. 1979. "Regional and Partisan Bases of Congressional Support for the Changing Agenda of Civil Rights Legislation," *Journal of Politics* 41: 665–79.

Black, Merle, and Earl Black. 1982. "The Growth of Contested Republican Primaries in the American South, 1960–1980." In Laurence W. Moreland, Tod A. Baker, and Robert P. Steed, eds., *Contemporary Southern Political Attitudes and Behavior*. New York: Praeger.

———. 1990. "The South in the Senate: Changing Patterns of Representation on Committees." In Robert P. Steed, Laurence W. Moreland, and

Tod A. Baker, eds., *The Disappearing South?* Tuscaloosa: University of Alabama Press.

Bobo, Lawrence, and Franklin D. Gilliam, Jr. 1990. "Race, Socio-Political Participation, and Black Empowerment." *American Political Science Review* 84: 377–93.

Bowman, Lewis, William E. Hulbary, and Anne E. Kelley. 1990. "Party Sorting at the Grass Roots: Stable Partisans and Party-Changers among Florida's Precinct Officials." In Robert P. Steed, Lawrence W. Moreland, and Tod A. Baker, eds., *The Disappearing South?* Tuscaloosa: University of Alabama Press.

Boynton, George Robert. 1965. "Southern Conservatism: Constituency Opinion and Congressional Voting." *Public Opinion Quarterly* 29: 259–69.

Brace, Kimball, Bernard Grofman, and Lisa Handley. 1987. "Does Redistricting Aimed to Help Blacks Necessarily Help Republicans?" *Journal of Politics* 49: 167–85.

Brady, David W. 1978. "Critical Elections, Congressional Parties, and Clusters of Policy Change." *British Journal of Political Science* 8: 79–99.

———. 1988. *Critical Elections and Congressional Policy Making*. Palo Alto, Calif.: Stanford University Press.

Brady, David W., and Charles S. Bullock. 1980. "Is There a Conservative Coalition in the House?" *Journal of Politics* 42: 549–59.

———. 1981. "Coalition Politics in the House of Representatives." In Lawrence C. Dodd and Bruce I. Oppenheimer, eds., *Congress Reconsidered*. 2d ed. Washington, D.C.: Congressional Quarterly Press.

Brooks, Gary H. 1982. "Black Political Mobilization and White Legislative Behavior." In Laurence W. Moreland, Tod A. Baker, and Robert P. Steed, eds., *Contemporary Southern Political Attitudes and Behavior*. New York: Praeger.

Bullock, Charles S. 1981. "Congressional Voting and the Mobilization of a Black Electorate in the South." *Journal of Politics* 43: 662–82.

———. 1985. "Congressional Roll Call Voting in a Two-Party South." *Social Science Quarterly* 66: 789–804.

———. 1988. "Creeping Realignment in the South." In Robert H. Swansbrough and David M. Brodsky, eds., *The South's New Politics*. Columbia: University of South Carolina Press.

———. 1995. "The Impact of Changing the Racial Composition of Congressional Districts on Legislators' Roll Call Behavior." *American Politics Quarterly* 23: 141–58.

————. 1997. "The South in the House, Version '96." *Extension of Remarks* (January).

Bullock, Charles S., and David W. Brady. 1983. "Party, Constituency, and Roll Call Voting in the U.S. Senate." *Legislative Studies Quarterly* 8: 29–43.

Bullock, Charles S., and Susan A. MacManus. 1981. "Policy Responsiveness to the Black Electorate: Programmatic versus Symbolic Representation." *American Politics Quarterly* 9: 357–68.

Bullock, Charles S., III, and Mark Rozell. 1998. "Southern Politics at Century's End." In Charles S. Bullock III and Mark Rozell, eds., *The New Politics of the Old South*. Lanham, Md.: Rowman and Littlefield.

Burnham, Walter Dean. 1971. *Critical Elections and the Mainsprings of American Politics*. New York: Norton.

Cameron, Charles, David Epstein, and Sharyn O'Halloran. 1996. "Do Majority-Minority Districts Maximize Substantive Black Representation in Congress?" *American Political Science Review* 90: 794–812.

Campbell, Bruce A. 1977a. "Change in the Southern Electorate." *American Journal of Political Science* 21: 37–64.

————. 1977b. "Patterns of Change in the Partisan Loyalties of Native Southerners." *Journal of Politics* 39: 730–61.

Carmines, Edward G., and James H. Kuklinski. 1990. "Incentives, Opportunities, and the Logic of Public Opinion in American Political Representation." In John A. Ferejohn and James H. Kuklinski, eds., *Information and Democratic Processes*. Urbana: University of Illinois Press.

Carmines, Edward G., and Harold W. Stanley. 1990. "Ideological Realignment in the Contemporary South." In Robert P. Steed, Lawrence Moreland, and Tod A. Baker, eds., *The Disappearing South?* Tuscaloosa: University of Alabama Press.

Carmines, Edward G., and James A. Stimson. 1989. *Issue Evolution: Race and the Transformation of American Politics*. Princeton: Princeton University Press.

Carsey, Thomas M. 1995. "The Contextual Effects of Race on White Voter Behavior: The 1989 New York City Mayoral Election." *Journal of Politics* 57: 221–28.

Cash, W. J. 1941. *The Mind of the South*. New York: Knopf.

Clausen, Aage R. 1967. "Measurement Identity in the Longitudinal Analysis of Legislative Behavior." *American Political Science Review* 61: 1020–35.

————. 1973. *How Congressmen Decide: A Policy Focus.* New York: St. Martin's Press.

Clausen, Aage R., and Richard B. Cheney. 1970. "A Comparative Analysis of Senate-House Voting on Economic and Welfare Policy, 1953–1964." *American Political Science Review* 64: 138–52.

Cobb, James C. 1982. *The Selling of the South: The Southern Crusade for Industrial Development.* Baton Rouge: Louisiana State University Press.

————. 1984. *Industrialization and the Transformation of Southern Society.* Lexington: University Press of Kentucky.

Combs, Michael W., John R. Hibbing, and Susan Welch. 1984. "Black Constituents and Congressional Roll Call Votes." *Western Political Quarterly* 37: 424–34.

Conway, M. Margaret. 1991. *Political Participation in the United States.* Washington, D.C.: Congressional Quarterly Press.

Cosman, Bernard. 1962. "Presidential Republicanism in the South, 1960." *Journal of Politics* 24: 303–22.

————. 1966. *Five States for Goldwater: Continuity and Change in Southern Presidential Voting Patterns.* University: University of Alabama Press.

————. 1967. "Republicanism in the South: Goldwater's Impact upon Voter Alignment in Congressional, Gubernatorial, and Senatorial Races." *Southwest Social Science Quarterly* 48: 13–23.

Cotter, Cornelius P., James L. Gibson, John F. Bibby, and Robert J. Huckshorn. 1984. *Party Organizations in American Politics.* New York: Praeger.

Cotter, Patrick R., and James Glen Stovall. 1990. "The Conservative South?" *American Politics Quarterly* 18:103–19.

Cox, Gary W., and Mathew D. McCubbins. 1993. *Legislative Leviathan: Party Government in the House.* Berkeley: University of California Press.

CQ Almanac. 1993. "Clinton Keeps Southern Wing on His Team in 1993." *CQ Almanac*: 22C–27C.

Crook, Sara Brandes, and John R. Hibbing. 1985. "Congressional Reform and Party Discipline: The Effects of Changes in the Seniority System on Party Loyalty in the House of Representatives." *British Journal of Political Science* 15: 207–26.

Dalton, Russell J. 1988. *Citizen Politics: Public Opinion and Political Parties in the United States, United Kingdon, France, and West Germany.* Chatham, N.J.: Chatham House.

Davidson, Chandler, ed. 1984. *Minority Vote Dilution.* Washington, D.C.: Howard University Press.

Davidson, Chandler, and Bernard Grofman, eds. 1994. *Quiet Revolution in the South: The Impact of the Voting Rights Act, 1965–1990.* Princeton: Princeton University Press.

Dawson, Michael C. 1994. *Behind the Mule: Race and Class in African-American Politics.* Princeton: Princeton University Press.

Downs, Anthony. 1957. *An Economic Theory of Democracy.* New York: Harper and Row.

Ehrenhalt, Alan. 1987. "Changing South Perils Conservative Coalition." *Congressional Quarterly Weekly Report,* August 1, 1699–1705.

Elazar, Daniel. 1972. *American Federalism.* 2d ed. New York: Thomas Y. Crowell.

Enelow, James, and Melvin J. Hinich. 1984. *The Spatial Theory of Voting.* New York: Cambridge University Press.

Erikson, Robert. 1971. "The Electoral Impact of Congressional Roll Call Voting." *American Political Science Review* 65: 1018–32.

Erikson, Robert S., Gerald C. Wright, and John P. McIver. 1989. "Political Parties, Public Opinion, and State Policy in the United States." *American Political Science Review* 83: 729–50.

Feagin, Joe R. 1972. "Civil Rights Voting by Southern Congressmen." *Journal of Politics* 34: 484–99.

Feagin, Joe R., and Harlan Hahn. 1970. "The Second Reconstruction: Black Political Strength in the South." *Social Science Quarterly* 51: 42–56.

Feig, Douglas G. 1990. "Dimensions of Southern Opinion on Prayer in Schools." In Robert P. Steed, Laurence W. Moreland, and Tod A. Baker eds., *The Disappearing South?* Tuscaloosa: University of Alabama Press.

Fenno, Richard F. 1973. *Congressmen in Committees.* Boston: Little, Brown.

———. 1978. *Home Style: House Members and Their Districts.* Boston: Little, Brown.

Fiorina, Morris P. 1973. "Electoral Margins, Constituency Influence, and Policy Moderation: A Critical Assessment." *American Politics Quarterly* 2: 479–98.

———. 1974. *Representatives, Roll Calls, and Constituencies.* Lexington, Mass.: Lexington Books.

Fleisher, Richard. 1993. "Explaining the Change in Roll–Call Voting Behavior of Southern Democrats." *Journal of Politics* 55: 327–41.

Frendreis, John, James L. Gibson, and Laura L. Vertz. 1990. "The Electoral Relevance of Local Party Organizations." *American Political Science Review* 84: 226–35.

Friedrich, Robert J. 1982. "In Defense of Multiplicative Terms in Multiple Regression Equations." *American Journal of Political Science* 26: 797–833.

Froman, Louis. 1963. *Congressmen and Their Constituencies.* Chicago: Rand McNally.

Gibson, James L., Cornelius P. Cotter, John F. Bibby, and Robert J. Huckshorn. 1983. "Assessing Party Organizational Strength." *American Journal of Political Science* 27: 193–222.

———. 1985. "Whither the Local Parties? A Cross-Sectional and Longitudinal Analysis of the Strength of Party Organizations." *American Journal of Political Science* 29: 139–60.

Gibson, James L., John P. Frendreis, and Laura L. Vertz. 1989. "Party Dynamics in the 1980s: Change in County Party Organizational Strength, 1980–1984." *American Journal of Political Science* 33: 67–90.

Giles, Michael W. 1977. "Percent Black and Racial Hostility: An Old Assumption Revisited." *Social Science Quarterly* 58: 820–35.

Giles, Michael W., and Melanie Buckner. 1993. "David Duke and Black Threat: An Old Hypothesis Revisited." *Journal of Politics* 55: 702–13.

Giles, Michael, and Kaenan Hertz. 1994. "Racial Threat and Partisan Identification." *American Political Science Review* 88: 317–26.

Gilliam, Franklin D., Jr., and Kenny J. Whitby. 1989. "Race, Class, and Attitudes toward Social Welfare Spending: An Ethclass Interpretation." *Social Science Quarterly* 70: 88–100.

Gilligan, Thomas W., and Keith Krehbiel. 1989. "Asymmetric Information and Legislative Rules with a Heterogeneous Committee." *American Journal of Political Science* 33: 459–90.

———. 1990. "Organization of Informative Committees by a Rational Legislature." *American Journal of Political Science* 34: 531–64.

Glaser, James M. 1994. "Back to the Black Belt: Racial Environment and White Racial Attitudes in the South." *Journal of Politics* 56: 21–41.

———. 1996. *Race, Campaign Politics, and the Realignment in the South.* New Haven: Yale University Press.

Glenn, Norval. 1975. "Recent Trends in White-Nonwhite Attitudinal Differences." *Public Opinion Quarterly* 38: 596–604.

Grantham, Dewey W. 1965. *The Democratic South.* New York: Norton.

Green, John C., and James L. Guth. 1990. "The Transformation of Southern Political Elites: Regionalism among Party and PAC Contributors," In Robert P. Steed, Lawrence W. Moreland, and Tod A. Baker, eds., *The Disappearing South?* Tuscaloosa: University of Alabama Press.

Grofman, Bernard, and Chandler Davidson, eds. 1992. *Controversies in Minority Voting: The Voting Rights Act in Perspective.* Washington, D.C.: Brookings Institution.

Grofman, Bernard, Robert Griffin, and Amihai Glazer. 1992. "The Effect of Black Population on Electing Democrats and Liberals to the House of Representatives." *Legislative Studies Quarterly* 17: 365–79.

Grofman, Bernard, and Lisa Handley. 1989. "Minority Population Proportion and Black and Hispanic Congressional Success in the 1970s and 1980s." *American Politics Quarterly* 17: 436–45.

Hall, Richard L. 1995. *Participation in Congress.* New Haven: Yale University Press.

Hall, Richard L., and Colleen Heflin. 1994. "The Importance of Color in Congress: Minority Members, Minority Constituencies, and the Representation of Race in the U.S. House." Paper presented at the Annual Meeting of the Midwest Political Science Association, Chicago.

Hawkey, Earl W. 1982. "Southern Conservatism, 1956–1976." In Laurence W. Moreland, Tod A. Baker, and Robert P. Steed, eds., *Contemporary Southern Political Attitudes and Behavior.* New York: Praeger.

Heard, Alexander. 1952. *A Two-Party South?* Chapel Hill: University of North Carolina Press.

Herrnson, Paul S. 1988. *Party Campaigning in the 1980s.* Cambridge, Mass.: Harvard University Press.

———. 1990. "Reemergent National Party Organizations." In L. Sandy Maisel, ed., *The Parties Respond: Changes in the American Party System.* Boulder, Colo.: Westview Press.

———. 1996. *Congressional Elections: Campaigning at Home and in Washington.* Washington, D.C.: Congressional Quarterly Press.

Hill, Kevin A. 1995. "Does the Creation of Majority Black Districts Aid Republicans? An Analysis of the 1992 Congressional Elections in Eight Southern States." *Journal of Politics* 57: 384–401.

Hill, Kim Quaile, and Patricia A. Hurley. 1999. "Dyadic Representation Reappraised." *American Journal of Political Science* 43: 108–37.

Hood, M. V., III, Quentin Kidd, and Irwin L. Morris. 1999. Of Byrd[s] and Bumpers: Using Democratic Senators to Analyze Political Change in the South, 1960–1995." *American Journal of Political Science* 43: 431–64.

Hood, M. V., III, and Irwin L. Morris. 1998. "Boll Weevils and Roll Call Voting: A Study in Time and Space." *Legislative Studies Quarterly* 23: 245–69.

Huckfeldt, Robert, and Carol Weitzel Kohfeld. 1989. *Race and the Decline of Class in American Politics*. Urbana: University of Illinois Press.

Huntington, Samuel. 1950. "A Revised Theory of American Party Politics." *American Political Science Review* 44: 669–77.

Inter-University Consortium for Political and Social Research. 1991. *United States Congressional Roll Call Voting Records, 1789–1991* [computer file]. Ann Arbor, Mich.: Inter-University Consortium for Political and Social Research.

Jackman, Mary R., and Michael J. Muha. 1984. "Education and Intergroup Attitudes: Moral Enlightenment, Superficial Democratic Commitment, or Ideological Refinement?" *American Sociological Review* 49: 751–69.

Jacobson, Gary C. 1992. *The Politics of Congressional Elections*. 3d ed. New York: HarperCollins.

———. 1996. "The 1994 House Elections in Perspective." *Political Science Quarterly* 111: 203–24.

Jacobson, Gary C., and Samuel Kernell. 1983. *Strategy and Choice in Congressional Elections*. New Haven: Yale University Press.

Jaynes, Gerald David, and Robin M. Williams, eds. 1989. *A Common Destiny: Blacks and American Society*. Washington, D.C.: National Academy Press.

Jelen, Ted. 1982. "Sources of Political Intolerance: The Case of the American South." in Laurence W. Moreland, Tod A. Baker, and Robert P. Steed, eds., *Contemporary Southern Political Attitudes and Behavior*. New York: Praeger.

Jennings, Edward T. 1977. "Some Policy Consequences of the Long Revolution and Bifactional Rivalry in Louisiana." *American Journal of Political Science* 21: 225–46.

Katznelson, Ira, Kim Geiger, and Daniel Kryden. 1993. "Limiting Liberalism: The Southern Veto in Congress, 1933–1950." *Political Science Quarterly* 108: 283–306.

Kazee, Thomas A., and Mary C. Thornberry. 1990. "Where's the Party? Congressional Candidate Recruitment and American Party Organizations." *Western Political Quarterly* 43: 61–80.

Keech, William R. 1968. *The Impact of Negro Voting: The Role of the Vote in the Quest for Equality*. Chicago: Rand McNally.

Keefe, William J. 1994. *Parties, Politics, and Public Policy in America*. 7th ed. Washington, D.C.: Congressional Quarterly.

Keefe, William J., and Morris Ogul. 1993. *The American Legislative Process: Congress and the States*. New York: Prentice–Hall.

Kellstedt, Lyman A. 1990. "Evangelical Religion and Support for Social Issue Policies: An Examination of Regional Variation." In Robert P. Steed, Laurence W. Moreland, and Tod A. Baker, eds., *The Disappearing South?* Tuscaloosa: University of Alabama Press.

Kernell, Samuel. 1973. "Comment: A Re-evaluation of Black Voting in Mississippi." *American Political Science Review* 67: 1307–18.

Key, V. O. Jr. 1949. *Southern Politics in State and Nation.* New York: Knopf.

———. 1955. "A Theory of Critical Elections." *Journal of Politics* 17: 3–18.

———. 1959. "Secular Realignment and the Party System." *Journal of Politics* 21: 198–210.

Kingdon, John W. 1973. *Congressmen's Voting Decisions.* New York: Harper and Row.

———. 1989. *Congressmen's Voting Decisions.* 3d ed., Ann Arbor: University of Michigan Press.

Klinkner, Philip. 1992. "Race and the Republican Party: The Rise of the Southern Strategy in the Republican National Committee, 1960–1964." Paper presented at the Annual Meeting of the American Political Science Association, Chicago.

Knoke, David, and N. Kyriazis. 1977. "The Persistence of the Black Belt Vote: A Test of Key's Hypotheses." *Social Science Quarterly* 57: 900–906.

Krehbiel, Keith. 1991. *Information and Legislative Organization.* Ann Arbor: University of Michigan Press.

———. 1993. "Where's the Party?" *British Journal of Political Science* 23: 235–66.

Kuklinski, James H., and Gary M. Segura. 1995. "Endogeneity, Exogeneity, Time and Space in Political Representation." *Legislative Studies Quarterly* 20: 3–21.

Ladd, Everett Carl, Jr., with Charles D. Hadley. 1978. *Transformations of the American Party System.* 2d ed. New York: Norton.

Lamis, Alexander P. 1984. *The Two-Party South.* New York: Oxford University Press.

———. 1990. *The Two-Party South.* Rev. and expanded ed. New York: Oxford University Press.

Lawson, Steven F. 1976. *Black Ballots: Voting Rights in the South, 1944–1969.* New York: Columbia University Press.

Lerche, Charles O. 1964. *The Uncertain South.* Chicago: Quadrangle Books.

Lublin, David. 1997. *The Paradox of Representation: Racial Gerrymandering and Minority Interests in Congress.* Princeton: Princeton University Press.

McDonald, Laughlin. 1992. "The 1982 Amendments of Section 2 and Minority Representation." In Bernard Grofman and Chandler Davidson, eds., *Controversies in Minority Voting: The Voting Rights Act in Perspective*. Washington, D.C.: Brookings Institution.

MacRae, Duncan, Jr. 1952. "The Relation between Roll Call Votes and Constituencies in the Massachusetts House of Representatives." *American Political Science Review* 46: 1046–55.

―――. 1958. *Dimensions of Congressional Voting*. Berkeley: University of California Press.

―――. 1970. *Issues and Parties in Legislative Voting*. New York: Harper and Row.

Manley, John F. 1973. "The Conservative Coalition in Congress." *American Behavioral Scientist* 17: 223–47.

Mann, Thomas E., and Raymond Wolfinger. 1980. "Candidates and Parties in Congressional Elections." *American Political Science Review* 71: 166–76.

Marshall, F. Ray. 1967. *Labor in the South*. Cambridge, Mass.: Harvard University Press.

Matthews, Donald R., and James W. Prothro. 1963. "Social and Economic Factors and Negro Voter Registration in the South." *American Political Science Review* 57: 24–44.

―――. 1966. *Negroes and the New Southern Politics*. New York: Harcourt, Brace, and World.

Mayhew, David R. 1966. *Party Loyalty among Congressmen: The Difference between Democrats and Republicans*. Cambridge, Mass.: Harvard University Press.

―――. 1974. *Congress: The Electoral Connection*. New Haven: Yale University Press.

Miller, Phillip L. 1982. "The Impact of Organizational Activity on Black Political Participation." *Social Science Quarterly* 62: 82–98.

Miller, Warren E., and Donald E. Stokes. 1963. "Constituency Influence in Congress." *American Political Science Review* 67: 55–72.

Miller, Warren E., and the National Election Studies. 1991. *American National Election Studies Cumulative Data File, 1952–1990* [computer file]. 6th release. Ann Arbor: University of Michigan, Center for Political Studies [producer]. Ann Arbor: Inter-University Consortium for Political and Social Research [distributor].

Miller, Warren E., Donald R. Kinder, Steven J. Rosenstone, and the National Election Studies. 1993. *American National Election Study, 1992: Pre- and Post-Election Survey [Enhanced with 1990 and 1991 Data]* [computer file].

Conducted by University of Michigan, Center for Political Studies. ICPSR ed. Ann Arbor: University of Michigan, Center for Political Studies, and Inter-University Consortium for Political and Social Research [producers]. Ann Arbor: Inter-University Consortium for Political and Social Research [distributor].

Moore, Barrington, Jr. 1966. *Social Origins of Dictatorship and Democracy: Lord and Peasant in the Making of the Modern World*. Boston: Beacon Press.

Nadeau, Richard, and Harold W. Stanley. 1993. "Class Polarization in Partisanship among Native Southern Whites." *American Journal of Political Science* 37: 900–919.

Nesbit, Dorothy Davidson. 1988. "Changing Partisanship among Southern Party Activists." *Journal of Politics* 50: 322–34.

Nixon, C. H. 1946. "The Politics of the Hills," *Journal of Politics* 8: 123–33.

Oppenheimer, Bruce I., James A. Stimson, and Richard W. Waterman. 1986. "Interpreting U.S. Congressional Elections: The Exposure Thesis." *Legislative Studies Quarterly* 11: 227–48.

Overby, L. Marvin. 1993. "Political Amateurism, Legislative Inexperience, and Incumbency Behavior: Southern Republican Senators 1980–1986." *Polity* 25: 401–20.

Overby, L. Marvin, and Kenneth Cosgrove. 1996. "Unintended Consequences? Racial Redistricting and the Representation of Minority Interests." *Journal of Politics* 58: 540–50.

Page, Benjamin I., and Robert Y. Shapiro. 1983. "Effects of Public Opinion on Policy." *American Political Science Review* 77: 175–90.

———. 1992. *The Rational Public: Fifty Years of Trends in Americans' Policy Preferences*. Chicago: University of Chicago Press.

Palazzolo, Dan, and Andrew O. Rich. 1992. "Partisanship and Deficits: Is There a Relationship?" Paper presented at the Annual Meeting of the Midwest Political Science Association, Chicago, Illinois.

Palmer, Bruce. 1980. *"Man over Money": The Southern Populist Critique of American Capitalism*. Chapel Hill: University of North Carolina Press.

Patterson, James T. 1967. *Congressional Conservatism and the New Deal*. Lexington: University of Kentucky Press.

Patterson, Samuel C., and Gregory A. Caldeira. 1984. "The Etiology of Partisan Competition." *American Political Science Review* 78: 691–707.

———. 1988. "Party Voting in the United States Congress." *British Journal of Political Science* 18: 111–31.

Perkins, Jerry. 1982. "Ideology in the South: Meaning and Bases among Masses and Elites." In Laurence W. Moreland, Tod A. Baker, and Robert

P. Steed, eds., *Contemporary Southern Political Attitudes and Behavior*. New York: Praeger.

Petrocik, John R. 1981. *Party Coalitions: Realignments and the Decline of the New Deal Party System*. Chicago: University of Chicago Press.

———. 1987. "Realignment: New Party Coalitions and the Nationalization of the South." *Journal of Politics* 49: 347–75.

Petrocik, John R., and Scott Desposato. 1998. "The Partisan Consequences of Majority-minority Districting in the South." *Journal of Politics* 6: 613–33.

Poole, Keith T. 1981. "Dimensions of Interest Group Evaluation of the U.S. Senate: 1969–1978." *American Journal of Political Science* 25: 49–67.

———. 1988. "Recent Developments in Analytical Models of Voting in the U.S. Congress." *Legislative Studies Quarterly* 13: 117–34.

Poole, Keith T., and R. Steven Daniels. 1985. "Ideology, Party, and Voting in the U.S. Congress." *American Political Science Review* 79: 373–99.

Poole, Keith T., and Howard Rosenthal. 1985. "A Spatial Model for Legislative Roll Call Analysis." *American Journal of Political Science* 29: 357–84.

———. 1991. "Patterns of Congressional Voting." *American Journal of Political Science* 35: 228–78.

———. 1997. *Congress: A Political-Economic History of Roll Call Voting*. New York: Oxford University Press.

Prothro, James, and Charles Grigg. 1960. "Fundamental Principles of Democracy." *Journal of Politics* 22: 276–94.

Prysby, Charles L. 1989. "The Structure of Southern Electoral Behavior." *American Politics Quarterly* 17: 163–80.

———. 1992. "Ideological Sorting among Southern Grassroots Party Activists." Paper presented at the Annual Meeting of the American Political Science Association, Chicago, Illinois.

Rae, Nicol C. 1989. *The Decline and Fall of the Liberal Republicans: From 1952 to the Present*. New York: Oxford University Press.

———. 1994. *Southern Democrats*. New York: Oxford University Press.

Reed, John Shelton. 1972. *The Enduring South: Subcultural Persistence in a Mass Society*. Lexington, Mass: Lexington Books.

———. 1986. *The Enduring South: Subcultural Persistence in a Mass Society*. 2d ed. Chapel Hill: University of North Carolina Press.

Rohde, David W. 1979. "Risk-bearing and Progressive Ambition: The Case of the United States House of Representatives." *American Journal of Political Science* 23: 1–26.

———. 1989. "'Something's Happening Here; What It Is Ain't Exactly Clear': Southern Democrats in the House of Representatives." In Morris P. Fiorina and David W. Rohde, eds., *Home Style and Washington Work: Studies of Congressional Politics*. Ann Arbor: University of Michigan Press.

———. 1991a. "The Electoral Roots of the Resurgence of Partisanship among Southern Democrats in the House of Representatives." Paper presented at the 1991 Annual Meeting of the American Political Science Association, Washington, D.C.

———. 1991b. *Parties and Leaders in the Postreform House*. Chicago: University of Chicago Press.

———. 1994a. "Partisanship, Leadership, and Congressional Assertiveness in Foreign and Defense Policy." In David Deese, ed., *The Politics of American Foreign Policy*. New York: St. Martin's Press.

———. 1994b. "Presidential Support in the House of Representatives." In Paul E. Peterson, eds., *The President, the Congress, and the Making of Foreign Policy*. Norman: University of Oklahoma Press.

———. 1995a. "Consensus, Conflict, and the Domain of Partisanship in House Committees." Paper presented at the Annual Meeting of the Midwest Political Science Association, Chicago.

———. 1995b. "Parties and Committees in the House: Member Motivations, Issues, and Institutional Arrangements." In Kenneth A. Shepsle and Barry R. Weingast, eds., *Positive Theories of Congressional Institutions*. Ann Arbor: University of Michigan Press.

———. 1996. "The Inevitability and Solidity of the 'Republican Solid South.'" *American Review of Politics* 17: 23–46.

Rosenstone, Steven J., Donald R. Kinder, Warren E. Miller, and the National Election Studies. 1997. *American National Election Study, 1996 Pre- and Post-Election Survey* [computer file]. Conducted by University of Michigan, Center for Political Studies. Ann Arbor: University of Michigan, Center for Political Studies, and Inter-University Consortium for Political and Social Research [producers]. Ann Arbor: Inter-University Consortium for Political and Social Research [distributor].

Rosenstone, Steven J., Warren E. Miller, Donald R. Kinder, and the National Election Studies. 1995. *American National Election Study, 1994: Post-Election Survey [Enhanced with 1992 and 1993 Data]* [computer file]. Conducted by University of Michigan, Center for Political Studies. 2d ICPSR ed. Ann Arbor: University of Michigan, Center for Political Studies, and Inter-University Consortium for Political and Social

Research [producers]. Ann Arbor: Inter-University Consortium for Political and Social Research [distributor].

Rozell, Mark J., and Clyde Wilcox. 1995. *God at the Grass Roots: The Christian Right in the 1994 Elections*. Lanham, Md.: Rowman and Littlefield.

Salamon, Lester, and Stephen Van Evera. 1973. "Fear, Apathy, and Discrimination: A Test of Three Explanations of Political Participation." *American Political Science Review* 63: 1288–1306.

Scammon, Richard. 1973. *America Votes 10.* Washington, D.C.: Congressional Quarterly Press.

———. 1975. *America Votes 11.* Washington, D.C.: Congressional Quarterly Press.

———. 1977. *America Votes 12.* Washington, D.C.: Congressional Quarterly Press.

Scammon, Richard, and Alice V. McGillivray. 1979. *America Votes 13.* Washington, D.C.: Congressional Quarterly Press.

———. 1981. *America Votes 14.* Washington, D.C.: Congressional Quarterly Press.

———. 1983. *America Votes 15.* Washington, D.C.: Congressional Quarterly Press.

———. 1985. *America Votes 16.* Washington, D.C.: Congressional Quarterly Press.

———. 1987. *America Votes 17.* Washington, D.C.: Congressional Quarterly Press.

———. 1989. *America Votes 18.* Washington, D.C.: Congressional Quarterly Press.

———. 1991. *America Votes 19.* Washington, D.C.: Congressional Quarterly Press.

Schattschneider, E. E. 1942. *Party Government.* New York: Rinehart.

———. 1960. *The Semi-Sovereign People.* New York: Holt, Rinehart, and Winston.

Schlesinger, Joseph A. 1966. *Ambition and Politics: Political Careers in the United States.* Chicago: Rand McNally.

———. 1985. "The New American Political Party." *American Political Science Review* 70: 1152–69.

———. 1991. *Political Parties and the Winning of Office.* Chicago: University of Chicago Press.

Schneider, Jerrold E. 1979. *Ideological Coalitions in Congress.* Westport, Conn.: Greenwood Press.

Schuman, Howard, Charlotte Steeh, and Lawrence Bobo. 1985. *Racial Attitudes in America*. Cambridge, Mass.: Harvard University Press.

Schwab, Larry M. 1988. *The Impact of Congressional Reapportionment and Redistricting*. Lanham, Md.: University Press of America.

Schwarz, John E., Barton Fenmore, and Thomas J. Volgy. 1980. "Liberal and Conservative Voting in the House of Representatives: A National Model of Representation." *British Journal of Political Science* 10: 317–29.

Seagull, Louis M. 1975. *Southern Republicanism*. New York: Wiley.

Shaffer, Steven D., and David Breaux. 1992. "Generational Differences among Southern Grassroots Party Workers." Paper presented at the Annual Meeting of the American Political Science Association, Chicago, Illinois.

Shaffer, William R. 1980. *Party and Ideology in the United States Congress*. Lanham, Md.: University Press of America.

———. 1982. "Party and Ideology in the U.S. House of Representatives," *Western Political Quarterly* 35: 92–106.

———. 1987. "Ideological Trends among Southern U.S. Democratic Senators: Race, Generation, and Political Climate." *American Politics Quarterly* 15: 299–324.

Shannon, Joseph Berry. 1949. *Toward a New Politics in the South*. Knoxville: University of Tennessee Press.

Shannon, Wayne. 1968. *Party, Constituency, and Congressional Voting*. Baton Rouge: Louisiana State University Press.

———. 1972. "Revolt in Washington: The South in Congress." In William C. Havard, ed., *The Changing Politics of the South*. Baton Rouge: Louisiana State University Press.

Shelley, Mack C., II. 1983. *The Permanent Majority: The Conservative Coalition in the United States Congress*. University: University of Alabama Press.

Sheppard, Burton D. 1985. *Rethinking Congressional Reform*. Cambridge, Mass.: Schenkman.

Shepsle, Kenneth A. 1979. "Institutional Arrangements and Equilibrium in Multidimensional Voting Models." *American Journal of Political Science* 23: 27–59.

Sigelman, Lee, and Susan Welch. 1991. *Black Americans' Views of Racial Equality: The Dream Deferred*. New York: Cambridge University Press.

Sinclair, Barbara. 1977. "Party Realignment and the Transformation of the Political Agenda: The House of Representatives, 1925–1938." *American Political Science Review* 71: 940–53.

———. 1981. "Agenda and Alignment Change: The House of Representatives, 1925–1978." In Lawrence C. Dodd and Bruce I. Oppenheimer, eds., *Congress Reconsidered*. 2d ed. Washington, D.C.: Congressional Quarterly Press.

———. 1982. *Congressional Realignment*. Austin: University of Texas Press.

———. 1983. *Majority Party Leadership in the U.S. House*. Baltimore: Johns Hopkins University Press.

———. 1989. "House Majority Party Leadership in the Late 1980s." In Lawrence C. Dodd and Bruce I. Oppenheimer, eds., *Congress Reconsidered*. 4th ed. Washington, D.C.: Congressional Quarterly Press.

———. 1995. *Legislators, Leaders, and Lawmaking: The U.S. House of Representatives in the Postreform Era*. Baltimore: Johns Hopkins University Press.

Smith, Steven S., and Christopher Deering. 1984. *Committees in Congress*. Washington: Congressional Quarterly Press.

———. 1990. *Committees in Congress*. 2d ed. Washington: Congressional Quarterly Press.

Smith, Steven S., and Bruce A. Ray. 1983. "The Impact of Congressional Reform: House Democratic Committee Assignments." *Congress and the Presidency* 10: 219–40.

Sorauf, Frank J. 1984. *Party Politics in America*. 5th ed. Boston: Little, Brown.

Sorauf, Frank J., and Scott A. Wilson. 1990. "Campaigns and Money: A Changing Role for the Political Parties?" In L. Sandy Maisel, ed., *The Parties Respond: Changes in the American Party System*. Boulder, Colo.: Westview Press.

Stanley, Harold W. 1987. *Voter Mobilization and the Politics of Race*. New York: Praeger.

———. 1988. "Southern Partisan Changes: Dealignment, Realignment, or Both?" *Journal of Politics* 50: 64–88.

Stanley, Harold W., and David S. Castle. 1988. "Partisan Changes in the South: Making Sense of Scholarly Dissonance." In Robert H. Swansbrough and David M. Brodsky, eds., *The South's New Politics*. Columbia: University of South Carolina Press.

Stanley, Harold W., and Richard Niemi. 1991. *Vital Statistics on American Politics*. Washington, D.C.: Congressional Quarterly Press.

Steed, Robert P., Laurence Moreland, and Tod A. Baker. 1990. "Searching for the Mind of the South in the Second Reconstruction." In Robert P. Steed, Laurence W. Moreland, and Tod A. Baker, eds., *The Disappearing South?* Tuscaloosa: University of Alabama Press.

Stern, Mark. 1982. "Assessing the Impact of the 1965 Voting Rights Act: A Microanalysis of Four States." In Laurence W. Moreland, Tod A. Baker, and Robert P. Steed, eds., *Contemporary Southern Political Attitudes and Behavior.* New York: Praeger.

Stimson, James A. 1985. "Regression in Space and Time: A Statistical Essay." *American Journal of Political Science* 29: 914–47.

———. 1991. *Public Opinion in America: Moods, Cycles, and Swings.* Boulder: Westview Press.

Stone, Walter J. 1979. "Measuring Constituency-Representative Linkages: Problems and Prospects." *Legislative Studies Quarterly* 4: 623–40.

———. 1980. "The Dynamics of Constituency Electoral Control in the House," *American Politics Quarterly* 8: 399–424.

———. 1982. "Electoral Change and Policy Representation in Congress: Domestic Welfare Issues from 1956–1972." *British Journal of Political Science* 12: 95–115.

Stouffer, Samuel. 1955. *Communism, Conformity, and Civil Liberties.* New York: Doubleday.

Strain, Judith A. 1963. "The Nature of Political Representation in Legislative Districts of Intense Party Competition." B.A. thesis, Chatham College.

Strong, Donald S. 1956. *The 1952 Presidential Election in the South.* University: University of Alabama Bureau of Public Administration.

———. 1960. *Urban Republicanism in the South.* University: University of Alabama Bureau of Public Administration.

Sullivan, John L., and Eric M. Uslaner. 1978. "Congressional Behavior and Electoral Marginality." *American Journal of Political Science* 22: 536–53.

Sundquist, James L. 1983. *Dynamics of the Party System.* Washington, D.C.: Brookings Institution.

Sutton, C. David. 1982. "Party Competition in the South's Forgotten Region: The Case of Southern Appalachia." In Laurence W. Moreland, Tod A. Baker, and Robert P. Steed, eds., *Contemporary Southern Political Attitudes and Behavior.* New York: Praeger.

Swain, Carol M. 1993. *Black Faces, Black Interests: The Representation of African-Americans in Congress.* Cambridge, Mass.: Harvard University Press.

Tate, Katherine. 1993. *From Protest to Politics: The New Black Voters in American Elections.* Cambridge, Mass.: Harvard University Press.

Theilmann, John, and Allen Wilhite. 1990. "Labor Money in Southern Elections: Continuation of an Old Trend." In Robert P. Steed, Lawrence

W. Moreland, and Tod A. Baker, eds., *The Disappearing South?* Tuscaloosa: University of Alabama Press.

Timpone, Richard J. 1995. "Mass Mobilization or Government Intervention? The Growth of Black Registration in the South." *Journal of Politics* 57: 425–42.

Tindall, George B. 1967. *The Emergence of the New South, 1913–1945.* Baton Rouge: Louisiana State University Press.

———. 1972. *Disruption of the Solid South.* New York: Norton.

Turner, Julius. 1951. *Party and Constituency: Pressures on Congress.* Baltimore: Johns Hopkins University Press.

Turner, Julius, and Edward V. Schneier, Jr. 1970. *Party and Constituency: Pressures on Congress.* 2d ed. Baltimore: Johns Hopkins University Press.

U.S. Census. 1972. *Congressional Districts of the 93rd Congress.* Washington, D.C.: Government Printing Office.

———. 1974. *Congressional Districts of the 94th Congress.* Washington, D.C.: Government Printing Office.

———. 1982. *Congressional Districts of the 98th Congress.* Washington, D.C.: Government Printing Office.

———. 1984. *Congressional Districts of the 99th Congress.* Washington, D.C.: Government Printing Office.

Voss, D. Stephen. 1996. "Beyond Racial Threat: Failure of an Old Hypothesis in the New South." *Journal of Politics* 58: 1156–70.

Wald, Kenneth D. 1997. *Religion and Politics in the United States.* 3d ed. Washington, D.C.: Congressional Quarterly Press.

Wattenberg, Martin P. 1991. *The Rise of Candidate-centered Politics.* Cambridge, Mass.: Harvard University Press.

Weilhouwer, Peter W., and Brad Lockerbie. 1994. "Party Contacting and Political Participation, 1952–1990." *American Journal of Political Science* 38: 211–29.

Weilhouwer, Peter W., and James L. Regens. 1993. "Political Parties as Transaction Cost Minimizers." Paper presented at the Annual Meeting of the American Political Science Association, Washington, D.C.

Weiner, Jonathan M. 1982. *Social Origins of the New South.* Baton Rouge: Louisiana State University Press.

Weingast, Barry R. 1979. "A Rational Choice Perspective on Congressional Norms." *American Journal of Political Science* 32: 245–62.

Weingast, Barry R., and William Marshall. 1988. "The Industrial Organization of Congress." *Journal of Political Economy* 96: 132–63.

Weisberg, Herbert F. 1978. "Evaluating Theories of Congressional Roll Call Voting," *American Journal of Political Science* 22: 554–77.

West, Darrell M. 1988. "Activists and Economic Policymaking in Congress." *American Journal of Political Science* 32: 662–80.

Whitby, Kenny J. 1985. "Effects of the Interaction between Race and Urbanization on Votes of Southern Congressmen. *Legislative Studies Quarterly* 10: 505–17.

———. 1987. "Measuring Congressional Responsiveness to the Policy Interests of Black Constituents." *Social Science Quarterly* 69: 367–77.

———. 1997. *The Color of Representation: Congressional Behavior and Black Interests.* Ann Arbor: University of Michigan Press.

Whitby, Kenny J., and Franklin D. Gilliam, Jr. 1991. "A Longitudinal Analysis of Competing Explanations for the Transformation of Southern Congressional Politics." *Journal of Politics* 53: 504–18.

Wilcox, Clyde, and Aage Clausen. 1991. "The Dimensionality of Roll Call Voting Reconsidered." *Legislative Studies Quarterly* 16: 393–406.

Wolfinger, Raymond, and Robert B. Arsenau. 1978. "Partisan Change in the South 1952–1976." In Louis Maisel and Joseph Cooper, eds., *Political Parties: Development and Decay.* Beverly Hills, Calif.: Sage.

Wolfinger, Raymond, and Joan Hollinger. 1971. "Safe Seats, Seniority, and Power in Congress." In Raymond E. Wolfinger, ed., *Readings on Congress.* Englewood Cliffs, N.J.: Prentice-Hall.

Wright, Gavin. 1986. *Old South, New South: Revolutions in the Southern Economy since the Civil War.* New York: Basic Books.

Wright, Gerald C., Jr. 1977. "Contextual Models of Electoral Behavior: The Southern Wallace Vote." *American Political Science Review* 71: 497–508.

Wyman, Hastings, Jr. 1997. "Southern GOP Grapples with Christian/ Mainstream Tensions." *Southern Political Report*, September 30.

Zaller, John R. 1992. *The Nature and Origins of Mass Opinion.* Cambridge: Cambridge University Press.

INDEX

Abortion, 18, 31, 41, 43, 44, 54, 59,
    68, 69, 74, 77, 83, 89, 91-93, 97,
    99, 100, 101, 106, 107, 121,
    136–38, 141, 142, 164, 165, 173,
    174, 179, 184–87, 196
Activists, 18, 90–99, 104–107,
    140–42, 165, 174, 176, 179,
    181–83, 189, 215n.2
Adams, Greg D., 93
AFL-CIO, 49. *See also* Labor unions.
African Americans: as members of
    Congress, 36, 120, 140, 144, 148,
    158, 161, 163, 164, 166, 170, 172,
    173; mobilization of voters, 30,
    31, 32, 35, 36, 39, 40, 41, 42, 46,
    52, 63, 69,70, 71, 73, 76, 117, 145,
    146, 149, 156, 175, 176, 178–80,
    190, 196, 217nn.2,3; and New
    Deal programs, 114; partisan
    loyalties, 75, 76, 158, 188, 190;
    political attitudes, 31, 41, 43, 44,
    46, 49, 71, 78, 82, 86–89, 103,
    106, 107, 123, 139, 144, 158, 163,
    164, 172, 176, 178, 196, 203,
    214n.1; southern Democrats'

responsiveness to, 110, 124,
    139–41, 144–46, 156, 158, 163,
    217n.3; voting rights, 145, 175,
    179, 180, 216n.1
Agenda setting, 11, 12, 13, 26, 134,
    141, 183
Agriculture, 47, 48, 113, 216n.4
Aistrup, Joseph A., 189
Alabama, 197, 213n.2
Ambition, 191
American Indians, legal claims of,
    130
Americans for Democratic Action,
    34
Anti-Ballistic Missile Treaty, 132
Appropriations. *See* Budget,
    federal
Appropriations Committee,
    House, 185
Arkansas, 213n.2
Arrow's paradox, 27

B-1 bomber, 132
Balanced budget amendment, 195
Ballistic missile defense, 132, 134